D0918370

ARTHUR KOESTLER

GARLAND REFERENCE LIBRARY
OF THE HUMANITIES
(VOL. 612)

ARTHUR KOESTLER
A Guide to Research

Frank Day

GARLAND PUBLISHING, INC. • NEW YORK & LONDON
1987

Library of Congress Cataloging-in-Publication Data

Day, Frank, 1932–
  Arthur Koestler : a guide to research.

  (Garland reference library of the humanities ;
v. 612)
  Includes indexes.
  1. Koestler, Arthur, 1905–   —Bibliography.
I. Title. II. Series.
Z8467.1774.D39 1987   016.828′91209   85-45122
[PR6021.04]
ISBN 0-8240-8670-8

Printed on acid-free, 250-year-life paper
Manufactured in the United States of America

To Patricia, with Love

CONTENTS

PREFACE

The plan of this book is simple. I have taken Reed Merrill and Thomas Frazier's *Arthur Koestler: An International Bibliography* and annotated all of the items included in it. I have added *Bricks to Babel* to the list to make the primary bibliography complete, and I have picked up and annotated the most important secondary sources published since Merrill and Frazier's book came out in 1979. As a result, a user of this book can be confident that the primary bibliography is essentially complete and that the secondary bibliography is reliable through 1978. My book differs from Merrill and Frazier's in that they list all of the many editions, translations, and diverse appearances of Koestler's works in print but do not provide any annotations, whereas I have customarily listed only the first publication of a book but have summarized its contents in detail. Anyone seeking information about the publishing history of Koestler's works will want to consult Merrill and Frazier; anyone interested in the contents of these works will find lengthy annotations in this book. (See my annotation of Merrill and Frazier's bibliography in Item No. 291.)

I have accumulated a number of debts in writing this book. Marian Withington, Julie Pennebaker, and Dale Simmons of the Clemson University library staff were efficient and obliging in obtaining books and articles through interlibrary loan. I am extremely grateful to them for all of their work. Rob Roy MacGregor proved an excellent sleuth when I asked him to track down a Latin quotation. Victor Rudowski, Chantal Mauldin, and Rose Marie Cothran gave me indispensable help with translation crises, and I want to say thank you in several languages to them. Over the course of two summers, my graduate assistant, Len McCall, did a lot of legwork for me in the library, and she has my gratitude for executing those many chores.

INTRODUCTION

Arthur Koestler was born September 5, 1905, in Budapest,
Hungary, the only child of Hungarian-Jewish parents. He was a
precocious child, especially adept in mathematics and the
sciences. His father was a rather eccentric, self-taught
businessman, who moved the family to Vienna during Koestler's
teens. From 1922 to 1926 Koestler studied science at the polytechnic in Vienna. During these college years, he became a
devoted Zionist, and he left the university without a degree to
go to Palestine in the service of the Revisionist Party. His
experience in Palestine--drawn on in his novel *Thieves in the
Night*--was not satisfying to him, but in 1927 he was hired by
Ullstein's, the German newspaper chain, and soon moved to
Paris. In 1930 he moved again, this time to Berlin, where he
was named science editor of *Vossische Zeitung* and foreign
editor of *Berliner Zeitung am Mittag*. His rapid success as a
journalist contributed to his becoming the only newspaperman
to accompany the *Graf Zeppelin* on its flight to the North Pole
in 1931.

In 1931 Koestler joined the German Communist Party, and less
than a year later he gave up his position with Ullstein's and
took an extended tour of the Soviet Union to study that
nation's Five-Year Plan. In 1933 he returned to Paris for
three years where he worked for the Comintern. He married
Dorothy Asher in 1935; they separated after two years and were
divorced in 1950. At the outbreak of the Spanish Civil War in
1936, Koestler went to Spain as a correspondent for the *London
News Chronicle*. He was soon arrested by the Nationalists,
imprisoned in Seville, and sentenced to death. He was released
largely as the result of efforts by the British press, and he
turned his prison experience into *Spanish Testament* (1938),
later revised as *Dialogue with Death* (1942). A significant
period in his life ends in 1938 with his resignation from the
Communist Party in disillusionment with Stalinism and the
Moscow show trials.

Back in Paris in 1939, he was once again imprisoned, this
time in a French internment camp for aliens. This imprisonment
also became the subject of an autobiographical book, *Scum of
the Earth* (1941). After release by the French, Koestler joined

the French Foreign Legion as a ruse to hide his identity and finally escaped to England, where he spent 1941 and 1942 in the British Pioneer Corps. *Darkness at Noon* was first published in 1940, translated into English by Daphne Hardy. It appeared in French in 1946 under the title of *Le zéro et l'infini*, and it created an uproar among Parisian intellectuals of the Left. Koestler was living in Paris at the time, and he became one of the villains in Simone de Beauvoir's *roman à clef*, *The Mandarins* (1956).

With his reputation as an apostate to Communism firmly established after the war, Koestler became one of the principal spokesmen among anti-Communist intellectuals. He made two lecture tours of America and was a Chubb Fellow at Yale University during 1950-1951. In *The God That Failed* (1950), Koestler gave personal testimony of his disillusionment with Communism, and his account was accompanied by similar confessions from André Gide, Louis Fischer, Stephen Spender, Richard Wright, and Ignazio Silone. After his divorce from Doroth Asher in 1950, Koestler married Mamaine Paget in the same year, and they went to live in America on a farm along the Delaware River. The marriage lasted three years. Koestler returned to England to live in 1952, and in 1955 he announced in *The Trial of the Dinosaur and Other Essays* (1945-1954) that he was through with political writing.

In 1957 Koestler was named a Fellow of the Royal Society of Literature, and he began his new writing career in 1959 with the unexpected publication of a long history of astronomy, *The Sleepwalkers: A History of Man's Changing Vision of the Universe*. *The Sleepwalkers* was followed by two companion volumes on the psychology of creativity, *The Act of Creation* (1964) and *The Ghost in the Machine* (1967). In 1965 Koestler married his secretary, Cynthia Jefferies. They lived in London (Koestler became a naturalized citizen of England), and he wrote books and essays on a number of topics until they both committed suicide on March 3, 1983.

The Fiction

In his Postscript to the Danube edition of *The Gladiators*, Koestler explains that it forms, along with *Darkness at Noon* and *Thieves in the Night* a trilogy "whose leitmotif is the central question of revolutionary ethics and of political ethics in general: the question whether, or to what extent, the end justifies the means." This key question is answered in the affirmative in *The Gladiators*, which was suggested by the Slave War of 73-71 b.c. The slave leader, Spartacus, is advised by a wise Essene that of all God's curses on man, "the worst curse

of all is that he must tread the evil road for the sake of the
good and right, that he must make detours and walk crookedly
so that he may reach the straight goal." The "law of detours"
is soon exemplified by Crixus, a co-leader with Spartacus, in
his decision to lead an unruly, troublesome faction into a
battle that will mean their sure death. By sacrificing the
unruly in this cynical act of policy, Crixus has ironically
supported the idealism of the movement by ridding it of its
discordant element and he has done it with tacit support of
Spartacus. But Spartacus himself cannot meet the moral demands
of the law of detours. Challenged by the Celts in a rebellion
against his command, Spartacus fails to exercise the necessary
ruthlessness that would preserve order. In clinging to the
idealism with which he began the revolution, Spartacus lets the
revolution slip away. Koestler explains Spartacus's failure in
his 1965 Postscript: "Yet he shrinks from taking the last
step--the purge by crucifixion of the dissident Celts and the
establishment of a ruthless tyranny; and through this refusal
he dooms his revolution to defeat."

Two themes dominate Koestler's masterpiece, *Darkness at
Noon*: the argument that, contra the Essene in *The Gladiators*,
the end does not justify the means, and the conviction that
the individual ego, the I, is not a mere "grammatical fiction"
with its outline blurred by the sweep of the historical
dialectic. Whereas its support for the position that the end
justifies the means makes *The Gladiators* a subtle apologia for
Communism, *Darkness at Noon* turns on this proposition and
attacks it forcefully. The old Bolshevik, Rubashov, finds that
he can no longer connive with the Party in the devious detours
it takes on the road to Socialist Utopia. The individual is
real, not abstract, and he cannot be brutalized in the name of
History. The arguments given by Rubashov are essentially those
given by Koestler himself in *The God That Failed*.

The novel inspired interesting critical responses. The
French Marxist Maurice Merleau-Ponty insisted that Koestler was
a poor student of Marxism who misrepresented Marxist Communism
in *Darkness at Noon*. Admittedly, said Merleau-Ponty, Marxist
policies might involve "dialectical detours but at least could
not entirely ignore human purposes." (See Item No. 360.) In
Merleau-Ponty's reading of history, humanism and violence go
together: "Each humanitarian reform is accompanied by violence
and death."

George Orwell rejected the theory of what he called "catastrophic gradualism," or the theory defined in the banality
that you cannot make an omelet without breaking eggs--which is
what Merleau-Ponty's argument reduces to. Orwell maintains
that Koestler is correct to ignore the omelet cooked by Stalin.
(See Item No. 372.)

John Strachey interprets the Russian Revolution--and
Stalinist oppression--as a natural outgrowth of the Enlightenment. (When Ivanov lectures Rubashov on the revolutionary
ethic, he tells him that the Party's acts follow from "logical
deduction.") Thus for Strachey *Darkness at Noon* should be read
as "the starting point of the literature of reaction" to rationalism. (See Item No. 395.) Strachey's point is not easily
dismissed.

Koestler's third novel, *Arrival and Departure* (1943), is a
study of the revolutionary mentality and does not deal directly with the theme of ends versus means. Its hero, Peter
Slavek, is a young Eastern European and a former Communist who
finds himself in Portugal in 1940, wondering what path he
should commit himself to. Through a psychiatrist, Dr. Sonia
Bolger, Peter learns that his motives for political action can
be traced to childhood guilt feelings. This knowledge under-
cuts much of the idealism underlying his career as a political
activist. Although the novel seems at first depressing in its
deconstruction of human behavior into a series of grudges and
neuroses, Koestler holds out hope. He says, "You can explain
the messages of the Prophets as epileptic foam and the Sistine
Madonna as the projection of an incestuous dream. The method
is correct and the picture in itself complete. But beware of
the arrogant error of believing that it is the only one."
Revolutionary motives cannot, then, be reduced exclusively to
dissection by psychoanalysis and psychobiography.

The reactions to *Thieves in the Night* (1946) were mixed. It
tells the story of the establishment of Ezra's Tower, a commune
in Palestine. In the character of Joseph, a young English-born
Jew through whose eyes much of the narrative is presented,
Koestler created one of his most convincing characters. The
novel depicts well the stresses of communal life and the effects
on Palestine of international politics in the period from 1937
to 1939. Many critics were disturbed, however, by its endorsement of terrorism, as Joseph joins a terrorist group at the
novel's close. It is ironic that although Koestler is well
known for rejecting in *Darkness at Noon* and *The God That Failed*
the ethic that the end justifies the means, in two of his three
novels that treat the theme--*The Gladiators* and *Thieves in the
Night*--the law of detours is upheld. Thus in the final analysis
Koestler often appears close to accepting that Orwell called
"catastrophic gradualism" and the close relationship between
humanism and terror that Merleau-Ponty explicates.

No such grand philophic themes dominate *The Age of Longing*
(1951), a story of spiritual disillusionment and longing for an
age of faith. The setting is Paris on Bastille Day--projected
into the middle 1950s--and events center around three characters:
Hydie, a lapsed Catholic seeking a new faith; Fedya Nikitin, a

Communist security officer with a rigid commissar mentality; and Julien Delattre, a poet and former Party member who in many ways is Koestler himself. Delattre tells Hydie at one point, "My generation turned to Marx as one swallows acid drops to fight off nausea."

The Age of Longing is notable for the unity of mood Koestler develops in depicting a period of despair and pessimism. Gerard Irvine commented on how the novel can be seen as a "resetting of Dostoevsky's legend of the Grand Inquisitor: "What men of the age long for is the certainty and the authority of faith to save them from the intolerable burden of freedom." (See Item No. 462.) Koestler also satirizes quite effectively the Marxist-existentialist philosopher Jean-Paul Sartre in the person of Professor Pontieux. The professor is the author of a fashionable text of postwar despair, "Negation and Position." The professor "can prove everything he believes, and he believes everything he can prove."

Koestler waited over twenty years before he published another novel, *The Call Girls* (1972). The title refers to the prominent intellectuals who travel the world expounding their ideologies at international conferences. As a work of art, *The Call Girls* is a slight production, but it effectively dramatizes the philosophical concerns Koestler had become preoccupied with after giving up political writing. The conferees he brings together in a Swiss mountain resort divide into behaviorists and nonbehaviorists. Koestler himself attacked behaviorist psychology for over two decades, and *The Call Girls* is an entertaining psychomachy, a battle between the soulless behaviorists and the advocates of man's existential freedom. In this respect it illustrates once again Koestler's fondness for staging his intellectual dramas in the dress of of irreconcilable opposites--the yogi and the commissar, ends versus means, etc. *The Call Girls* is a novel of ideas in the manner of Aldous Huxley.

Although *Darkness at Noon* has been translated into thirty-three languages and reprinted many times, Koestler has not achieved a high reputation for his six novels. Only the sensational subject matter of *Darkness at Noon* has kept it alive. The critical consensus has always been that Koestler is strong in ideas but weak in artistry as a novelist. A few critics (see Peter Steele's analysis of the literary techniques in *Darkness at Noon* in Item No. 393) have praised Koestler's creative talents--and Philip Toynbee even called him "probably the cleverest novelist writing in English today" (Item No. 445)--but his fiction no longer attracts much attention. In the 1940s some readers found his novels of ideas stimulating relief from the preciosities of the Bloomsbury novel of personal relationships, but that historical circumstance has not helped

them to endure. It is likely that *Darkness at Noon* will
continue to be read for its documentary value, but his other
novels will be of interest only to specialists pursuing particular interests.

Israel and the Jews

One of the most interesting of the strands that Koestler's
thought is woven of is his attitude toward Jews and Jewishness.
He never quite seemed to know what to make of being a Jew.
Lionel Abel says that Koestler's relationship to his Jewishness
is "hardly clear" either to him or to us (Item No. 296). His
youthful experience at the polytechnic in Vienna led to an
interest in Zionism and Jabotinsky's revolutionary politics
that took him to Palestine. But he realized as soon as he got
there that settling down on a commune was not congenial to his
temperament, and he quickly settled into the role of the
observer.

His Palestine sojourn provoked a lot of reflection on Jews
and history, their culture, manners, and psychology. His
descriptions of European Jews were not flattering. The *TLS*
reviewer of *Thieves in the Night* commented that Koestler seemed
"almost over-anxious to concede familiar psychological observations about Jews" (Item No. 455). Orville Prescott condemned
the apparent support of terrorism in *Thieves in the Night* and
concluded that Palestine "confused his moral vision" (Item No.
377). Many of his Jewish critics were severe with *Thieves in
the Night*. Nathan Glazer, writing in *Commentary*, charged that
"for the Jews themselves this book can be harmful" (Item No.
448). Clement Greenberg dismissed the novel and sneered at
Koestler's "newfound Anglophilia" that led him to turn on
European Jews with contempt. (See Item No. 450.) Evaluation
of the novel as a work of art and judgment of its political
stance are both clouded by the problematic attitude toward Jews
that it demonstrates.

Promise and Fulfillment (1949), Koestler's account of modern
Palestine, predictably provoked a variety of impassioned
responses. The sharpest attack on Koestler as a historian of
the area came from G.L. Arnold, whose scholarly condemnation
has an authoritative ring in many places. (See Item No. 556.)
The Palestine issue was so clearly a Rorschach test of political orientation that readers of Koestler's book will need to
pick their way carefully through the responses.

One point was very clear, though, in *Promise and Fulfillment*:
Koestler's insistence that modern Jews should choose between
migrating to Israel or assimilating into the culture they live
and giving up the Jewish faith. Critics attacked this rigid

either-or position passionately. Lillian Feinsilver described
Koestler's ultimatum as "incredibly naive" and based on a false
premise. (See Item No. 557.) Leslie Fiedler doubted the
ability of Western Jews to assimilate as easily as Koestler
thought they could. (See Item No. 558.)

The most detailed analysis of Koestler's attitude toward
Jews came from Lothar Kahn in *The Chicago Jewish Forum* (Item
No. 345). Kahn traced Koestler's "obvious need for belonging
in some larger and impersonal groups" to his "barren childhood." His claim that Koestler is both a cold rationalist and
an "inveterate romanticist" is probably quite accurate. Koestler's ambivalence toward Jews appears in the revulsion he feels
for Jewish ethnocentrism on one hand, and his strong support
for the civil rights of Jews on the other hand. Kahn notes
very perceptively that Koestler's support for Zionism derives
from his conviction that a return to the soil would purge
Ghetto Jews of their "habitual over-smugness." Many of Koestler's Jewish readers would probably share Kahn's final judgment: "The story of Koestler is that of an incomplete Jew who,
though he leaned over backward to develop one phase of Jewishness, was too deficient in others ever to achieve fullness."

Sixteen years after Kahn's analysis, Koestler wrote *The
Thirteenth Tribe* (1976), a study of the history of the Khazars
that many interpreted as his final act of apostasy against his
Jewish birth. In "Judah at the Crossroads" (Item 16), Koestler
had repeated his thesis that Jews should either assimilate or
go to Israel, asserting that "[e]thnic assimilation is impossible with maintaining the Mosaic faith; and the Mosaic faith
becomes untenable with ethnic assimilation." He based part of
his argument on genes, finding only "a small and somewhat
hypothetical 'hard core' of Jewish characteristics in the sense
of biological heredity, and a vast complex of physical and
mental characteristics which are of environmental origin and
transmitted through social inheritance." (In light of Koestler's fascination with Lamarckism, one should note the belief
here in "physical" traits transmitted socially. The remark
also raises the question of how much of Koestler's Lamarckist
sympathy was prompted by speculations about Jews and race.) In
The Thirteenth Tribe Koestler came back to these concerns and
tried to demonstrate that Ashkenazic Jews were not of Semitic
racial stock, after all. He expresses the possibility that
"the majority of eastern Jews--and hence of world Jewry--might
be of Khazar, and not of Semitic origin." (See Item No. 30.)
Given this new view of the Jews' racial origins, Koestler says
that "the term 'anti-Semitism' would become void of meaning."
Although Koestler believes that the question of Jewish origins
is irrelevant to the issues in modern Israel, Edward Grossman
is probably right in taking Koestler's underlying thesis to be

that if the Jews are Khazars, they should either go to Israel or assimilate. (See Item No, 689.)

Several reviewers pointed out a fallacy in Koestler's reasoning. Establishing the Khazars as the ancestors of Polish Jews will not hurt the notion of the "Chosen Race," says Hyam Maccoby, for "[t]here has never been a 'Chosen-Race' doctrine in Judaism." Jews, instead, continues Maccoby, regard them-selves as a "chosen *people*." Maccoby describes *The Thirteenth Tribe* as "one more stage in Koestler's struggle to exorcise his own Jewishness."

Leon Wieseltier's long review of *The Thirteenth Tribe* at-tacked Koestler's scholarship, accusing him of taking a hack-neyed thesis discredited by most historians and stringing together a flimsy narrative "with a medley of quotations from better-known historians, all of which combine to make him appear learned." (See Item No. 700.) This charge was support-ed by another historian, Henry R. Huttenbach. (See Item No. 690.) For Wieseltier, *The Thirteenth Tribe* is "[a] barely veiled and singularly defeasible argument about the character and prospects of the contemporary Jewish community." Wieseltier concludes that "only a Jew would have taken so much trouble to come up with an alibi for his own self-effacement." Even Philip Toynbee, one of Koestler's greatest admirers over the years, admitted that *The Thirteenth Tribe* is a "mischievous book" because it damages the Jews' sense of a unique heredity. (See Item No. 699.)

But the book also had its admireers. Karl Meyer thought it was "important and rigorously argued" (Item No, 696), Fitzroy MacLean called it "excellent," "readable," and "thought-provok-ing" (Item No. 695), and Chaim Raphael described it as "a delight," observing that in terms of race it makes no difference whether or not Jews are of Khazar origin since "[t]he Jews have always known that physically they are a mixed people."

There can be no clear-cut verdict on the Khazar thesis or any certainty about Koestler's motives, but *The Thirteenth Tribe* is an excellent demonstration of what Koestler had a special knack for: taking an obscure scholarly issue, writing it up with a tendentious edge, and forcing everybody to look at it all over again.

Toads and Telepathy

In *The Case of the Midwife Toad* (1971) Koestler once again enlivens an old argument. This time he takes the story of Dr. Paul Kammerer, the Austrian biologist who committed suicide after it was shown that his key specimen of Alytes obstetricans, the midwife toad, had been reconstructed with ink. (See the

full summary in Item No. 26.) Again, most reviewers praised
the deftness with which Koestler resurrected the story, but the
scholarly reviewers were generally hard on Koestler insofar as
he tried to vindicate Kammerer. Indeed, his book probably will
convince few readers that Kammerer proved much about the inheritance of acquired characteristics, but it does raise successfully the question of who exactly midwifed the bogus specimen.
Koestler himself made no large claims for Lamarckism on the
basis of his story.

Koestler was not content, however, to tell an interesting
story about science and fraud, but used his discussion of
Kammerer's obsession with coincidences as a basis for speculation about parapsychological phenomena. Kammerer's coincidences were bound together under his theory of "seriality,"
which Koestler describes as a belief in "a force of attraction
comparable to universal gravity."

From Kammerer's seriality Koestler moves easily into the
subject of his next book, *The Roots of Coincidence: An Excursion into Parapsychology* (1972). The result is lamentable in
many ways. It is embarrassing to see him open his defense of
the scholarly respectability of ESP studies with a roll call of
prestigious scholars who have served as presidents of the
British Society for Psychical Research. The book is interesting mostly for its anecdotal accounts of events taken to illustrate ESP. He rehearses in detail the arguments suggested by
Kammerer, as well as the similar theory expounded by C.G. Jung
under the heading of "synchronicity," concluding that "Synchronicity and Seriality are modern derivatives of the archetypal
belief in the fundamental unity of all things, transcending
mechanical causality." Furthermore, he suggests an analogy
between Lamarckism and ESP, speculating that just as almost all
traces of acquired characteristics may be filtered out in
heredity, so may almost all traces of extra-sensory communication be filtered out in the organs of perception. That is
extreme speculation, but bracing and imaginative.

To imply, however, that the paradoxes of contemporary
science, especially as they emerge in quantum physics, in some
way legitimize the study of parapsychology is pretty courageous.
Koestler says, "The rapprochement between the conceptual world
of parapsychology and that of modern physics is an important
step towards the demolition of the greatest superstition of our
age--the materialistic clockwork universe of early nineteeth-
century physics." Such a claim is hardly reasonable. Physics
has always had a frontier, but it is pushed ahead a little
further every day. Parapsychology has the same frontier it has
always had. The analogy is terribly strained by the weight of
Koestler's almost hysterical search for more things on heaven
and earth than are dreamt of in our science.

Science History and Theories of Creativity

Koestler's works in the history of science cannot be separated from his theory of creativity because it is his theory that energizes his history. The two books for which he will be longest remembered are probably *Darkness at Noon* and *The Sleepwalkers: A History of Man's Changing Vision of the Universe.* *The Sleepwalkers* is a spendidly readable history of ancient and medieval astronomy. The treatment of Galileo was generally received by scholars as excessive in its debunking, but the long section on Kepler, Koestler's hero, is absolutely engrossing and fired with insights and imagination. It was highly praised and has been reprinted separately. What so fascinated Koestler in Kepler's story is the way the astronomer's work demonstrated Koestler's main thesis about creativity: that it is often a kind of sleepwalking in which the rational processes in scientific thought are largely under the control of some little-understood irrational instrument.

This thesis was elaborated at great--and unnecessary--length in two companion volumes, *The Act of Creation* and *The Ghost in the Machine.* Central to these two works was Koestler's notion of "bisociation" (although one reviewer said he could not see how it was different from mere association) and his evolving concept of the "holon," a "Janus-faced" entity that is omnipresent in nature and articulates those more complex entities superior to it with those that lie beneath it in the chain of unity. These terms are more metaphorical than scientific, but they have an honest usefulness. The same judgment applies to the works themselves: they are stimulating and often very readable, but few scientists would admit them to their canons.

Stephen Toulmin, an acute reader of Koestler's works, has identified the "three positions on which Koestler concentrates his destructive fire": behaviorist psychology, neo-Darwinist evolution theory, and the belief in historical coincidences. (See Item No. 397.) Only the most determined fools would rush in to do battle on these shell-pocked fields, and the military history is all recorded in the following annotations. But one inconsistency does not seem accounted for in Koestler's grand plan (what Toulmin calls his theodicy). In his attacks on behaviorism, Koestler is intent on freeing man from his strait jacket, but in his abhorrence of randomness he tries to put him back in it but garb him in a different cut of cloth. The resolution perhaps lies in his longing for a supernatural principle that would free man from the terror of an aimless creation and give him more dignity than is found in the tyranny of behavioral conditioning. Thus man could be seen as existentially free but at the same time under the governance of sufficient reason.

Koestler's last book was *Bricks to Babel: A Selection from 50 Years of His Writings, Chosen and with New Commentary by the Author* (1980). He divides this omnibus into two sections, the titles of which suggest how he saw his life. Book One, "In Search of Utopia," testifies to what was undoubtedly a life of both physical and moral courage. No one has reported more effectively on the viciousness of Soviet Communism, or done so with better authority. *Darkness at Noon* and *The God That Failed* were indispensable texts in history and political theory for at least one generation. He was a first-rate observer--in Spanish prisons, in Palestine, and in the haunts of yogis and Zen masters--and his reports on what he saw were always vivid and informed by a provocative point of view. His autobiographical writings depict a restless spirit and a hunger for experience, and they are invaluable documents of twentieth-century history.

In Book Two, "In Search of Synthesis," he excerpts those works in which he contributed to the ongoing dialogue over what life means and how it should be lived. It is not to be expected that all readers will agree with his conclusions or regard him as a seminal thinker in science. But it would be petty to deny that he had an unmistakable voice.

Primary Sources

A

NOVELS

1 *The Gladiators.* Trans. from the German by Edith
   Simon. London: Jonathan Cape, 1939.

   Based on the Slave War of 73-71 B.C. as
described by the historians Livy, Plutarch,
Appian, and Florus--only four thousand words
all told. The narrative divides into four books.
Book One, "Rise," traces the revolt hatched by
Spartacus, a Thracian gladiator, and his ruthless
co-leader, a Gaul named Crixus. Their march
through Campania provides them with loot and attracts more followers. Book Two, "The Law of Detours," describes the rebels' destruction of the
towns Nola, Suessula, and Calatia. At their
strongest, the insurgents number twenty thousand,
but the undisciplined ransacking of villages by
the outlaw members destroys the idealism of the
movement. Spartacus struggles with a hard decision, whether to let the unruly faction go on to
certain slaughter in combat against the Roman
troops of Varinius (a decision that would re-
lieve him of his problem elements) or to try to
win them to a policy of restraint and caution.
He is told by a wise Essene that "the worst curse
of all is that he must tread the evil road for
the sake of the good and right, that he must make
detours and walk crookedly so that he may reach
the straight goal." So Spartacus follows the "law
of detours," allowing Crixus to lead the lawless
to their deaths in battle and making of them a
cynical sacrifice. But Spartacus fails later to
be sufficiently ruthless. When his troubled Sun
State is threatened with rebellion by its dissat-
isfied Celtic elements, he rejects the law of detours. In a 1965 Postscript Koestler explains

3

Spartacus's mistake:"Yet he shrinks from taking
the last step--the purge by crucifixion of the
dissident Celts and the establishment of a ruthless tyranny; and through this refusal he dooms
his revolution to defeat." In Book Three, "The
Sun State," Spartacus is overcome by the force of
accumulated conflicts, and in Book Four, "Decline,"
the gladiators suffer humiliation and crucifixion.
In Spartacus's coping with the law of detours, *The
Gladiators* dramatizes well the difficulties inherent in the principle that the end justifies the
means.

2   *Darkness at Noon*. Trans. from the German by
    Daphne Hardy. London: Jonathan Cape, 1940.

Describes the interrogations of an old Bolshevik, Rubashov, who is accused of heresy against
the Communist Party. His questioners are Ivanov,
who is later executed, and Gletkin. The result is
Rubashov's own execution. The story is told in
three parts, one for each hearing Rubashov is
given, and a brief epilogue on "The Grammatical
Fiction." Flashbacks and extracts from Rubashov's
diary fill in the background. Of those accused in
the so-called Moscow Trials held by Stalin in the
1930's, Nikolai Bukharin was closest in his thinking to the fictional Rubashov. Gletkin also has a
counterpart in the actual trial prosecutor, Andre
Vishinsky. *Darkness at Noon* rejects the doctrine
that the end justifies the means and asserts the
authenticity of the individual ego, the I, in the
workings of history. Rubashov's doubts about the
Party result from the way various loyal members
are sacrificed to the law of detours. Little
Loewy, the Belgian dockworkers' leader, is de-
ceived by the Party and forced into unloading
Russian ships carrying materials for the German
war machine. He eventually hangs himself. And
Arlova, Rubashov's secretary and lover, is called
back to oblivion in Russia simply because her
brother married a foreigner. Rubashov observes
these examples of the law of detours in operation,
and he becomes an apostate to the Faith. Ivanov
lectures him on the Party's philosophy: "But you
must allow that we are as convinced that you and
they would mean the end of the Revolution as you
are of the reverse. That is the essential point.

The methods follow by logical deduction. We can't afford to lose ourselves in political subtleties."

(See Chapter XXXVII of *The Invisible Writing.*)

3 *Arrival and Departure.* London: Jonathan Cape; New York: Macmillan, 1943.

Peter Slavek, a twenty-two-year-old Eastern European, stows away on a freighter to Neutralia (Portugal) in 1940. He has been a Communist, has been tortured by Fascists, and must now make a hard choice among four possible courses of action: reluctant reunion with the Party; even more reluctant alliance with the Fascists; flight to America; or enlistment with the British. He meets two women in Neutralia. Dr. Sonia Bolgar provides him with a room, and her lover, Odette, a young French war widow, also has a brief affair with Peter. When Odette leaves for America, Peter experiences a psychosomatic paralysis in one leg. Thanks to Sonia's psychoanalysis of his behavior, Peter finds that his political acts have motives rooted in childhood guilt feelings. With his paralysis cured by this self-insight, Peter joins the British military forces.

4 *Thieves in the Night: Chronicles of an Experiment.* London and New York: Macmillan, 1946.

Thieves in the Night describes the founding of the commune of Ezra's Tower in Palestine. Joseph, a young Englishman with a Jewish father and an English mother, is the central character, and he copes with the problems involved in cultural assimilation. The novel dramatizes the tensions in communal life and focuses on the international politics that Palestine was caught up in during 1937-1939. The British decision made in the 1939 White Paper is exposed in its cruel shutting down of the flow of vulnerable European Jews into Palestine. Joseph finally joins the terrorist movement and helps smuggle Polish Jews off Romanian cattle boats. The treatment of terrorism offers another perspective on Koestler's old ethical conundrum of the ends and the means.

5   *The Age of Longing*. London: Collins; New York:
    Macmillan, 1951.

    The Age of Longing is set in Paris in the
    1950's, an age of longing for spiritual faith.
    Three characters dominate the plot. A young
    American girl, Hydie, struggles to recover the
    faith she once had in Catholicism, but only
    complicates her life by her affair with Fedya
    Nikitin, a Russian security officer. Fedya has
    the rigid commissar mentality to be expected
    from the son of proletarian revolutionaries
    from Baku. His mentality is governed by Party
    slogans and clichés. When he and Hydie become
    lovers, he treats her so unfeelingly that she
    tries to kill him after learning that he is a
    spy. Koestler puts much of himself into the
    third major character, Julien Delattre, an
    apostate to communism who explains that "My
    generation turns to Marx as one swallows acid
    drops to fight off nausea." DeLattre takes satis-
    faction in explicating the traps in Party ideol-
    ogy. When Delattre takes Hydie to a Rally for
    Peace and Progress, Koestler skewers Jean-Paul
    Sartre in the person of Professor Pontieux, au-
    thor of *Negation and Position*, who can "prove
    everything he believes, and believes everything
    he can prove."

6   *The Call Girls: A Tragicomedy with Prologue and
    Epilogue*. London: Hutchinson, 1972.

    The "call girls" of the title are fashionable
    intellectuals--in this case mostly scientists but
    including a poet and a priest--who star on the
    international conference circuit. They meet in a
    Swiss mountain resort and exchange ideas on "ap-
    proaches to survival," a topic chosen by Nikolai
    Solovief, the physicist who organizes the session.
    Little good will is achieved, as the meetings
    become a series of rancorous debates between
    behaviorists and their opponents. Only Nikolai
    himself and Tony, the priest, can reconcile the
    claims of both faith and reason. As a novel of
    ideas, *The Call Girls* effectively dramatizes the
    struggle between the yearning for spirit and the
    inescapability of matter.
    Published in the United States without the
    prologue and the epilogue.
    (See No. 25.)

B

DRAMA

7   *Twilight Bar: An Escapade in Four Acts*. New York:
    Macmillan, 1945.

   Explains in a note that he began this play in 1933
   in Moscow, and soon sold it to the leading theater
   for modern plays in Budapest, but that it was never
   performed because of the political climate. After
   forgetting about the play for eleven years, he re-
   wrote the published version in 1944 when he was
   again trying to escape from reality.

   The Twilight Bar is a little watering hole on any
   island republic at any time, tended by Sam, the bar-
   man, and patronized by such as Glowworm, a poet and
   political columnist. The characters are the regular
   cast of any populist rebellion against capitalist
   oppression: a rich planter named Gonzales; a police
   colonel; Mary, the dynamic young leader of the rebel
   Coolies; a detective inspector; and various platitud-
   inizing Cabinet ministers. The island is visited by
   two strangers from outer space, Alpha and Omega, who
   are an advance party assigned to check on the hospit-
   ability of Earth and the success its inhabitants have
   made of civilization here. The panicked citizens are
   given forty-eight hours to create a reign of peace
   and happiness that will convince the strangers to
   spare the planet. Everything goes well the first day,
   with rapidly rising happiness quotients reported from
   all over the globe, but human greed and meanness gain
   control and things return to normal: i.e., oppression
   and revolution. The play ends with Glowworm and Sam
   pondering life's paradoxes and waiting out the last
   hour before the visitors' judgment on Earth is made
   clear.

C

AUTOBIOGRAPHY

8   *Spanish Testament*. Trans. n.g. London: Victor
     Gollancz, 1937.

Koestler explains in *The Invisible Writing*
(p. 337): "In all foreign editions, including the
American, *Dialogue with Death* appeared as a self-
contained book. In the original edition, however
(Gollancz and Left Book Club, 1937), it formed the
second part of *Spanish Testament*, the first part of
which consisted of the earlier propaganda book on
Spain that I had written for Muenzenburg. *Spanish
Testament* is (and shall remain) out of print.
Dialogue with Death has been re-issued in England
under that title, in the form in which it was
originally written."

CONTENTS

Part I

Part II

Part I. Describes his arrival in Lisbon in August,
1936, where he obtains a visa for Spanish rebel
territory and proceeds to Seville, only to be recognized by a Nazi journalist who knows his liberal
background. Sketches the factors leading to the Civil
War, and gives an account of its beginning. Analyzes
the structure and characteristics of the opposing
military forces, and their ways of treating the
civilians. Comments on German involvement. Discusses
the Catholic Church's role in the war, finding it
split in its support. Summarizes the propaganda an-
nouncements of both sides, noting the many atrocity
reports. Describes reports of fighting in city of
Toledo, judging that the government lost the fight
because of its reluctance to do serious damage to
the city. Describes the damage done to Madrid by
Franco's air attacks, estimating civilian casualties
at 1,000 dead and 2,800 to 3,000 injured between
October 24 and November 19. Stresses the bomb damage
done to art museums, public buildings, and churches
by the bombing. Recounts the fall of Malaga in
February, 1937, including his own personal experiences, which are described more fully in Part Two.
Concludes with the story of his waiting at the house
of Sir Peter Chalmers Mitchell, expecting arrest.
For Part II, *Dialogue with Death,* see No. 8a.

8a   *Dialogue with Death.* Trans. Trevor and Phyllis
      Blewitt. New York: Macmillan, 1952.

Narrates his experiences as a correspondent for
the London *News Chronicle* in the Spanish Civil War,
featuring the story of his capture and imprisonment
under sentence of death by Franco's army. Arrives in
Malaga on January 28, 1937, to find the city heavily
damaged from air and artillery bombardment. Visits
Sir Peter Chalmers-Mitchell in Malaga (see No. 733).
and is with him during the fall of the city to the
rebels on February 8, 1937; they are arrested the
next day in a dramatic scene in which Koestler is
nearly executed on the spot. Witnesses torture of
prisoners in jail. Describes his 102 days in prison
cells, having been transferred to Seville on the
fourth day. Summarizes the small events that con-
stituted prison life: finally getting books to read,
getting shaved, chancing upon a cigarette, etc.,
and learning that he got his way best if he made a
fuss. Analyzes the psychology of the prisoner (e.g.,

"I cannot help looking on the warders as superior
beings").
(See Chapter XXXII, "Arrest," in *The Invisible
Writing*.)

9   *Scum of the Earth*. London: Jonathan Cape, 1941.

An account of his experiences in Europe during
1939-1940. Divided into four books.
Agony. Takes up residence in August, 1939, in a
run-down villa near Monaco with a woman friend
referred to as G. Reacts with great dismay to news
of German-Soviet non-aggression pact, which destroys
the last vestiges of his good feeling about Russia.
Learns of German invasion of Poland on his way with
G. to Paris, where he learns the police are after
him. Spends a month in Paris before his eventual
arrest as an alien.
Purgatory. Confined with other foreigners--"the
scum of Paris"--first in the Roland Garros Stadium
in Paris and then in a camp in Le Vernet near the
Pyrenean frontier, a brutal incarceration site for two
thousand people: "As regards food, accommodation and
hygiene, Vernet was even below the level of Nazi
concentration camps." Released by British influence
on January 17, 1940. This section is particularly
rich in its inventory of the anomalous internees,
with vivid sketches of individuals, and an engrossing study of the psychology and sociology of men
penned up under cruel conditions.
Apocalypse. Returns to Paris, endures a nightmarish
ordeal with bureaucrats in an attempt to renew his
identity card, and finishes *Darkness at Noon*. Arrested again but bluffs his way out. Sneaks out of
Paris and joins the Foreign Legion under false name
in Limoges. Makes arduous passage to Bayonne on
days following armistice, avoiding advancing German
occupational troops, finally marching out to non-
occupied France just ahead of Germans. Separates
from G.
Aftermath. Records day-by-day events as soldiers
wait for demobilization amid extreme confusion and
conflicting rumors. Gets demobilized on August 11,
1940, and makes his way in six weeks via Africa and
Lisbon to London, but does not give details of his
trip. Rejoins G. Attributes the humiliation of
France to its falling behind England and Germany
in industrializing, and its provincial struggle to

preserve the status quo.

Epilogue. A. Letter to Colonel Blimp. Appreciates, even during six weeks' imprisonment in Pentonville, feeling safe for the first time since the war began. Expresses the unity he and his fellow Europeans feel for England: "if one of us dies, the other will be burnt alive with the corpse."
B. Letter to Comrade Blump. Pleads for system combining a planned economy with a democratic polity.
   (In Chapter XXXVII of *The Invisible Writing*, Koestler explains that G. was Daphne Hardy, who translated *Le Zéro et l'Infini* into English.)

10   *The God That Failed.* Ed. Richard Crossman. New York: Harper Brothers; London: Hamish Hamilton, 1949.

   Part I *The Initiates* includes essays by Koestler, Ignazio Silone, and Richard Wright. Part II *Worshipers from Afar* includes essays by André Gide (presented by Dr. Enid Starkie), Louis Fischer, and Stephen Spender. Each essay explains why its author was drawn initially to Communism and why he eventually renounced it.
   Koestler confesses he became a Communist convert "because I was ripe for it and lived in a disintegrating society thirsting for faith." Calls himself a rather typical product of the disillusioned middle class of his time and place, shocked by capitalist tactics to maintain high prices during the depression. Describes his introduction while living in Berlin in 1931 to a Party functionary named Ernst Schneller, who negotiated his Party membership. Recalls the series of events involving von E., a young man under his supervision in the Party, that forced him to resign his position with the Ullstein publishing house. Chronicles the events of 1932 as Communists and Nazis clashed in Berlin. Summarizes his trip to Russia in 1932-1933 and the disillusionment it bred in him. Names the Seventh Congress of the Comintern in 1934, a congress that revitalized the anti-Fascist effort, as a "second honeymoon with the Party" that boosted his faith anew. Realizes after his imprisonment in Spain and escape to England that he has lost his faith, a realization that is clinched by the news of the arrests in Russia of his friends Alex and Eva Weissberg. Resigns from the Party in the spring of 1938.

11   *Arrow in the Blue: An Autobiography (1905-31).*
      London: Collins; Hamish Hamilton; New York:
      Macmillan, 1952.

Part I. Ahor and Babo. 1905-1921. Traces his
early years in Budapest, stressing his lonely childhood and his sense of "Ahor" ("the irrational, archaic Horror") and Ahor's conqueror, "Babo," or the
"Baron in the Bog," a Munchausen character who
grabs himself by the hair of his head and pulls
himself out of a bog. Describes his preoccupation
with math and physics and his subsequent fascination with infinity. "You could shoot a super-arrow
into the blue with a super-force which could carry
it beyond the pull of the earth's gravity, past the
moon, past the sun's attraction--and what then?"
This questing for the Infinite drove him, he says,
to the Promised Land and into the Communist Party.
Recalls the brief period under the Hungarian Commune in 1919. As a counterpart to the Arrow in the
Blue of the Infinite, he develops the Paradox of
the Ego Spiral in which insistent self-consciousness
drives the ego deeper and deeper into the infinite
self.
    Part II. The Arrow Splits. 1922-1926. Provides in
the story of his school years an absorbing account
of the dueling societies at the Technische Hoch-
schule in Vienna: "during those three years, from
seventeen to twenty, and only during those three
years, I was able to enjoy myself without a feeling
of guilt." Describes the two forces of action and
contemplation that he felt pulling at him, explaining that the contemplative moods "dictated the
really important decisions" of his life. The conflicting tugs of these two forces on a Central European of his time make his books "the chart of an
experimental neurosis produced in the laboratory
of our time." Recalls the circumstances of his attraction to Zionism and especially to the influence
of Vladimir Jabotinsky. Abandons engineering studies
with less than a year to go and departs for Palestine in 1926.
    Part III. A Vagabond at Large. 1926-1927. Summar-
izes his unsuccesful attempt at communal life in
Palestine, and the story of his down-and-out days
in Haifa. Odd jobs in Tel Aviv, an aimless existence
ended by an invitation to help edit a newspaper in
Cairo. After the Cairo paper folds quickly, he goes

to Berlin to work for Jabotinsky's Revisionist
movement. Finally gets a job in 1927 with the Ullstein newspaper chain as its Jerusalem correspondent.

Part IV. The Road to Respectability. 1927-1930.
Interviews King Faisal of Iraq; writes prolifically
and very successfully for two years in Jerusalem;
transfers to Paris in July, 1929. Describes Parisian bawdy house of the 1930's, lamenting their
closing in 1946. Returns to Berlin in 1930 as science editor for Ullstein papers, and in 1931 becomes foreign editor of the *B.Z. am Mittag* as well.
Confesses to the "phantom chase" that dominated his
erotic life--a lifelong case of "emotional measles."

Part V. The Road to Marx. 1930-1931. Describes
his conversion to Communism, with sketches of the
two "gurus" who brought him into the Party. Analyzes the psychology of the convert, finding his
own conversion to Communism followed a "typical,
almost conventional pattern of that time." Defends
himself and other converts to Communism in his day:
"To be attracted to the new faith was, I still believe, an honourable error." Sums up the events in
science that destroyed the determinist philosophy
of his youth, and explains how he applied his new
indeterminist views to social behavior. Describes
his first attempts at research into occult phenomena. Recalls vividly his trip to the North Pole as
the only journalist on the *Graf Zeppelin*. Concludes
with his joining the Communist Party on December
31, 1931.

12   *The Invisible Writing: An Autobiography.* London:
      Collins with Hamish Hamilton, 1954.

Carries his life story forward from the day he
joined the Communist Party (December 31, 1931)
through his escape from France to England in the
Fall of 1940. Divides the account into four sections.

Euphoria. Decides--at Party urging--to continue
his journalism, keeping secret his Party membership.
Soon loses his job when he reveals his Party ties.
Describes his Party cell ("one among several thousand in Berlin") and its feuds with the Nazis in
1932. Learns the rules of order governing the Party's closed system, as well as its vocabulary ("a
caricature of the revolutionary spirit"). Masters

the tactics of double-think necessary to Party survival. Recalls his self-abasement in the spirit of romanticizing the proletariat. Expresses contempt for Bertold Brecht. Leaves in July 1932 for a tour of Russia.

Utopia. Witnesses mass famine in the Ukraine. Writes series of censored essays on the Five-Year Plan. Takes long trip through the Caucasus, Armenia, and Turkestan, much of it in the company of Langston Hughes, and observes much of the political and cultural life of the regions. Completes *Red Days*, a book about his trip, but it is heavily censored and published only in German in a small Ukrainian printing. Receives orders--to his relief-- to go to Paris to help in the anti-Fascist propaganda effort. Writes *Bar du Soleil* and leaves Moscow to spend several months in Budapest before going on to Paris in late summer 1933.

Exile. Despairs over the Fascist triumphs of the Thirties and sees himself as a Cassandra. Participates in the machinations of Willy Muenzenberg's propaganda group in Paris as they write the *Brown Book* and conduct a "counter trial" finding Communists innocent in the Reichstag fire and the Nazis themselves guilty. Realizes that he does not want to be a Muenzenberg hack ("I wanted to be an amateur Communist, not a professional") and early in 1934 resigns from his Party job to keep his independence and self-respect. Writes, in part, the first of three books on sexology under the pseudonym Dr. Costler, books which made him but very little money even though they became enormous best sellers and had been commissioned by two of his cousins who ran a publishing house in Budapest. Helps out in a home for children of dead Party members, and writes his first novel (never published). Contemplates suicide after the severe Party criticism of the unpublished novel, but is reinvigorated by a chance to work for the Institute for the Study of Fascism. Continues a lonely, meager life as a refugee in Paris. Teaches himself the discipline of work as the only cure for his manic-depressive mood swings. Resigns from the Institute (which soon closes) as a result of "internal maneuvering." Lives with Dorothy, who became his first wife, and works on his first published novel, *The Gladiators*. Goes to the Saar in late 1934 on Party's orders to edit a comic weekly--

an enterprise that folds after one issue. Spends
1935-36 wandering "like a hobo." Marries Dorothy
in Zurich in March, 1935. Separates from Dorothy
a few months later. Supports himself with prolific
hack writing, living in Budapest while writing the
second sex book under the Dr. Costler pseudonym.
Spends a month on Lake Lugano with Maria Kloepfer,
and reproaches himself afterwards for leaving her
while she was struggling against madness. Spends a
brief period in Paris in 1936 working for a phony
Party news agency.

   The Invisible Writing. Goes to Spain in 1936 at
Muenzenberg's urging and with contrived press
credentials, to snoop for the Party and check on
German and Italian intervention in the Civil War
on Franco's side. Escapes to Gibraltar an hour before a warrant for his arrest is signed in Seville,
after his having been recognized as a Communist.
Goes to Malaga with Gerda Grepp, a Norwegian correspondent; stays with Sir Peter Chalmers-Mitchell
(see No.733) in his house; arrested on February 9,
1937. Suffers imprisonment as recounted in *Dialogue
with Death.* Describes his psychological state while
imprisoned in Seville, stressing the mystical peace
he arrived at. Rejects utilitarian ethics and comes
to believe in an occult dimension, a text for life
written in invisible ink. Rejoins his estranged
wife, Dorothy, in England for several months after
release from prison in Seville. Meets Thomas Mann
in Switzerland, finding him lacking in human
warmth. Visits parents in Belgrade. Goes to Greece
and Palestine on intelligence-gathering mission
for the Party. Early in 1938 makes lecture tour in
England for the Left Book Club. Delivers heretical
speech in Paris in spring of 1938, alienating Party
members, and soon resigns from Party. Completes *The
Gladiators* in July, 1938, and begins writing *Darkness at Noon.* Later reads General Krivitsky's *I Was
Stalin's Agent* and is struck by similarities to
Darkness at Noon. Visits Freud in London. Edits
for a few months in 1938-39 a German weekly, *Die
Zukunft,* in Paris. Suffers the internment in France
described in *Scum of the Earth;* gets back to England and is interned in Pentonville for six weeks.

D

BOOKS AND COLLECTIONS OF ESSAYS

13   *The Yogi and the Commissar and Other Essays (1941-45)*. London: Jonathan Cape, 1945.

"The Yogi and the Commissar." Places the Yogi—who believes in change from within, values only means and ignores ends, and practices mysticism—on the opposite end of the political spectrum from the Commissar, who attempts change from without, argues that the end justifies the means, and approaches life through utilitarian logic. Perceives in history patterns of displacement back and forth across the spectrum defined by their two positions.

"The French 'Flu." Diagnoses the French 'flu as the typical British reader's uncritical acceptance of a work of literature if it comes from France. Deplores Gide for his "arrogant spiritualism," Louis Aragon for his preciosity, and Vercors for "a mixture of inferiority complex and arrogance" in *Le Silence de la Mer*.

"The Novelist's Temptations." Warns novelists against (1) shutting out the world, (2) becoming too involved in it, and (3) limiting themselves to a restricted view of it.

"The Reader's Dilemma." Advises "Corporal Jeff" on how to read the periodical reviews, defining as "the main and ultimate task of socialism" the creation of a society in which there is no longer an educated elite separated by a wall from the educated working class. Warns against the temptation of anti-intellectualism ("Your opponent is not the highbrow, but the rich") and urges reading only for pleasure.

"The Great Crank." A profile of Hitler as Crank, figured as a key which met the right kind of lock in his country's "embittered populace."

"In Memory of Richard Hillary." Explores the significance of the death at 23 of Richard Hillary, the pilot and author of *The Last Enemy*, who insisted on flying again even after being grotesquely maimed in combat. "When all isms become meaningless and the world an alley of crooked query-marks, then indeed a man's longing for the Holy Grail may become so strong that he flies like a moth into the flame; and having burned his wings, crawls back into it again."

"The Intelligentsia." Ascribes the formation of an intelligentsia to a social process beginning with the French Revolution. Poses the question of how true progressive movements "invariably find the right ideology waiting for them at the right moment." Answers that political economy and cultural development are two aspects of the same basic process. Diagnoses neurosis as a "professional disease" among the intelligentsia.

"Scum of the Earth--1942." (Not included in the Danube edition; see Macmillan edition.) Looks back on his experiences two years earlier in the French concentration camp at Le Vernet. Recounts the fate of the inmates after the camp was turned over to the Nazis: extradition to the Gestapo or deportation into the Sahara. "And crusaders they were, the pride and the heroes of a declining Continent, pioneers in the fight to safeguard the dignity of man."

"On Disbelieving Atrocities." Speculates on the psychology underlying the human inability to connect the accounts of atrocities to their daily lives. Recommends two minutes a day of silent concentration on evil.

"Knights in Rusty Armour." Judges that "the coming victory will be a conservative victory and lead to a conservative peace," but that the "knights in rusty armour" will finally be on the winning side. Holds out hope for the future.

"The Fraternity of Pessimists." Laments the
collapse of "horizontal structures," of Socialism's missed opportunities, but predicts a revival of "horizontalism" in "an irresistible global
mood" marked by renewed "balance between rational
and spiritual values."

"Le Roi est Mort...." (Not included in the Danube
edition; see Macmillan edition.) Warns that Fascism
won't die with Hitler and that constitutional guarantees do not warrant complacency.

"Anatomy of a Myth." Accuses political science
of ignoring the irrational elements in human behavior. Finds that the "irrational craving for an
Absolute" that marked pre-nineteenth-century revolutionary movements was neglected by the founders
of modern socialism, and that this craving made its
inevitable return after World War I in Fascism and
the Soviet myth. Describes Soviet Russia as the
revival of an archetype previously expressed in the
Golden Age, the Land of Promise, and the Kingdom of
Heaven.

"Soviet Myth and Reality." Identifies six defensive measures adopted by Soviet leaders to perpetu-
ate the Soviet myth, and exposes the reality behind
each one. Seeks to discover whether the Soviet system is really socialistic or not. The defensive
measures are:
   (1) A "deafening propaganda barrage." The Russian
victory at Stalingrad, for instance, which was pub-
licized as evidence of the superiority of the Soviet
system.
   (2) Camouflage or denial of facts. Cites the
famine in the Ukraine in 1932-33, a tragedy that
he witnessed while living in Kharkov.
   (3) The doctrine of "esoteric" and "exoteric"
truth. "Official statements which sound too fantastic to the Western mind are justified as being
aimed at home consumption only, with a reference
to the backwardness of the Russian masses. E.g.:
Zinoviev an agent of the British Intelligence
Service."
   (4) Distinction between socialist strategy and
tactics. Any act that seems reactionary is explained
away as a "temporary expedient."

(5) The end justifies the means.

(6) The doctrine of the unshaken foundations. The argument that failures and weaknesses are surface phenomena only, and that the "fundamentally progressive nature" of the Soviet Union remains sound and healthy.

Koestler gives detailed evidence of inequalities among classes, revealing the Soviet Union's failure to achieve socialist equality despite nationalization of the means of production and the institutionalization of state planning. He concludes that the Russian Revolution failed to produce the much hoped-for new human society."The ultimate reason for its failure was the arid nineteenth-century materialism of its doctrine. It had to fall back on the old opiates because it did not recognise man's need for spiritual nourishment."

"The End of an Illusion." Continues the discussion begun in "Soviet Myth and Reality," defining Soviet Russia as "a State-capitalistic totalitarian autocracy." Explains that Russian power politics is energized by contempt for bourgeois ethics and its capacity for forming working alliances whereever it is to the state's advantage. Outlines the severe measures the Soviets took to nullify independent socialist movements, mainly the mass deportations of political activists. Predicts continued Soviet expansion: "the demarcation line between the Russian and Western zones of influence has already shifted from the Vistula to the Elbe; from the Black Sea to the Adriatic and Mediterranean, from east of Warsaw to west of Prague." Anticipates that socialists will have to wean themselves of their devotion to Russia.

"The Yogi and the Commissar." Reviews the history of the antinomy of freedom and determinism and recapitulates much of current knowledge in experimental embryology. Concludes with a cataloging of "degenerated" ethical systems deriving from the confusion of mixing levels of understanding.

14 *Insight and Outlook: An Inquiry into the Common
    Foundations of Science, Art, and Social Ethics.*
    New York and London: Macmillan, 1949.

TABLE OF CONTENTS

Appendix I A Note on Nature and the Visual Arts
Appendix II Other Theories of the Comic: Bergson
            and Freud

States his two aims: (1) "to present a unifying
theory of humour, art and discovery," and (2) to
propose an ethical system "derived from the same
integrative tendency in the evolutionary process
to which the creative activities of art and discovery are traced."
    Part One. The Comic. Describes laughter as a
spontaneous "luxury reflex," a "specifically human
property," like weeping. Defines the "cognitive
geometry" of jokes as two intersecting streams of
associated ideas. Develops his notion of an "operative field," or a "system of mental processes acquired by habit," and introduces the concept of
bisociation as a link between operative fields in
humor, art, and discovery. Surveys theories of
humor, finding malice and self-assertion common to
them. Agrees with Herbert Spencer that laughter is
a way of discharging nervous energy, often "emotion
cast off by the intellect." Declares that laughter
signifies "man's departure from the rails of instinct." Piles up examples of bisociation in form
and function, form and content, etc.
    Part Two. Self-Assertion and Self-Transcendence.
Identifies seven situations in which we cry, and
defines crying as "a discharge reflex for redundant
or frustrated self-transcending emotions." Dismisses
Freud's Eros and Thanatos as "biological novelties
which only appear at a relatively high level of
complexity." Discovers only one fundamental principle applicable to all biology: "the polarity be-
teen the integrative and self-assertive tendencies."
Explores parallels between social and biological
behavior, anticipating the discipline of sociobiol-
ogy: "Sooner or later biology and sociology...will
appear as branches, or rather levels, of one discipline...." Traces what is known of the way children and primitive peoples achieve self-transcendence:
perceptual projection, empathy, the altruism that is
an aspect of group psychology, and extra-sensory
perception. Contends that the nineteenth century
stressed the self-assertive over the self-transcending emotions, and analyzes in detail the psychological and physiological processes involved in their
interrelationships. Rejects the conservative Freudian

thesis that civilization is achieved at the cost of
human happiness, and denounces the notion of harmful "instinct-renunciation." Asserts the wrongheadedness of Freud's vision of civilized achievements
as substitutes for "goal-inhibited sexual desire,"
finding instead that history discloses a "general
tendency towards higher integration." Counters
Freudian theory with these arguments: (1) destructive
behavior is not instinctive, (2) the sexual drive is
only a branch of the integrative tendency, and (3)
"the processes of the sublimation and internalization
of impulses are continuous with biological evolution."
Clears the way for much of his argument with the conclusion that "the amount and type of discontent in a
given civilization is determined by specific conditions, and is not an inherent consequence of social
evolution as such." Offers the aspiration to self-
transcendence of Eastern philosophies as proof of
their being basic to human nature, while having their
own drawbacks in "intellectual stagnation and social
resignation." Interprets the "Western crisis" (characterized by "ruthless competition, war, and political fanaticism") as products of environmental stress
brought on by rapid social change, not as evidence
of a destructive instinct. Rejects rationalism, optimism, and utilitarianism as agents of social regeneration, discovering them lacking in anything for the
self-transcending tendencies to fasten on.

Part Three. The Neutral Arts: Invention and Discovery. Seeks to apply the findings in Part Two about
the quality of emotions to those of Part One on the
creative mental processes. Defines the "exploratory
drive" as a well-balanced mixture of self-assertive-
ness and self-transcendence. Traces the bisociations
made by Darwin as he worked out his own "Eureka process" with natural selection. Finds a challenge for
education in the need to make students relive important bisociative discoveries.

Part Four. The Emotive Arts. Elaborates the many
diverse bisociative acts that he identifies in
aesthetic experience. Traces the bisociations common in illusion to primitive worship practices, calling artistic illusion "the most important vehicle
of self-transcendence." Details the importance to
metaphor, simile, and poetic imagery of originality,
implicitness, and relevance. Stresses the way particular metaphors work by "grounding," that is, by
relating the particular to the universal. Speculates

interestingly on the manic speech of patients enduring brain surgery, and the relation of their
speech to creative speech. Compares the scientist's
exploratory drive with the poet's creative stress:
the scientist resolves his tension via the eureka
process, the poet his by regressing into "more primitive fields of expression." Sums up: "Poetic experience is a bisociation of fields of ideational
content and rhythmic pattern. The content itself is
the product of a fusion of abstract ideation with
sensory imagery, rooted in the archetypal layers of
the past. The implicit rhythmic pattern focuses conscious attention and draws it into the vortex of
even more archaic forms of experience." Lists numerous archetypal conflicts common in literature, and
explicates the death and rebirth archetype (the
"Night Journey") in terms of absorption in the
"Trivial Plane" followed by emergence on to the
"Tragic Plane."

15 *Promise and Fulfillment: Palestine 1917-1949.*
    New York and London: Macmillan, 1949.

    Divided into three books: "Background," Close-Up,"
and "Perspective."
    BACKGROUND. Part One: "Conception and Gestation
(1917-1939)." Accepts that Palestine belonged to the
Arabs who lived there: "the country was no doubt
'theirs' in the generally accepted sense of the
word." Judges the "romantic" notion of a "National
Home" a political absurdity impossible to administer.
Describes the muddle that resulted: the British were
more like the Arabs in temperament and the Arabs
often came to feel they had tacit British support
for their actions. Assesses eloquently the concept
of "historic justice," finding it a function of two
variables: "the point in time chosen, and the criteria of value applied." Concludes that the injustice
done to Palestinian Arabs remains an "undeniable
fact" but "a relatively mild injustice compared with
historical precedents." Stresses that Arabs sold land
freely to Jews, who then led the way to great increases in prosperity, including agriculture, hous-
ing, and health care; but notes the Jews' rigidity
and self-righteousness made difficult the later
development of the State of Israel. Concludes that
"It was a fair and humane conquest, but a conquest
nevertheless." Denies that Jewish High Finance

provided the money for land purchases, insisting it came instead from contributions by the Jewish masses all over the world.

BACKGROUND. Part Two. "Suspense (1939-1945)." Condemns the Chamberlain White Paper of 1939 but insists it be seen in the context of the time. Recounts the harrowing story of the many ships bringing refugees to Palestine, only to be turned back with their helpless cargoes, and attributes the rise of terrorism to this tragic policy. Surveys the rise of Haganah, the Jewish defense army, stressing the duplicitousness of British policy in ignoring the Haganah at times, prosecuting it at others, and secretly using it in the war at still others. Identifies the origin of terrorism in Irgun and the Stern Gang, both of whom were unofficially fought by Haganah until late 1945.

BACKGROUND. Part Three. "The Birth Pangs (1945-1948)." Summarizes the terrible plight of the 700,000 surviving Jews in Europe--Displaced Persons. Traces the evasiveness and betrayal of Bevin and the British Labour Party in denying Jews entry into Palestine in post-war years, a policy that led to disaster for the British. Argues that Labour's post-war policy change toward Palestine was not prompted by expediency but rather by the Foreign Secretary's "irrational bias." Gives examples of the ruthlessness of both the British government and the Jewish terrorists, noting that "Without Mr. Bevin there would probably be no State of Israel today." Disentangles the confusion surrounding the U.N. vote for the partition of Palestine, and laments the viciousness of the last phase of Anglo-Jewish fighting. Sketches the main events in the Civil War of 1948. Spells out the ways by which the British deliberately dismantled Palestine before leaving--suspending postal service, destroying equipment, etc. Blames Bevin's "determination to destroy Zionism" for the total collapse of Britain's Arab policy.

CLOSE-UP. Based on diary entries from June 4, 1948, till the next June, beginning with his impressions of life in the new-born State of Israel and full of sharp observations on the psychological and sociological effects of war. Tells the story of the Israelis' capture of Safed from the Arabs, and in a chapter on "David and Goliath" narrates in vivid detail the courage and initiative of the underdog

Israelis in defending against attacks on such settle-
ments as Dagania, Ein Geb, Ramat Naphtali, and
Sha'ar Hagolan. Notes that the only effective Arab
fighting force was the Transjordan Legion, trained,
equipped, and led by British officers. "Had it been
withdrawn from the battlefield the war in Palestine
would have been over in a week." Gives, all in all,
a picture of Israeli heroism that compels great ad-
miration. Describes his visit to Jerusalem and of
the chaos there during its period under siege. Un-
ravels the story of the dissolution of Irgun after
the government trap sprung on them during the at-
tempted unloading of the arms-laden *Altalena*, concluding that the event served Ben Gurion's government by making Irgun the whipping-boy in Israel's
need to breach the truce to protect itself. Summarizes the moral issues in Israeli terrorism by carefully separating Irgun from the ruthless Stern Gang
and judging its actions--with two exceptions--morally
defensible under the dictum that the End justifies
the Means within certain narrow limits; concludes
that Irgun often became scapegoats for Haganah and
that the government's position was stiff and ungen-
erous toward Irgun. Reveals his impatience with the
tone adopted by much of the Israeli hierarchy--as in
his comment on Ben Gurion's "cultural claustrophilia"
being "perhaps the most general common denominator of
the population of Israel." Provides throughout the
section a rich series of impressions of life in the
new State of Israel.

PERSPECTIVE. Notes the difficulties of creating a
social pyramid "from the top downward": that is,
turning "middlemen, petty traders and social para-
sites, with a crust of intellectuals," into a "normal
social pyramid with a broad base of farmers and man-
ual workers." Explains the workings of the anomalous
Histadruth, or General Federation of Labour: "both a
Trade Union and the greatest single capitalist em-
ployer in Israel." Analyzes the roles played by the
different Israeli political parties, especially the
Labour Party and the United Workers' Party. Comments
on the problems involved in establishing Hebrew as a
national language, and advocates latinization of the
"cumbersome" alphabet. Expresses dismay over his
perception that Israel is "under the sway of cleri-
calism to a degree unequalled in any other country
of our contemporary world."

16   *The Trail of the Dinosaur and Other Essays (1945-*
      1954). London: Collins; New York: Macmillan, 1954.

Koestler says that these essays mark "a farewell
to politics and a return to my earlier interests, as
a student, in psychology and the sciences of life."
They also trace, he adds, his "evolution" from left
to right.

"The Challenge of Our Time." Defines the challenge
of the time as "the conflict between expediency and
morality," reiterating his much-discussed problem
of the Ends vs. the Means. Admits that "a certain
admixture of ruthlessness is inseparable from human
progress," but will allow the End to justify the
Means only within very narrow limits. "I am not sure
whether what the philosophers call ethical absolutes
exist, but I am sure that we have to act as if they
existed."

"A Way to Fight Suspicion." (Not in the Danube
edition.) Explains that the Soviet need to conceal
Western prosperity from its own people led to an
information blackout that inevitably bred suspicion
of the West. Urges the Western Powers to demand
psychological disarmament of the Russians, encourag-
ing free circulation of information and abolishment
of travel restrictions.

"Land of Virtue and Gloom." Decides the Labour
Government has failed to provide any inspiration or
sense of a new era.

"Land of Bread and Wine." Claims that France's
post-war recovery will have to be in the framework
of an economically integrated Western Europe.

"The Candles of Truth." Maintains that the dangers
of war would be much reduced if everybody had access
to Soviet reality. Urges publishers and editors of
the Left to "awaken to their responsibilities" and
dispel the "pink fog of half-truths."

"The Seven Deadly Fallacies." Enumerates his list
of seven deadly fallacies. (1) The confusion of
Left and East. Reminds that Liberals are not all
alike, and that the Soviet Union is not a socialist
country. (2) The soul-searching fallacy: Refusing

to resist Russian aggression because our own hands
are not completely clean. (3) The fallacy of the
false equation: Equating Soviet totalitarianism and
American imperialism. (4) The anti-anti attitude.
This is the mistake of not wanting to be identified
with anti-Communist witch-hunting. (5) The sentimental fallacy. After struggling with Communists
against Nazis for years, it is hard to give up past
loyalties. (6) The fallacy of the perfect cause.
It is a mistaken notion that "Only absolutely clean
hands have a right to reach out to protect and save
what remains of Europe." (7) The confusion between
short-term and long-term aims.

"Chambers, the Villain." Assumes Alger Hiss's
guilt ("though I believe he did what he is accused
of, I see it in the light of his then decent motives"). Defends Whittaker Chambers, an "unfrocked
priest," for performing "a service of great social
utility."

"The Little Flirts of St. Germain des Près." The
"little flirts" are the "pink intellectuals." They
are "the semi-virgins of totalitarian flirtations;
the Peeping Toms who watch History's debauches
through a hole in the wall; the *tricoteuses*, dili-
gently knitting their novels and editorials in the
shadow of the Lubianka." Praises Manes Sperber's
novel *Et Le Buisson Devint Cendre* (1949).
(Not in the Danube edition.)

"An Anatomy of Snobbery." Suggests that the essence
of cultural snobbery is "unconsciously applying to
any given field a judgment derived from an alien
system of values" (e.g., judging a painting by the
fame of its creator, not by its innate aesthetic
qualities). Argues that all appreciation of art has
a legitimate element of thrilling to the work's context, but that allowing the context to dominate one's
response constitutes snobbery. Perceives the root of
social snobbery to lie in the need to improve one's
standing in history by association with those who
make it. (Not in the Danube edition.)

"The Future of the Novel." Identifies archetypes
as constant factors, the culture of the time as a
variable in novels. Predicts more "Realism, Relevance,
Rhythm" in the novel, and finds the British novel

falling behind the French in realism and relevance, and behind the American in realism and rhythm.

"A Rebel's Progress: To George Orwell's Death." "Thus, the greater the distance from intimacy and the wider the radius of the circle, the more warming became the radiations of this lonely man's great power of love."

"Judah at the Crossroads: An Exhortation." "This essay follows to their conclusion certain thoughts and suggestions tentatively expressed in *Promise and Fulfilment*." Argues broadly that Jews should choose between assimilation and migration to Israel. Quotes from letters and editorials that attack him for his position. Insists that "Ethnic assimilation is impossible with maintaining the Mosaic faith; and the Mosaic faith becomes untenable with ethnic assimilation." Concludes that there is only "a small and somewhat hypothetical 'hard core' of Jewish characteristics in the sense of biological heredity, and a vast complex of physical and mental character- istics which are of environmental origin and trans- mitted through social inheritance." Asserts that the Jew's conviction that God speaks to him directly and specially is "a metaphysical snobbery based on gene- alogical assumptions as untenable as Houston Stewart Chamberlain's myth of the Nordic Man." Rejects Isaiah Berlin's contention that there are irrational but universally human motives built into the Jewish in- sistence on a special identity ("you must grant the same right to their adversaries").

"The Boredom of Fantasy." Describes the rise of the "new craze for science fiction" in the United States, judging it as at least partly a symptom of atomic-age malaise. Doubts that science fiction ("good entertainment") will ever grow into the lit- erature of the future. Believes that science fiction is literature only to the extent that it is not science fiction.

"The Shadow of a Tree." A futuristic fantasy set in a Russia that has been defeated in a world war.

"The Right to Say 'No': Four Contributions to the
Congress for Cultural Freedom." Writes a manifesto
enunciating fourteen points defining freedom. Berates
the 'moderate Left' for not having been outspoken
against Soviet Communism ("McCarthyism represents the
wages of the American liberals' sins"). Surveys the
variety of ideologies calling themselves Socialist,
finding that "Socialism has lost its claim to represent the internationalist trend of humanity." Asserts
that the antinomy between Capitalism and Socialism
"is rapidly becoming as antiquated and meaningless
as the dispute between Jansenists and Jesuits or the
War of the Roses." Identifies the new set of choices
as "total tyranny against relative freedom."

"The European Legion." Expresses pessimism about
the condition of Western Europe, and proposes a pan-
European elite military force, the "Legion of Liberty." (Not in the Danube edition.)

"A Guide to Political Neuroses." Warns against
believing that individuals are rational in their
political behavior: "our political libido is just
as complex-ridden, repressed and twisted" as our
sexual libido. Identifies in post-war Germans a
"neurosis" of collective guilt, and a repression of
German atrocities that has to be brought out in the
memory if a cure is to be effected. The French
evince a collective amnesia that promotes the com-
fortable delusion that they were more heroic during
the occupation in World War II than they really were.
Diagnoses the British neurosis as "escape from
reality," pretending for too long that Hitler was
up to nothing and repeating the mistake with Stalin.
Finds a number of analogies between sexual and political neuroses: flag fetishism, the eternal adoles-
cence of some aging radicals (Sartre's sect at *Les
Temps Modernes* is characterized as "incestuous"),
the "nymphomaniac" of a busybody on every "progressive" committee, and the masochist "whose self-
hatred and craving for self-punishment has turned
into hatred for his country or social class." Sums
up with the observation that twentieth-century man's
political neurosis comes from his lack of metaphysical security.

"The Trail of the Dinosaur." Points to an unprece-
dented recent surge in the range and power of man's
sensory and motor organs, accompanied by a "marked
deterioration" in spiritual maturity and social
ethics; sees this as alarming. Surveys the options
available for defending against atomic aggression.
Recommends a "quasi pan-European army with a pan-
European spirit and flag." Argues that a new spiritual climate is necessary, along with a balance of
military power, if peace is to endure. Traces the
rise since the Renaissance of the split between the
spiritual and the empirical sensibilities, expressing
hope they will eventually be rejoined. "The next few
decades, or the next half century at the outmost,
will decide whether *homo sapiens* will go the way of
the dinosaur, or mutate towards a stabler future."

17   *Reflections on Hanging*. London: Gollancz, 1956.

TABLE OF CONTENTS

Part One: Tradition and Prejudice. Notes the strong
support for capital punishment in English history,
stressing that around 1800 the so-called "Bloody
Code" applied to over two hundred offenses, many of
them as innocuous as stealing turnips and associating
with gypsies. Finds this code rooted in the popular-
ity of grisly public executions in the eighteenth
century. ("According to Lord Templewood, there were
about one hundred public executions a year in London
and Middlesex alone.") Stresses the carnival atmos-
phere of the public hangings, calling them "a kind
of medieval St. Vitus's dance." ("For distinguished

onlookers grandstands were erected as at contemporary
football games.") Documents the cruelty of the spec-
tacles in which the hangman often botched his work so
that some victims had to be hanged two or even three
times. Offers examples of the unusual cruelty of the
executions of children. Traces the origin of the
Bloody Code to (1) England's lead in the Industrial
Revolution, (2) the English tradition of civil rights
that made Englishmen wary of an effective police force,
and (3) the English Common Law that fostered a hide-
bound class "with the authority of oracles" and devoted to established precedents. "Faced by the choice
between the cop and the hangman, England chose the
hangman." Cites the first Reform Bill (1832) as the
decisive revolt against capital punishment, when the
number of capital statutes was reduced from 220-odd
to fifteen, and praises Samuel Romilly for his en-
lightened role in the struggle for abolition of the
death penalty. Identifies a major dilemma associated
with capital punishment: "Whenever social progress
outpaces the Law, so that its penalties appear dis-
proportionately severe to the public conscience, juries
become reluctant to convict, and reprieves, instead of
being an exceptional act of mercy, become virtually
the rule, so that only a small proportion of the sen-
tences are actually carried out and the threat accord-
ingly loses its deterrent effect." Indicts the "oracles" of the Common Law—Sir Edward Coke, Sir William
Blackstone, et al.—as the chief causes of the endurance of the harsh tradition of capital punishment.
("The history of English criminal law is a wonderland
filled with the braying of learned asses.") Attacks
the argument that capital punishment deters others
from committing murder, citing the dates on which many
other countries and American states abolished the
death penalty and quoting the conclusion of the British
Parliamentary Select Committee of 1929-30 that "capital punishment may be abolished in this country without
endangering life or property, or impairing the security
of Society." Rejects the claims that statistics are
unreliable and that foreign experience does not apply.
  Part Two. The Law. Reviews the cases of capital punishment of animals: "The last recorded case is the
trial and execution of a dog for having participated
in a robbery and murder, in Délémont, Switzerland,
1906." Tells the story of "Donald Martin" and why and
how he came to murder his wife in 1950, using the case
as an example of the illogicality of the laws; even

though Martin's act met all the requirements of the definition of murder, all involved concurred in having him detained as insane. Analyzes at length the philosophical issues raised about free will and determinism, concluding that the law relating to capital punishment "could only be reformed at the price of undermining the concept of criminal responsibility by such deterministic notions as 'irresistible impulse' or 'diminished responsibility'--that is, *by making determinism statutory*, as it were." States his own position on free will: "I believe in the unprovable existence of a factor *x*: an order of reality beyond physical causation, about whose nature only a negative statement is possible: namely, that in its domain the present is *not* determined by the past." Lists and discusses the main sources of error in murder trials: "(a) fallibility of witnesses; (b) fallibility of experts; (c) coincidence; (d) to (h) fallibility of juries, judges, appeal judges and Home Secretaries; (i) carelessness of solicitors and counsel; (j) unworkability of the M'Naghten rules."

Part Three. The End of the Nightmare. Rejects vigorously the usual euphemistic accounts of the actual execution procedures, insisting that "nightmare scenes are not exceptional." Identifies public opinion as giving the greatest support to the death penalty, citing its ignorance, prejudice, and repressed cruelty. Concludes with a plea for charity--defined as a mixture of humility and imagination.

18 *The Sleepwalkers: A History of Man's Changing Vision of the Universe.* London: Hutchinson; New York: Macmillan, 1959.

(Versions entitled *The Watershed* are the Kepler chapters published separately.)

Offers a "personal and speculative account of a controversial subject" developed around two major *leitmotifs*: a history of the long relationship between science and religion, and the role of the discovery process in creative thought ("the manner in which some of the most important individual discoveries were arrived at reminds one more of a sleepwalker's performance than an electronic brain's").

Part One: The Heroic Age.

I. Dawn. Notes accomplishments in astronomy of the Babylonians and Egyptians (e.g., the belt of the Zodiac); stresses the speculative insights of the

Ionians of the sixth century B.C.: Thales of Miletos,
Anaximander (the notion of an infinite universe), and
Anaximenes. Despite the diversity of their theories,
each sought explanations rooted in natural causes.

II. The Harmony of the Spheres. Praises Pythagoras
("the founder of Science") for his unifying vision
of the wholeness of all knowledge, of the balance
and order of the creation as revealed in mathematics.
Finds in Pythagorean number mysticism a union of
religious fervor and intellectual excitement that
after several centuries dissolved with unfortunate
results for civilization.

III. The Earth Adrift. Stresses that Aristarchus
taught in the third century B.C. that the universe
is heliocentric.

IV. The Failure of Nerve. Emphasizes the historical
importance of Plato's "doctrine that the world is a
copy of models in heaven," and especially of his
teaching that the world is shaped like a perfect
sphere, and all heavenly objects travel in perfect
circles at uniform speed. Explains Aristotle's contribution to cosmology as the reassertion of the
concept of a universe of nine heavenly spheres, with
God, the Prime Mover, on the outside spinning the
world; and with the earth and moon consigned to the
sub-lunary region subject to the corruptions of
mutability. Koestler's final word on Aristotle and
Plato is severe, as he speaks of their "throwing
grotesque shadows which are to haunt mankind for a
thousand years and more."

V. The Divorce from Reality. Describes the Ptolemaic
universe ("the work of a pedant with much patience
and little originality"), charging the Greeks with
inventing hypotheses merely "to explain away the
scandal of non-circular motions in the sky." Thus,
the "myth of the perfect circle" crippled astronomers
for centuries.

Part Two: Dark Interlude.

I. The Rectangular Universe. Quotes St. Augustine
in illustration of Christianity's repression of scientific knowledge. "Thus by the eleventh century
A.D., a view of the universe had been achieved
roughly corresponding to that of the fifth century
B.C."

II. The Walled-In Universe. Argues that through
much of the Middle Ages a split mentality governed
thought: a pious a priori teaching derived from the
church alongside a rough practical understanding
based on observation. Medieval cosmology reveals
much about the age: "the projections of its conflicts, prejudices and specific ways of double-
think onto the graceful sky."

III. The Universe of the Schoolmen. Sums up medieval obstacles hindering science: (1) the mental
split; (2) the geocentric dogma; (3) the dogma of
uniform motion in perfect circles; (4) separation
of science and mathematics; (5) the failure to grasp
that moving bodies tend to remain in motion.

Part Three. The Timid Canon.

I. The Life of Copernicus. Sketches Copernicus's
life, attributing his reluctance to publish his
heliocentric theory to his fear of ridicule. Summarizes the role of Rheticus in getting Copernicus's
theories into print, concluding that Copernicus knew
about the preface that Osiander wrote for *On the
Revolutions of the Heavenly Spheres*. Makes much of
the eccentricity and passion for secrecy of Copernicus: "In the Frankonian local dialect, '*Koepper-
neksch*' still means a far-fetched, cockeyed proposition."

II. The System of Copernicus. Analyzes the *Revolutions*, noting its "supreme unreadability" that made
it "an all-time worst seller." Explodes the common
assumption that Copernicus reduced the number of epi-
cycles from what Ptolemy's system required: Ptolemy's
system had forty, not eighty, as Copernicus claimed,
and Copernicus's system demanded forty-eight. Concludes that "the Copernican system (as opposed to
the heliocentric idea) is hardly worth bothering
about." Explains that the *Revolutions* opens with an
account of a finite sun-centered universe, but that
by the end of the book "there is hardly anything left
of the original doctrine." The earth eventually circles around a point in space; thus, the Copernican
system was "vacuocentric" instead of truly heliocentric. The result was "a confused nightmare." Concludes several things from this summary. (1) Copernicus was too timid in his respect for authority
(Kepler said, "Copernicus tried to interpret Ptolemy
rather than nature"). (2) Doubts about his system
reinforced Copernicus's fear of ridicule and made

him reluctant to publish. (3) Despite his inconsistencies, it is Copernicus's "lasting merit" that he was the first to develop the heliocentric universe with a comprehensive system. (4) Copernicus "unwittingly" destroyed the Aristotelian vision of a centralized universe with a fixed up and down, for the Copernican system "has no natural center of orientation to which everything else can be referred."

Part Four. The Watershed.
I. The Young Kepler. Traces admiringly the early life of Johannes Kepler.
II. The Cosmic Mystery. Reconstructs the fascinating story of Kepler's obsession with the five perfect solids (tetrahedron, cube, octahedron, dodecahedron, icosahedron) and his conviction that the spheres (orbits) of the five planets (Saturn, Jupiter, Earth, Venus, Mercury) nested in an elaborate construction of spheres within spheres, each circumscribing one of the perfect solids. Stresses that in a second edition of *Mysterium Cosmographicum* published twenty-five years later Kepler still reveals an attachment to this conceit; this "misguided belief" even worked as "the spur of his immortal achievements." Summarizes the *Mysterium*, showing that part one develops "fantastic" a priori deductions that give way in part two to serious observation: "Without transition, in a single startling jump, we have traversed the frontier between metaphysical and empirical science." Makes these points about the *Mysterium*: (1) it reaffirms the heliocentric system, rejecting Copernicus's teaching that the center of the world is the center of the earth's orbit; (2) it speaks of a "force emanating from the sun" that drives the planets along their paths; (3) it rejects Aristotle and embraces Pythagoras and Plato in restoring to the sun all the "mystic attributes and physical powers" of the universe.
III. Growing Pains. Gives an account of Kepler's marriage and of his introduction to Tycho de Brahe.
IV. Tycho de Brahe. Sketches the successful career of Tycho, focusing on the large body of precise astronomical measurements he had accumulated and which were so necessary to Kepler.
V. Tycho and Kepler. Describes the friction between Tycho and Kepler during their association at Tycho's quarters in Benatek: Tycho's bullying and Kepler's inability to get the astronomical data hoarded by Tycho.

VI. The Giving of the Laws. Extremely important chapter. Follows the complicated series of steps that led to the discovery of Kepler's first two laws and the writing of his magnum opus, *New Astronomy*. Seeking to discover the orbit of Mars, Kepler made three "revolutionary innovations": he anticipated Newton in identifying the two forces acting on each planet (the force of the sun--what we call gravity--and a force in the planet itself--what we call inertia), leading to his treating the sun as both the physical and the geometrical center of his system; he dismissed the Ptolemaic-Copernican claim that the plane of Mars oscillates in space, proving that the angle between the planes of Mars and Earth stays always at one degree and fifty minutes; he rejected the traditional belief in the uniform speed of planets. Using Tycho's measurements, Kepler then analyzed the orbit of Mars in nine hundred folio pages of small handwriting, only to find out that he was wrong. He threw out his theory because it produced a discrepancy of an eight-minute arc with the observed positions, an act which Koestler says began a "new era" in the history of thought. Importantly, "It was *his introduction of physical causality into the formal geometry of the skies* which made it impossible for him to ignore the eight minutes arc." Koestler outlines the sequence of false starts leading to Kepler's formulation of the Second Law, a story that provides rich support for Koestler's thesis: "It is perhaps the most amazing sleepwalking performance in the history of science...." The steps in the discovery of the First Law are just as amazing: Kepler stumbled by chance onto the elliptical orbit of Mars ("I felt as if I had been awakened from a sleep"). "*But he still did not realize that this formula specifically defined the orbit as an ellipse*." Koestler's observations are provocative. Speaking of the saturation of Kepler's unconscious with all the problems of the Martian orbit, he speculates, "It is perhaps this intermittent flicker of an overall vision which accounts for the mutually compensatory nature of Kepler's mistakes, as if some balancing reflex or 'backfeed' mechanism had been at work in his unconscious mind."

VII. Kepler Depressed. Recounts Kepler's difficulties in publishing the *New Astronomy*.

VIII. Kepler and Galileo. Debunks the popular understanding of Galileo's accomplishments: "the fame of this outstanding genius rests mostly on discoveries he never made, and on feats he never performed." Credits Galileo with founding the modern science of dynamics, which "provided the indispensable complement to Kepler's laws for Newton's universe." Traces the early relationship between Kepler and Galileo, making clear that Galileo believed early in a heliocentric universe but concealed his belief not out of a fear of the Church but out of a fear of ridicule. Expresses distaste for Galileo's personality: "Vanity, jealousy and self-righteousness combined into a demoniac force, which drove him to the brink of self-destruction." Reviews the Kepler-Galileo correspondence, stressing Galileo's exploitation of the telescope and his refusal to share one with Kepler despite Kepler's generous published support for Galileo's work.

IX. Chaos and Harmony. Chronicles Kepler's misfortunes: removal from Prague to Linz in 1612, deaths of his wife and six-year-old son in 1611, and his mother's arrest for witchcraft in 1615. With these events troubling his life, Kepler completed the *Harmony of the World* in 1618, an attempt "to bare the ultimate secret of the universe in an all-embracing synthesis of geometry, music, astrology, astronomy and epistemology." Kepler's procedure was to perceive a mystical parallel between the musical harmonies and the perfect polygons (those that can be constructed by a compass and a ruler), giving him a series of harmonic ratios that he applied to everything. Eventually his search led to his Third Law (the harmonic law): Given any two planets, the squares of their periods of revolution will be in the same ratio as the cubes of their mean distances from the sun.

X. Computing a Bride. Summarizes Kepler's considerations in choosing a second wife.

XI. The Last Years. Narrates the story of Kepler's final travels to the Duchy of Sagan in the employ of Wallenstein.

Part Five. The Parting of the Ways.

I. The Burden of Proof. Admits finding Galileo unattractive and views the struggle between Galileo and the Church as a "clash of individual temperaments" rather than a "fatal collision between

opposite philosophies of existence." Identifies the
academic Aristotelians as Galileo's strongest foes
at the outset. Blames Galileo's "hypersensitivity"
for bringing on his troubles. Interprets Galileo's
Letter to the Grand Duchess as a subtle shifting of
the burden of proof: "It is no longer Galileo's
task to prove the Copernican system, but the theologians' to disprove it." Reminds that it was the
Copernican system with its forty-eight clumsy epi-
cycles that Galileo supported, and claims that he
persisted against the church mostly out of vanity
after he had once committed himself. Summarizes the
aftermath of Galileo's challenge, featuring Cardinal
Bellarmine's letter of 1615 shifting the burden of
proof back on to Galileo and Galileo's seething for
years over his inability to provide the proof.

II. The Trial of Galileo. Explicates Galileo's
theory of tides and stresses that Galileo's attacks
on Jesuit scholars, not his Copernican views, prompted
the hostility that led to his trial. Explains that
under the sympathetic Pope Urban VIII Galileo felt
encouraged to write *Dialogue on the Flux and Reflux
of the Tides* in 1626-1630, thus bringing on the
famous trial when Urban felt Galileo had betrayed
him. Reviews the events of the trial, concluding
that "from the purely legal point of view the sentence was certainly a miscarriage of justice." But
at the same time, the judgment carefully "hushes up"
the most damaging contents of the book, forcing
Koestler to conclude that the Church had no desire
to do more than teach Galileo a lesson and show him
he was not of the stuff that martyrs are made of.

III. The Newtonian Synthesis. Sums up the situation
inherited by Newton: "complete disagreement (*a*) on
the nature of the force which drives the planets
round and keeps them in their orbits, and (*b*) on the
question what a body in the vastness of space would
do with itself if it were left alone, that is, without external agents acting on it." Explains Newton's
synthesis as the joining of Kepler's Laws to Galileo's laws about the motion of projectiles.

19 *The Lotus and the Robot*. New York: Macmillan;
        London: Hutchinson, 1960.

    An account of his thoughts after traveling in
    India and Japan in 1958-1959--"one the most tradition-
    bound, the other the most 'modern' of the great coun-
    tries of Asia."

        Part One. INDIA.
        I. "Four Contemporary Saints."
        Acharya Vinoba Bhave. Arrives in Bombay and is
    shocked by the thousands of people sleeping on the
    streets at night. Shocked also by the noise and con-
    fusion in Indian places of worship. ("I found that
    there is more peace to be had in Manhattan than in
    any Indian town or village, temple or shrine.")
    Describes Acharya Vinoba Bhave: an Indian holy man
    who set out in 1951 to walk across India persuading
    landowners to give some of their land to the poor.
    Eight years later, Vinoba had marched about 25,000
    miles and won almost eight million acres, only half
    of it cultivable and only a fraction of it actually
    in the hands of the poor. After eight "bone-shaking"
    hours in a Land Rover, Koestler finds Vinoba in the
    primitive village of Raganathpur and accompanies him
    to the village center to hear his address, learning
    that it is not the guru's words but his presence
    that inspires his audience. "It was an amorphous,
    indifferent audience which became more fidgety as
    Vinoba talked on, and now hardly even pretended to
    listen--only their eyes kept feasting on him, re-
    turning every few seconds for another gulp." Sum-
    marizes Vinoba's life: born in 1895; devoted to
    Gandhi's service from 1916 until Gandhi's death in
    1948; given title Acharya (preceptor) by Gandhi;
    gifted in mathematics and competent in a dozen
    languages; took up the Bhoodan movement of land for
    the poor after talking with Untouchables. Takes a
    long hike with Vinoba and his entourage. Judges the
    Bhoodan movement "a partial success, at worst a noble
    failure," and identifies its greatest significance as
    filling "millions of half-starved peasants and dis-
    illusioned intellectuals with a new hope...."
        Krishna Menon Atmananda. Explains that Krishna
    Menon (unrelated to the Foreign Minister) is a dis-
    ciple of Dhyana Yoga or Jnana Yoga--"the former
    meaning Union through meditation, the second through
    knowledge." Meets Krishna Menon in Trivandrum, the

capital of Kerala, which was then, in 1959, the only
Communist-governed Indian State: "a kind of tropical
Marxist Ruritania, where Cabinet Ministers were known
to consult their horoscopes to deduce the Party-line
from the stars...." Expresses his disappointment with
what he took to be the "arrogance" of Krishna Menon.
Refuses to address an anti-Communist meeting. Recounts a public meeting with Krishna Menon at which
the disciples were allowed to overhear the "bathroom
noises of the Swami's morning toilet" (Koestler was
too late to catch this phase of the devotion) and
admits to being "rather repelled by the type of
emotion reflected there." Quotes at length from
Krishna Menon's *Atma-Darshan: At the Ultimate*, and
Atma-Nirvriti: Freedom and Felicity in the Self,
both exploring old notions of radical empiricism
and explaining the world as a dream. Disapproves of
Krishna Menon's way of rolling words around "in a
game of Wonderland croquet with mobile hoops." Distinguishes European and Asian mysticism on this basis:
the Christian tradition with its roots in Greek
thought employed "sharply defined categories and
concepts," whereas in Asian thought "its categories
remained fluid, its grammar elusive, and its reasoning indifferent to contradiction." Leaves Trivandrum
under a cloud of confusion, with a newspaper reporting
that he was "hounded out" because of his politics, but
explains it was all due to a mistake in his hotel
reservation.

Sankaracharya of Kanchi. Seeks out in Madras the
Sankaracharya of Kanchi, Kamakoti Peetam, one of the
spiritual authorities of an important Traditionalist
sect of Hinduism. Admires the Sankaracharya's "charm
and sweetness." Feels that in their dialogue he and
the Sankaracharya are talking different languages.
Goes away impressed by the Sankaracharya's saintly
personality but depressed by the rigidity of his
conventional Hindu thought: "one would have to go
back several centuries to find a Christian mystic
of equal depth and stature; yet in his views on
religious practice he compared with the rigid eccle-
siastics of the nineteenth century."

Anandamayee Ma. Judges the sixty-three-year-old
Ma "an extraordinary personality." She is considered
by her devotees to be of divine origin. Quotes exten-
sively from *Mother As Revealed To Me*, a biography by
the disciple Bhaiji, giving stories of her fame and
spiritual astuteness. Finds in modern Hindu theolo-

gians a version of medieval Christian scholasticism.
Describes the "pathological" symptoms revealed by
Anandamayee Ma: her inability to eat much or to feed
herself, her fits of laughing and weeping, and her
playful cruelty. Visits her ashram in Benares and
later meets Anandamayee herself in Calcutta, enduring
an audience at which the Mother of the Universe sat
playing with her toes. Receives two tangerines from
her. "They were sticky and dirty, but sanctified by
Mother's touch, and I gave them to some urchins in
the street, hoping they would derive from them a
darshan that, for one reason or another, was denied
me."

II. "Yoga Unexpurgated." Explains that Yoga practice aims at the absorption of the subject in a pure
consciousness without object, a discipline laid out
in *Patanjali's Yoga Sutras* (second or third century,
B.C.), but that whereas this journey was originally
meant to be achieved through meditation it has become
in Hatha Yoga ("at least a thousand years old") an
experience achieved through physiological techniques.
(Hatha Yoga means literally "forced union.") True
disciples of Hatha Yoga believe in its promise of
supernatural powers and are reluctant to discuss it
with foreigners. Offers a summary of Hatha Yoga principles derived from the *Hatha Yoga Pradipika,* the
Siva Samhita, and the *Gheranda Samhita*. Lists the
steps of Yoga as given by Patanjali: "(1) and (2)
abstentions and observances (such as non-violence,
chastity, avoidance of human company, dietary rules);
(3) postures); (4) controlled breathing; (5) and (6)
sense-withdrawal and concentration; (7) meditation;
(8) samadhi--the complete absorption of the mind in
the atma." Points out that Hatha Yoga stresses headings (3) and (4), including eighty-four postures but
that advanced techniques must be preceded by cleansing practices such as (a) running a stalk of cane up
and down the gullet; (b) swallowing tepid water and
vomiting it up; and (c) swallowing a cloth twenty-two
and a half feet long and pulling it back up. Quotes
the *Gheranda Samhita* on the diverse practices for
cleansing the bowels, including the advanced technique for drawing out the long intestines and washing
them. Explains the jala-basti, in which water is
sucked up through the rectum and expelled, as well
as the very advanced vajroli mudra, in which liquids
are sucked up through the penis. Details the methods

for controlling breathing, the most sensational of
which demands gradually cutting back the lower ten-
don of the tongue so that the tongue can be extended
so far that it can close the nostrils. "This technique is often called the King of the Mudras. It is
still actively practiced." Explains that the king of
the mudras is important because it helps prevent the
loss of the vital fluid bindu (semen) which is sup-
posedly stored in a cavity in the skull. Elaborates
on the significance of Kundalini, the coiled serpent
slumbering at the base of the spine and the embodi-
ment of the vital force: when awakened, Kundalini
makes her way up the spine through various gates
until she reaches her consummation with Shiva (sym-
bolized by the phallus), thereby producing samadhi.
A permanent union is the ultimate samadhi. "Kundalini's painful journey, assisted by visceral acro-
bacies and respiratory intoxication, is one of the
most ancient symbols for the sublimation of the
libido."

   III. "Yoga Research." Identifies the three major
aspects of Yoga: the medical, the miraculous, and
the mystical. Investigates the medical claims of
Yoga, concluding that the statistics and terminology
are too vague to provide real support. Evinces a
general scepticism about the therapeutic values of
Yoga: "If it were difficult to prove that the simpler
Yoga exercises are dangerous to health, it would be
even more difficult to prove that they are beneficial
in preference to Western methods of physical train-
ing." Studies the stories of people who have sought
supernatural powers through Yoga, dismissing claims
of levitation for lack of hard evidence and finding
nothing truly supernatural in the experiments involving subjects buried in pits. Admits only that
Yoga demonstrates "the power of the mind over the
autonomous functions of the body more forcibly than
any Western school...." Summarizes several accounts
of samadhi (mystic union) and concludes that they
reveal a devotion to the annihilation of the ego in
death: "The dreamless, trance-sleep of samadhi is a
homage to Tanatos: an exercise in death while pre-
paring for the 'final samadhi' in which it is con-
sumed."

IV. "The Pressure of the Past." Analyzes the com-
plaints of Indian psychiatric patients, finding that
the most common one "turned out to be a highly unusual one by Western standards: male spermatorrhea--
seminal loss through nocturnal pollutions or pathological discharges." Attributes this "spermal anxiety" to the traditional preoccupation of Indians
with their vital fluid and to the example of Gandhi.
Observes that marriage by arrangement contributes
to the Indian male's resort to sex as the only way
he can "assert himself in the eyes of his stranger-
bride" and thereby helps set up with the prevalence
of spermal anxiety a contradictory attitude toward
sex that is psychologically debilitating. Notes that
the orthodox Hindu's preoccupation with digestion and
bowel function merges with sexual anxieties into one
clear complex of "compulsive ritual, pollution-phobia,
taboos on commensality, rigid social segregation."
Concludes that Indian family relations are the problem that "overshadows all others," especially the
dominance of the father over the sons. Cites Gandhi
as an example of one who "sat on his sons' shoulders
like the djini of the Arabian Nights, doing his best
to deprive them of their manhood...."

V. "The Crossroads." Decides India is at a crossroads at which it must choose between some kind of
democracy and its past. "I believe that the salvation
of India lies in a gradual transformation...dis-
carding the petrified elements in past tradition and
harnessing those spiritual resources which Gandhi
and Vinoba revealed, to create, not an artificial
pseudo-democracy, but...a home-grown 'Indiocracy'."

Part Two. JAPAN.
VI. "The Lotus and the Robot." Perceives in Japanese culture an exhilarating spirit of lotusland in
strong contrast to its other face as a regimented
robotland, producing a "dual culture." Traces this
ambivalence to the "Trojan horse" of Western science
and technology that invaded and conquered a culture
that did not have the gradual preparation for it
that Europe experienced. They were like "skin-grafts
from an alien donor which, though eagerly accepted,
never took." Characterizes the Japanese language as
a barrier between Japan and Western culture. Compares
the difficulties Japan experienced after its opening
up to the pains of a diver coming up with the bends.

VII. "The Unstable Crust." Sees in the "crustal
instability" of Japan's geophysical condition a
metaphor for its national character. Comments on
the "horrors of flower arrangement" and the minia-
turization of trees, traditions that "represent
Nature at a safe distance, seen through the reversed
lenses." Discerns in No drama an aesthetic which
puts all the burden of the emotional experience on
the spectator rather than on the actor.

VIII. "Character-Gardening." Describes traditional
Japanese education as "character-landscape garden-
ing," referring to the "axiomatic conviction that
the child in its innermost being *wants* to be properly
reconditioned that way, as the flower welcomes the
wire rack to display its petals to best advantage."
Notes that "Japanese madmen do not get mad" in the
sense of becoming violent, and that paranoid schizo-
phrenia is four times as common in the United States
as in Japan. Observes that Japanese patients get
abundant loving mother substitutes, and that Japanese
babies get close care from their mothers. Points to
the openness about erotic life that begins in childhood and extends through marriage. Contends that the
religious systems of Japan--Shinto, Buddhism, and
Confucianism--provide virtually no notions of sin,
guilt, and divine justice; thus, behavior is governed
by etiquette and the rules sometimes clash. Compares
what happened in Europe during the Renaissance to
what happened in Japan at about the same time: Europe
looked outward to "ever broader vistas in a transformed world," but Japan closed right up for two
hundred and fifty years.

IX. "The Comforts of Ambiguity." Suggests that
"the technique of ambiguity and evasion" functions
in Japanese life as an antidote to the rigidity of
Japanese conventions. Gives examples of ambiguous
poems. Condemns Japanese sensitiveness to any dis-
approval for its crushing effect on literary and
art criticism. "This stubborn reluctance to compete
in a competitive society, and the endless face-saving
manoeuvres which it entails, makes itself felt
throughout the cultural life of the nation: ambiguity
and evasion lie like a delicate mist over the Japanese landscape."

X. "The Road to Zen." Identifies many points of comparison between Japan and India, such as their family-based social structures. Whereas the Indian caste system has historically been rigid, in Japan it has been "relatively fluid." Whereas in India the authority of the father and the guru is religious, in Japan it is social. "The Indian is careless in his dealings with society, punctilious in his dealings with deity; in Japan, it is the reverse." Whereas for the Indian sexual intercourse is a harmful act made necessary by marriage, for the Japanese sex is a great satisfaction in its own right. Whereas in India suicide is rare, in Japan it is "a matter of social convention." Perceives that Zen is Japanese ambiguity at its "metaphysical peak"--"at best an existentialist hoax, at worst a web of solemn absurdities." Stresses the rudeness, directness, abruptness, and sarcasm of Zen. Quotes a number of mondos (quick exchanges between master and pupil) and koans (logically insoluble riddles presented to the pupil). Concludes that Zen teaching appears to be a counterweight against the influence in Japanese life of its strict codes of behavior.

XI. "Delusion and Self-Delusion." Defines key terms in Zen: satori, which is a burst of insight that leads to Awakening; and muga, the state in which the acting self and the self-observing self become one and "a mysterious 'It' has taken charge. Explains there is no formula for reaching satori; it can be induced by any number of experiences. Makes this distinction: "Samadhi is the elimination of the conscious self in the deep sleep of Nirvana; satori is the elimination of the conscious self in the wide-awake activities of intuitive living." Deplores the "hocus-pocus" of Zen, especially when it is mixed with European mysticism as in some writers. Spends several pages debunking Dr. Eugen Herrigel's *Zen in the Art of Archery*. Traces the decline of Zen, fixing the beginning in the monasteries in the sixteenth century. Attributes the decline to a confusion between "the spontaneous flash of creative originality, and the pseudo-spontaneity in exercising a skill which has become automatic. Deprecates the universal writing of haikus for its "tiresome permutations of crows perching on a branch, frogs leaping into a pond, drops sliding off bamboo-leaves, and autumn leaves rustling in the ditch."

XII. "A Stink of Zen." (The title is a phrase
often used in Zen literature.) Explains the principles of the Zen-influenced Morita therapy, a type
of psychotherapy popular in Japan: "a combination of
Behaviourism and Zen, of the Pavlov laboratory and
the doctrine of the no-mind." Remarks on a peril in
the tolerance of Zen: the abolition of the transcend-
ental element in Zen--the religious, doctrinal
"stink" of Zen--leaves it like the sound of one hand
clapping. Judges that neither state Shintoism nor
the other forms of Buddhism were able to give any
doctrinal guidance in ethical matters. "They were
unable, and even unwilling to do so, because of the
ethical relativism of their tradition, their denial
of a universal moral law, and a misguided tolerance
which had become indistinguishable from passive complicity."

XIII. "Epilogue." Rejects the tendency of some intellectuals to blame the growing materialism of Asia
on Western technological society. Describes the Kha-
sis of Assam, "who used to weave beautiful coloured
fabrics; they also used to sacrifice little boys to
the gods by pushing a two-pronged stick up their
nostrils and into the brain. Now they buy hideous
mass-produced textiles, and sacrifice no more little
boys." Emphasizes the point many Ruskin-influenced
critics miss: "these patterns of living hang together." Concludes that "our cherished habit of
contrasting the contemplative and spiritual East
with the crude materialism of the West is based on
a fallacy." Cites approvingly William S. Haas's
suggestion in *The Destiny of the Mind* that the
neologism "philousia" describes best the Oriental
approach to life: *ousia*, or essential Being, cap-
tures the Eastern preference of "intuition to reason,
symbols to concepts, self-realization through the
annihilation of the ego to self-realization through
the unfolding of individuality."

20   *Hanged by the Neck: An Exposure of Capital Punish-*
      ment in England. (With C.H. Rolph.) Harmondsworth,
      England, and Baltimore: Penguin Books, 1961.

      The Acknowledgement explains that "Roughly a third
      of this book (comprising parts of Chapters 2, 3, 5,
      and 7) appeared in a former volume by Arthur Koestler
      entitled *Reflections on Hanging*, published in 1956...."

CONTENTS

21 Editor, *Suicide of a Nation?* London: Hutchinson, 1963.

Also printed as a special issue of *Encounter,* 118 (July, 1963).

CONTENTS

Prelude: BLIND MAN'S BUFF

On the Comforts of Anger	Henry Fairlie
England, Whose England?	Malcolm Muggeridge

I. COLD CLASS WAR

Amateurs and Gentlemen	Goronwy Rees
The Comforts of Stagnation	Michael Shanks
The Plaintive Treble	Andrew Shonfield
Taboo on Expertise	Austen Albu
'A Red Under Every Bed?'	Aidan Crawley
The Price of Obstinacy	John Cole

II. ISLAND AND MAINLAND

Commonwealth, Common Market, Common Sense	Hugh Seton-Watson
The Logic of Survival	John Mander
A Cure for Westminster	John Grigg
The French Paradox	A Note from Paris

III. TOWARDS A NEW SOCIETY?

This Gale-swept Chip	Cyril Connolly
The Comforts of the Sick-bay	Marcus Cunliffe
Sex on these Islands	Alan McGlashan
Against the Stream	Elizabeth Young
The Tragedy of Being Clever	John Vaizey

22   *The Act of Creation.* New York: Macmillan; London:
      Hutchinson, 1964.

     Book One theorizes about "the conscious and uncon-
scious processes underlying scientific discovery,
artistic originality, and comic inspiration," arguing
that they reveal a common pattern. Develops much of
the material already treated in *Insight and Outlook*
(No. 14). Book Two tries to demonstrate that all
organisms reveal certain basic principles, and that
"phenomena analogous to creative originality can be
found on all levels."

BOOK ONE. THE ART OF DISCOVERY
AND THE DISCOVERY OF ART

PART ONE. THE JESTER

     I. "The Logic of Laughter." Depicts humor, discov-
ery, and art as a triptych comprising three columns
of creative activities--one for each realm--with the
activities merging gradually with those they bound:
e.g., comic comparison, objective analogy, poetic
image. Insists "there are no frontiers where the
realm of science ends and that of art begins. Defines
laughter as a luxury reflex, recognizing the great
range of the response. Identifies humor as *"the only
domain of creative activity where a stimulus on a
high level of complexity produces a massive and
sharply defined response on the level of physiological reflexes,"* making the study of humor a promising
approach to understanding the comic and other types
of creativity. Isolates "bisociation"--perceiving a
situation or idea in *"two self-consistent but habit-
ually incompatible frames of reference"*--as the
feature common to funny stories. Explains his use
of the words "matrix" and "code": a matrix is "any
ability, habit, or skill, any pattern of ordered
behaviour governed by a *'code'* of fixed rules";
"code" denotes a set of fixed rules operating in a
"compressed 'secret language.'" Codes are "fixed,
invariable," whereas a matrix is the "variable aspect" of a skill or habit. Codes are "hidden persuaders" of which we are barely conscious, from
which we escape by recourse to dream-like states
where the rational faculty is suspended, or by leaps
of bisociation that join unconnected matrices. Two
independent matrices may collide in laughter, fuse
in a new synthesis of ideas, or confront each other
in an aesthetic experience. Cites as example the
bisociation of 'man' and 'machine,' acknowledging

Bergson's metaphor of "the mechanical encrusted on
the living."

II. "Laughter and Emotion." Identifies an
aggressive-defensive element as the common denominator of humor, naming it the "self-asserting tendency," and identifies the "self-transcending tendency" as its counterpart in aesthetic experience.
Laughter is a "discharge mechanism" which neutral-
izes excitations that cannot be "consummated in any
purposeful manner." Gives examples of the "inertia"
of the emotions, of how the body's responses persist
beyond the control of reason, concluding that "the
grain of salt which must be present in the narrative
to make us laugh turns out to be a drop of adren-
aline." Analyzes the mechanism of laughter, finding
it to be "a phenomenon of the trigger-release type,
where a minute cause can open the tap of surprisingly
large stores of energy from various sources: repressed sadism; repressed sex; repressed fear; even
repressed boredom." Relates laughter to the ability
to see oneself from outside and to criticize oneself.

III. "Varieties of Humour." Analyzes a great number
of jokes and humorous situations under the following
headings: "Pun and Witticism," "Man and Animal,"
"Impersonation," "The Child-Adult," "The Trivial and
the Exalted," "Caricature and Satire," "The Misfit,"
"The Paradox of the Centipede," "Displacement,"
"Coincidence," "Nonsense," "Tickling," "The Clown."
Suggests three main criteria by which to judge the
comic: originality, emphasis, and economy.

IV. "From Humour to Discovery." Divides the bisociative surprise of discovery into an exploding
catharsis in which the self-asserting tendencies
are sublimated through the sympathico-adrenal system,
and a peaceful ebbing away of the self-transcending
feelings. Recognizes degrees of awareness in the
creation of bisociations: "the bisociative act, in
humour as in other branches of creativity, depends
in varying degrees on assistance from fringe-
conscious or unconscious processes." Separates the
experience of the discoverer of a bisociation from
that of the audience, judging any "Eureka" response
by the discoverer as a "minor gesture" of a "sublimated nature."

PART TWO: THE SAGE

V. "Moments of Truth." Cites examples of bisociative inventiveness in animals, and emphasizes the way in which playful activities have often assumed great practical importance in bisociative discoveries. Stresses the importance of "ripeness" in discovery-- the right climate of ideas, the right experience, etc.--but asserts that discovery still demands the spark of creative genius. Assesses the relative roles of logic and intuition in brilliant bisociations.

VI. "Three Illustrations." Analyzes the bisociative experience at work in Gutenberg's invention of print- ing with movable type, Kepler's synthesis of physics and astronomy, and Darwin's theory of evolution by natural selection.

VII. "Thinking Aside." Observes an "apparent para- dox": that the remarks of scientists reveal how much scientific thinking depends on "mental processes which are subjective, irrational, and verifiable only after the event." Attributes this apparent para- dox to the influence of Cartesian rationalism, pointing out with numerous examples the anti-Cartesian tradition of belief in the unconscious mind and its workings. Traces the role of habit in thinking, and puts it at the opposite end of the scale from creat- ive ideas. Contrasts the explorations of "the shal- lows" we do in ordinary thinking with the explorations of the depths in creative thinking, both in response to some manner of guidance. Describes Coleridge's account of the conception of "Kubla Khan" as an ex- ample of the artist's regressions to "earlier stages in mental evolution." Quotes passages from Friedrich August von Kekulé, Michael Faraday, Einstein, and the mathematician Jacques Hadamard, all in support of reasoning by means of mental images.

VIII. "Underground Games." Provides many examples of the bisociative process at work in the unconscious, most of them trivial but some of them leading to leaps of artistic and scientific insights: "In fact they may be likened to an immersed chain, of which only the beginning and the end are visible above the surface of consciousness. The diver vanishes at one end of the chain and comes up at the other end, guided by invisible links."

IX. "The Spark and the Flame." Admits that the Eureka act commonly produces false inspirations and intuitions that frequently lead to dead ends; also, even though insights present themselves, the bisociative act often fails to occur (e.g., Kepler discovered universal gravity only to reject it). Cites statistics on vocabulary growth as evidence of "a kind of diluted Eureka process."

X. "The Evolution of Ideas." Compares the crises experienced by individual scientists in working toward a discovery with those of a scientific discipline as a whole, both progressing in "jerky, unpredictable" ways. Stresses the "discontinuity" exhibited by twenty-six centuries of science, with periods of "creative anarchy" leading to new syntheses. Describes advances in scientific thought as products of "mental cross-fertilization between different disciplines," and stresses the importance of thinking about facts as opposed to merely compiling them. Discusses the factors that hinder progress in scientific thought, citing Aristotle's dominance up till the Renaissance, and "the conservatism of the scientific mind in its corporate aspect." Emphasizes that "scientific evidence can never confirm that a theory is *true*; it can only confirm that it is *more true* than another." Distinguishes between "progress in the precision of scientific statements and their explanatory power." Notes that scientific controversies can be "as subjective and emotional as fashions in art."

XI. "Science and Emotion." Identifies the three prevailing archetypes of the scientist: the Benevolent Magician (who expresses the self-transcendent element), the Mad Professor (who incarnates the self-assertive tendency), and the pedantic, uninspired bookworm or laboratory worker, finding that the real-life scientist incorporates features of them all. Maintains that both the self-assertive and the self-transcending drives motivate the scientist, but he puts them to use by sublimating them. Laments the boredom that has crept into scientific writing.

PART THREE: THE ARTIST

XII. "The Logic of the Moist Eye." Distinguishes weeping from crying, and compares the bodily changes in weeping and laughing. Identifies the causes of weeping: raptness, mourning, relief, sympathy, self-pity.

XIII. "Partness and Wholeness." Assigns to every living organism and social body "wholeness" and "partness": "It acts as an autonomous, self-governing

whole on its own subordinate parts on lower levels
of the organic or social hierarchy; but it is sub-
servient to the coordinating centre on the next
higher level."

XIV. "On Islands and Waterways." Describes one's
early sense of the individuality of objects as
"islands" located in the fluid universe of the self;
connections are made through artistic, religious,
and social communion leading to increased self-
transcendence. Lists some of the "more ordinary
phenomena through which the self-transcending emotions manifest themselves in everyday life": perceptual projection, projective empathy, transference,
introjection.

XV. "Illusion." Finds a self-transcending value in
illusions, stressing the self-transcendence in es-
capism, catharsis, and vicarious experience.

XVI. "Rhythm and Rhyme." Describes the bisociation
in poetic measure and meaning, with observations on
the role of rhythms, repetition, and punning in
creative bisociations.

XVII. "Image." Details the various kinds of imagery
that operate in bisociation: analogy, synesthesia,
pictorial thinking. The most powerful images are
archetypal with a force that grounds them in eternal
laws.

XVIII. "Infolding." Explains what he calls "infolding," the increasing implicitness of works of
art. Insists on originality, selective emphasis,
and economy as "a kind of handy mariner's compass
for the critic at sea."

XIX. "Character and Plot." Summarizes numerous
plot situations and conflicts in literature, concluding that "all these paradoxes and predicaments
arise from conflicts between incompatible frames of
experience or scales of value, illuminated in consciousness by the bisociative act."

XX. "The Belly of the Whale." Outlines the features of the death and rebirth motif ("the night
journey"), in which the hero experiences a crisis
from which he emerges purified--an example of the
"interlacing" of the Tragic and the Trivial planes
of existence.

XXI. "Motif and Medium." Compares the attitudes
towards nature of different cultures, concluding
*There is always a second matrix active behind, or
superimposed upon, the visual appearance.*" Notes
that we cannot express visual experiences in verbal

statements without their suffering "major impover-
ishment and distortion." Explains aesthetic pleasure
in visual perceptions as "a series of bisociative
processes involving the participatory emotions,"
stressing the artist's many gifts for achieving
illusion. Traces some of the "inferential processes"
exploited by artists: e.g., projective empathy,
synesthesia, the Rohrschach-like "projection of
meaning into the ambiguous motif." Emphasizes the
force of convention as a "hidden persuader."

XXII. "Image and Emotion." "Tastes and distastes
on the sensory level play, like consonances and
dissonances, only a subordinate role in the aesthetic
experience, as one among many patterns of unity-in-
variety. The pre-condition of the experience to
occur is once more that the emotive potentials of
the matrices participating in it should form an
ascending gradient, and provide a hint, however
tentative or teasing, of some hidden reality in the
play of forms and colours."

XXIII. "Art and Progress." Decides that art, like
science, evolves cumulatively, with bisociations
at "the great turning points." Repeats his claim for
the importance of economy of means and subtlety of
implication.

XXIV. "Confusion and Sterility." Instances the
cultural snob as someone confused by "a hotchpotch
of matrices."

BOOK TWO: HABIT AND ORIGINALITY

I. "Prenatal Skills." Analyzes the stages of embryonic development, discerning fixed rules in the
genetic code operating with various "fixed strategies." Spells out in much detail the principles of
cell differentiation, especially as the embryo is
manipulated experimentally.

II. "The Ubiquitous Hierarchy." Elaborates the
systems of hierarchy that govern the nervous system,
finding evidence contradictory to the claims of the
behaviorists' stimulus-response theories.

III. "Dynamic Equilibrium and Regenerative Potential." Defines equilibrium as a condition that exists
*"between the self-assertive tendencies of the part
and the restraints imposed by the controlling centre."*
Says of sexual reproduction that "the bisociation of
two genetic codes is the basic model of the creative
act."

IV. "Reculer Pour Mieux Sauter." (To Fall Behind in Order To Leap Ahead.) Gives many examples of regeneration in the animal kingdom--the more primitive the creature, the greater its regenerative powers--and finds that psychotherapy often proceeds by analogous ways of regressing in order to better leap ahead. "It seems that *reculer pour mieux sauter* is a principle of universal validity in the evolution of species, cultures, and individuals, guiding their progression by feedback from the past."

V. "Principles of Organization." Identifies four principles of organization at work in embryonic development: (1) motivation ("a subject for the metaphysician"), (2) code, (3) matrix, and (4) environment. Gives the term "Janus principle" to the way entities function as both parts of larger wholes and as wholes made up of their own parts. Two types of "input" govern the functions of all components of an organism: "The first consists of specific trigger signals from its superior controls in the hierarchy; the second are inputs and feedbacks from more or less random events in its environment." Stresses that code and matrix are "complementary aspects of a unitary process."

VI. "Codes of Instinct Behaviour." Surveys the remarkable variety of coded behavior among animals, producing "an interlocking of individual behaviour-patterns into a collective supercode which casts the individual bird or bee into the role of a part in the social whole."

VII. "Imprinting and Imitation." Reviews examples of imprinting and imitation among animals, noting the "overshooting" of evolution--a providing of surplus potential.

VIII. "Motivation." Considers much experimental evidence on motivation, concluding that the exploratory drive is vital to organisms and that behaviorism is an inadequate explanation of motivation.

IX. "Playing and Pretending." Describes play as the "purest manifestation" of the exploratory drive.

X. "Perception and Memory." Explicates the physics and physiology of aural experiences. Points out the apparent close relationship between visual learning and memory. Asserts that perception is active, not passive, and that "Nowhere are 'stimuli' and 'responses' neatly separable; they form hierarchies of loops within loops."

XI. "Motor Skills." Traces the behavior involved

in learning motor skills such as typing and playing
a piano, skills which "may have a high degree of
flexibility, but they nevertheless operate through
automatized sub-skills on the lower ranges of the
hierarchy, which manifest themselves in the individual 'touch' of the pianist, the 'style' of the
tennis-player, the fixed mannerisms, quirks, idio-
syncrasies, and unconscious rituals which are our
personal hallmarks."

XII. "The Pitfalls of Learning Theory." Sums up
the chaos in learning theory as taught by various
schools, dismissing behaviorist experiments on rats
for their shaky foundations.

XIII. "The Pitfalls of Gestalt." Identifies the
source of the "sad confusion" in Gestalt theory
in an ambiguity in Gestalt psychologists' use of
the word 'insight,' taking it sometimes to mean
intelligence, at others to describe a dramatic
acquisition of *new* understanding: "the position of
the Gestalt school boils down to the tautology that
the animal's behaviour is the more intelligent the
more insight it has into causal relations."

XIV. "Learning to Speak." Summarizes the process
of learning to speak as essentially one of attaching
verbal labels to pre-verbal concepts, which are
modified over the years, stressing that language
and thinking are different operations.

XV. "Learning to Think." Abstraction enables us
to create order "out of the chaotic stream of experience," whereas discrimination makes possible a
differentiation in our responses. Emphasizes the
importance of the concept of causality in a child's
learning to think. Lists various processes which
lead to understanding. Summarizes the steps in
learning mathematical reasoning, and describes the
development of logical reasoning as abstracting
the "explicit formulations of implicit relations."

XVI. "Some Aspects of Thinking." Outlines the
"hierarchic organization of levels of understanding,
levels of consciousness, and levels of habit and
flexibility...." Lists several types of language
matrices: phonetic matrices, chronological matrices,
classificatory codes, dogmatic matrices ("closed
systems with distorted feedback and impaired sub-
skills of reasoning"), and style codes. "The *total
matrix*, which comprises all these frames of behaviour, constitutes the personality structure."

XVII. "Association." Associative thinking proceeds

horizontally rather than hierarchically, is the "exercise of habit," and does not entail bisociation.

XVIII. "Habit and Originality." Tabulates the distinguishing features of habit (associative thinking) and originality (bisociative discovery).

Appendix I. "On Loadstones and Amber." Illustrates the way "previously separate branches of knowledge merge in a series of bisociative acts" by tracing developments in the understanding of magnetism and electricity.

Appendix II. "Some Features of Genius." Gives brief sketches of the sensibilities of a number of scientific geniuses (e.g., "Newton, Monster and Saint," "The Mysticism of Franklin," "The Atheism of Darwin") to illustrate their diverse motivations. Notes some of the characteristics of brilliant scientists: precociousness, scepticism and credulity, abstraction and practicality, multiple potentials.

23   *The Ghost in the Machine.* London: Hutchinson; New York, 1967.

PART ONE: ORDER

I. "The Poverty of Psychology." Ridicules behaviorism as "the philosophy of ratomorphism."

II. "The Chain of Words and the Tree of Language." Rejects the behaviorist view of language, finding language more fully explained by his theory of hierarchic systems, which also allows individual freedom: "on each level there is a variety of strategic choices: from the selection and ordering of the material, through the choice of metaphors and adjectives, down to the variety of possible intonations of individual vowels."

III. "The Holon." Introduces the term "holon" to describe the "Janus-faced entities" of hierarchies; holons look both up and down in a hierarchic system, serving as the whole for the parts of which they consist and which lie beneath them on the scale, and as a part of the holons above them in the hierarchy. The holon "also symbolizes the missing link-- or rather series of links--between the atomistic approach of the Behaviourist and the holistic approach of the Gestalt psychologist."

"Hierarchies are 'dissectible' into their constituent branches, on which the holons form the 'nodes.' The number of levels which a hierarchy comprises is called its 'depth,' and the number of holons on any given level its 'span.'

"Holons are governed by fixed sets of rules and
display more or less flexible strategies. The rules
of conduct of a social holon are not reducible to
the rules of conduct of its members."

Moreover, holons reveal their Self-Assertive tendency in their drive for autonomy, their Integrative
tendency in their need for dependence.

IV. "Individuals and Dividuals." Distinguishes
between "'structural' hierarchies, which emphasize
the spatial aspect" and "'functional' hierarchies,
which emphasize process in time." Provides detailed
examples of hierarchies at work in biological systems, emphasizing "the *integrative* potential of
holons to behave as parts of a more complex whole."

V. "Triggers and Filters." "To sum up: in motor
hierarchies an implicit intention or generalised
command is particularized, spelled out, step by step,
in its descent to the periphery. In the perceptual
hierarchy we have the opposite process: the input
of the receptor organs on the organism's periphery
is more and more 'de-particularised', stripped of
irrelevancies during its ascent to the centre. The
output hierarchy concretises, the input hierarchy
abstracts. The former operates by means of trigger-
ing devices, the latter by means of filtering or
scanning devices."

VI. "A Memory for Forgetting." Postulates "interlocking hierarchies of perception" that give experience its "multi-colouration." Storing memories involves stripping them to "bare essentials, which are
then dressed up again in recollection."

VII. "The Helmsman." Stresses the role of the
feedback mechanism (the cybernetic helmsman) in
maintaining homeostasis in organisms. Defines an
organism structurally and functionally as "a hierarchy of self-regulating holons which function (a)
as autonomous wholes in supra-ordination to their
parts, (b) as dependent parts in subordination to
controls on higher levels, (c) in co-ordination with
their local environment."

VIII. "Habit and Improvisation." Explains that
going upward in a hierarchy reveals "more complex,
flexible and less predictable patterns of activity."

PART TWO: BECOMING

IX. "The Strategy of Embryos." rehearses the steps
in embryonic development, finding analogies to hierarchic processes—especially in the presence of "hidden persuaders."

X. "Evolution: Theme and Variations." Argues
against the conventional view of evolution as the
blind working out of chance mutations, preferring
to describe it not as "a free-for-all, nor the execution of a rigidly predetermined computer programme," but as "a musical composition whose possi-
bilities are limited to the rules of harmony and
the structure of the diatonic scales...."

XI. "Evolution Ctd: Progress by Initiative."
Stresses the role of the exploratory drive in evolution, deciding that "evolution no longer appears
as a tale told by an idiot, but rather as an epic
recited by a stutterer...."

XII. "Evolution Ctd: Undoing and Redoing." Continues to support a modified evolutionary theory,
one marked by hierarchic controls and "the draw-
back-to-leap pattern of paedomorphosis."

XIII. "The Glory of Man." Returns to the theme of
The Act of Creation, repeating the arguments about
bisociation at work in art, scientific discovery,
and comic inventiveness.

XIV. "The Ghost in the Machine." "I have tried to
explain...the general principles of a theory of
Open Hierarchic Systems (O.H.S.), as an alternative
to current orthodox theories. It is essentially an
attempt to bring together and shape into a unified
framework three existing schools of thought--none
of them new. They can be represented by three symbols: the tree, the candle and the helmsman. The
tree symbolises hierarchic order. The flame of the
candle, which constantly exchanges its materials,
and yet preserves its stable pattern, is the simp-
lest example of an 'open system'. The helmsman represents cybernetic control. Add to these the two
faces of Janus, representing the dichotomy of partness and wholeness, and the mathematical sign of the
infinite (a horizontal figure of eight), and you
have a picture-strip version of O.H.S. theory."

PART THREE: DISORDER

XV. "The Predicament of Man." Emphasizes at length
the danger inherent in the self-transcending tendency as "it entails the partial surrender of personal responsibility and produces the quasi-hypnotic
phenomena of group psychology."

XVI. "The Three Brains." Argues for the presence
of "schizophysiology" built into the human species,
a theory based on Paul MacLean's study of the evolution of the human brain and the division of its

cortex into what Koestler calls "the reptilian, primitive mammalian and neo-mammalian brain." Concludes that "This would provide a physiological basis for the paranoid streak running through human history, and point the direction of the search for a cure."

XVII. "A Unique Species." Cites examples of man's uniqueness, his "unsolicited gift" being a brain with potential far beyond what man has yet done with it. Claims that with man *"intra-specific differences have become more vital than intra-specific affinities,"* resulting in the destructiveness wrought by the self-transcending tendency. Points to the bloodshed resulting from man's unique skill of language and the divisiveness it has produced. Finally, "The discovery of death by the intellect, and its rejection by the instinct became a paradigm of the split mind."

XVIII. "The Age of Climax." Finds two frightening features in modern life: the dizzying speed of growth in population and technology, combined with the possibility since Hiroshima of man's destroying himself. Urges a search for a biochemical solution to man's potentially fatal schizophysiology, distancing himself emphatically from drug cultists.

Appendix I. "General Properties of Open Hierarchical Systems (O.H.S.)." A long list.

Appendix II. "On Not Flogging Dead Horses." Defends his arguments against the "ratormorphic philosophy" of behaviorism.

24   *Drinkers of Infinity. Essays 1955-1967.* New York: Macmillan; London: Hutchinson, 1968.

"Gravity and the Holy Ghost." Traces Kepler's steps in formulating his three laws of planetary motion, noting his metaphysical inspiration ("a supposed analogy between the stationary sun, the stars and interstellar space on the one hand, and God the Father, the Son and the Holy Ghost on the other"); his "hesitant introduction of physical causation into man's vision of the skies"; his transition from a universe governed by spirit to one ruled by inanimate force; his groping toward "our contemporary, rather surrealistic concepts of electromagnetic and gravitational *fields*..."; his approach to the notion of universal gravity, only to forget it; and his status as the "founder of modern astronomy."

"The Walls of Jericho." Summarizes briefly the revolution in thought c. 1600 that replaced the notion of a closed universe with that of an open one, noting its "immediate impact on theology and philosophy."

"The Greatest Scandal in Christendom." Claims that Galileo had believed in the Copernican system for years while teaching the geocentric universe for fear of ridicule; that it was the scholars not the Church that opposed him originally; that it was Galileo's temperament that led to the showdown with the Church; "that the presumption of the theologians was matched by the *hubris* of an unbalanced genius and the vindictiveness of a benighted academic coterie."

"Artist on a Tightrope." Speculates that we live most of our lives on the trivial plane, rising at times to the tragic plane. "All true art is a tightrope walk on the line of intersection of the tragic and trivial planes of existence. When the acrobat slips, art degenerates into propaganda, or escapes into a bloodless cloud-cuckoo land."

"The Age of Discretion." Elaborates on his conviction that since Hiroshima man has possessed the power to write a last act to the human drama: "the necessity of getting reconciled with the idea of his possible extinction may breed a new humility, and may rid man of that biological jingoism which made him regard himself as the crown of creation."

"The Unreasonable Murderer." Summarizes the legal issues involved in the trial in 1956 of Clarence William Ward for murder.

"The Honourable Paradox: A Postscript to the Hanging Debate." Sums up the arguments that led to the House of Commons resolution in 1956 calling on the Government to introduce legislation to abolish capital punishment. The "ultimate cause" of the Commons' decision was "a revolt of moral conscience."

"Animals in Quarantine." Deplores the British law quarantining pets for six months upon their entry into the country.

"Dogs, Sticks and Smugglers." Follows up his call
for changes in the animal quarantine laws.

"When the Daydream Has To Stop." Attacks the class
barriers that he finds crippling to the whole society
in England.

"Reflections on a Peninsula." Describes the sixth
century B.C. as the "turning-point for the human
race," producing Confucius, Lao Tse, the Buddha,
the Ionian philosophers, and the Pythagorean brother-
hood. At the same time Europe and Asia went in different directions: the East toward intuition, the
West toward logic; the Easterner began striving for
depersonalization, the Westerner for individual fulfillment. But whereas the East remained oriented
toward intuition, the West alternated over the centuries. Defines "continuity-through-change" and
"unity-in-diversity" as "essential attributes of
an evolving culture." Affirms his pride in his
Europeanism.

"The Silent Generation." Characterizes the "silent
generation" of the fifties as disciples of Candide's
advice to cultivate one's own garden.

"Culture in Explosion." Three features distinguish
contemporary civilization: "it is explosive, osmotic,
and governed by feedback." Population and knowledge
are exploding, cultural osmosis is producing a global civilization, and feedback from the consumer
masses deletes the quality of culture.

"Words and Weapons." Laments the power of censor-
ship in totalitarian states, urging that "psychological armaments" be made into a serious international bargaining point.

"A Love Affair with Norway." Sketches some of the
unique features of Norwegian life, expressing great
appreciation for the country.

"Drifting on a River." Describes a canoe trip on
the Loire River in France.

"Tu Felix Austria." Comments on recent Austrian
history, noting the importance of Jews in pre-war
Austria, and judging Austria of the fifties as "a

symbol of Europe's phenomenal powers of moral regeneration."

"The Ubiquitous Presence." Points out the disper-
sal of Hungarian talent and genius: "I do not think
there has been a migration of scholars and artists
on a similar scale since the fall of Byzantium."
Notes that a "large proportion" of them were Jews,
many of them of Caucasian origin, not Semitic.

"Of Dogs and Men." Reviews of *Battle for the Mind*
and *The Unquiet Mind*, both by William Sargant. Dismisses *Battle for the Mind* with contempt for its
interpretation of the treatment of battle neuroses
in Pavlovian terms. Rejects Sargant's "physicalist-
ic" treatment of mental illness, reaffirming the
considerable evidence for "mentalistic" causes.

"Of Geese and Men." Review of *On Aggression* by
Konrad Lorenz. Criticizes Lorenz for treating "the
behaviour of the goose as a paradigm for the bonds
which unite human communities," but agrees that "the
remedies he has to offer mankind are wholly lauda-
ble."

"Of Apes and Men." Review of *The Naked Ape* by
Desmond Morris. "Strongly recommended" but with
reservations about some of Morris's conclusions.

"Mysterium Tremendum." Review of *The Living Stream*
and *The Divine Flame*, both by Sir Alister Hardy.
Sympathizes with Hardy's conviction that man "is
conscious of being in touch with some Power which
appears to be outside and beyond the individual
self and from which he can receive grace: help in
the conduct of his life and a sense of renewed
vitality" (Hardy's words). States his personal belief: "that only a fool would deny dimensions of
reality unknowable to man, which may add up to a
coherent whole; but that only a saint would attrib-
ute to it the qualities of benevolence and love."
Criticizes only Hardy's evasion of "the crucial
question of evil."

"The Patient's Dilemma." Review of *Fringe Medicine*
by Brian Inglis. Appreciates Inglis's critique of
conventional medical practice, but suspects him of
coming "perilously close to gullibility."

"The Patient as a Guinea Pig." Review of *Human Guinea Pigs* by M.H. Pappworth. Concludes that medical experimentation on humans comes down to the old question of when does the end justify the means, but judges Pappworth's position as alarmist.

"Daughter to Stalin." Review of *Twenty Letters to a Friend* by Svetlana Alliluyeva. Finds *Twenty Letters* valuable for its depiction of the "utterly depressing drabness, greyness, and banality" of Svetlana Alliluyeva's life with her father Stalin.

"Mistress to Picasso." Review of *Life with Picasso* by François Gilot and Carlton Lake. Admires Gilot for enduring ten years with Picasso.

"Books of the Years." Annotates his favorite books from 1955 through 1967.

"Return Trip to Nirvana." Describes his two experiences with psilocybin, rejecting the enthusiastic claims made by proponents of its use. (See No.

"The Poverty of Psychology." Argues that "these confluent trends in neurophysiology, neuropharmacology, experimental psychology and psychotherapy demonstrate that the concept of the 'human organism' as a bundle of conditional reflexes is an abstraction—the reality is the individual, an elusive entity with a blur of unpredictability at its core which determines the organism's reactions to the stimuli that impinge on it." Finds in experiments on flatworms evidence confirming "the transmission of acquired experience by asexual heredity." Praises J.B. Rhine's work in his Parapsychology Laboratory at Duke University.

"The Daemon of Socrates." Identifies himself as one of those who sympathize with the concept of a creative daemon "but deplore the ambiguity in the concept." Repeats arguments from *The Act of Creation* about bisociation and the role of the unconscious in creative thinking.

"Evolution and Revolution in the History of Science." Outlines four criteria of creativity: "originality, the improbability of the combination, its constructive-destructive aspect, and the intervention of extra-conscious factors." Stresses the alternation of revolutionary phases with peaceable phases in the history of science.

"Biological and Mental Evolution: An Exercise in Analogy." Disputes Sir Julian Huxley's description of evolution as a maze, citing paedomorphosis as one escape from the maze. (Paedomorphosis is "the appearance of some evolutionary novelty in the *larval or embryonic* stage of the ancestral animal, a novelty which may disappear before the adult stage is reached, but which reappears in the *adult* descendant.") Maintains that evolution reveals the capacity to step backward in order to leap ahead, and discovers an analogy in the power of the human mind to do the same: "the creation of novelty in mental evolution follows the same pattern of *reculer pour mieux sauter*, of a temporary regression to a naive or juvenile level, followed by a forward leap, which we have found in biological evolution."

"To Covet a Swallow." Summarizes a trivial contretemps prompted by his essay on "A Love Affair with Norway."

"*Darkness at Noon* and *The Strangled Cry*." Defends the psychology of confession in *Darkness at Noon*. Rejects John Strachey's thesis in *The Strangled Cry* that the works of Koestler, George Orwell, Whittaker Chambers, and Boris Pasternak represent the repudiation of rationalism, claiming that they instead reveal the shallowness of nineteenth-century optimism and utilitarianism.

"Between the Lotus and the Robot." An important postscript to *The Lotus and the Robot*. (See No. 19.) Quotes C.G. Jung's letter approving of Koestler's "debunking" of Yoga and Zen. Quotes a letter from Professor G. Scholem of the University of Jerusalem revealing that Eugen Herrigel, author of *Zen in the Art of Archery*, became a Nazi after World War II began. Rejects sharply the claims made for Zen irrationalism: "Inarticulateness is not a monopoly of Zen; but it is the only school which made a philosophy of it, whose exponents burst into verbal diarrhea to prove constipation." Spells out the reasons for the "intellectual and moral nihilism" of Zen:

"The first, because the emphasis is not on marrying intuition to reason, but on castrating reason. And the second, because its moral detachment has degenerated into complacency towards, and complicity with, evil."

25   *Beyond Reductionism. The Alpbach Symposium 1968: New Perspectives in the Life Sciences.* London: Hutchinson, 1969; New York: Macmillan, 1970.

Co-edited with J.R. Smythies, this volume collects the papers presented at a symposium organized by Koestler and held at Alpbach in the Austrian Tyrol. The object of Koestler's efforts, as he explains, was a confrontation with "the insufficient emancipation of the life sciences from the mechanistic concepts of nineteenth-century physics, and the resulting overly reductionist philosophy." Koestler's own contribution--"Beyond Atomism and Holism: The Concept of the Holon"--is a digest of the theories advanced in *The Ghost in the Machine.* The full program is outlined below.

Opening Remarks	Arthur Koestler
The Living System: Determinism Stratified	Paul A. Weiss
Chance or Law	Ludwig von Bertalanffy
Biochemical Approaches to Learning and Memory	Holger Hydén
The Gaps in Empiricism	Jean Piaget and Bärbel Inhelder
On Voluntary Action and Its Hierarchical Structure	Jerome S. Bruner
Beyond Atomism and Holism-- The Concept of the Holon	Arthur Koestler
Aspects of Consciousness	J.R. Smythies
The Paranoid Streak in Man	Paul D. MacLean
Empiricist and Nativist Theories of Language: George Berkeley and Samuel Bailey in the 20th Century	David McNeill
The Primacy of the Abstract	F.A. Hayek
New Perspectives in Psychopharmacology	Seymour Kety
The Theory of Evolution Today	C.H. Waddington
Reductionism and Nihilism	Viktor E. Frankl
General Discussion	
Retrospect	W.H. Thorpe

26   *The Case of the Midwife Toad*. London: Hutchinson;
      New York: Random House, 1971.

      Koestler tells the story of Dr. Paul Kammerer,
the gifted Austrian biologist who committed suicide
at 45 after the discovery that his key specimen of
a midwife toad had been injected with ink to give
it a false appearance. Kammerer was a native Vien-
nese who studied music before switching to zoology,
and he was a man of great personal charm who married twice and attracted a succession of female
admirers. Kammerer worked at the Institute for Experimental Biology in Vienna, where he succeeded in
breeding newts, lizards, and toads in a series of
experiments aimed at proving the Lamarckian thesis
that acquired characteristics can be inherited.
Koestler explains why Lamarck's theory has always
been so controversial: "In the Lamarckian view,
evolution is *cumulative*; in the Darwinian, *repeti-
tive*; it could go on for millions of generations
without any evolutionary progress." Much of Kammerer's work dealt with salamanders and sea-squirts,
but his most controversial experiments were with
Alytes obstetricans, the midwife toad. Most other
toads mate in the water, and during the mating
season the males develop spiny callosities, or nuptial pads, on their hands in order to grip the fe-
males better during copulation. But the midwife
toad--so-called because it wraps the fertilized
eggs around its hind legs and cares for them until
they hatch--is unusual in that it breeds on land
and has no need for nuptial pads. "Kammerer's claim
was that by inducing *Alytes* to copulate in water,
like other toads, for several generations, they
eventually developed nuptial pads as an acquired
hereditary feature." This was in 1909, and Kammerer
himself minimized the importance of his discovery,
judging his sea-squirt experiments far more crucial
in demonstrating the inheritance of acquired characteristics. The seeming simplicity with which Kammerer's results could be checked was destroyed by
several factors. First, breeding *Alytes* in water is
difficult under the best circumstances, and the experiment was not duplicated. Second, the callosities
develop only during the mating season, and therefore
specimens can not be produced on demand. Third, Kammerer's work was interrupted critically during the
upheaval of World War I. The eminent British

Mendelian biologist William Bateson began to question Kammerer's evidence as early as 1910 (the discovery of the nuptial pads occurred in 1909) and
continued an acrimonious assault on Kammerer well
into the 1920's. When Kammerer visited England in
1923 to lecture to the Cambridge Society and the
Linnean Society, he brought his only surviving
specimen of a midwife toad. It was preserved in
alcohol and presented nuptial pads on its right
hand, while the pad on its left hand had been cut
off for use in microscopic slides. Bateson did not
attend the lectures. "Neither Gadow nor Boulenger
or any other sceptic present at the Cambridge meet-
ings and demonstrations expressed doubts regarding
the authenticity of the specimens or the microscopic sections." After the war, Kammerer and Hans
Przibram, founder and director of the Biological
Institute, were destroyed financially by the mon-
strous inflation of the period. Partly as a result,
Kammerer made very popular lecture tours of the
United States and the continent, but even though he
was a charming, personable lecturer, the sensational
press notices were "definitely harmful to his scientific reputation." Finally, on August 7, 1926,
the prestigious journal *Nature* published an article
by G.K. Noble, Curator of Reptiles at the American
Museum of Natural History, maintaining that the
famous pickled toad was a fraud. Specifically,
Noble's examination "proved beyond doubt that the
specimen showed no nuptial pads, and that the black
colouration of its left hand was not due to natural
causes, but to the injection of Indian ink." Kammerer never replied to Noble, and shot himself six
weeks afterwards just before he was to assume an
important position in Moscow with the Pavlov Institute. Przibram argued credibly that the horny projections on the pads had obviously deteriorated,
but no one could offer a satisfying explanation of
the India ink. Przibram hinted at sabotage by a
jealous colleague. Koestler gives his own explanation of how the specimen passed inspection in England, only to fail with Noble: "The only plausible
explanation why they all failed to see what Noble
saw quasi at first glance three years later seems
to be that the doctoring was done *after* the specimen's return in its dilapidated state from Cam-
bridge--either to preserve the aspect of the already
near-vanished nuptial pads before the remaining

pigment vanished altogether, or to discredit Kammerer."

Koestler finds in Kammerer's story reasonable evidence to discomfit conventional neo-Darwinists, but at the same time holds off from serious endorsement of Lamarckism. "There seems to be every reason to believe that evolution is the combined result of a whole range of causative factors, some known, others dimly guessed, yet others so far completely unknown. And I do not think one is justified in excluding the possibility that within that wide range of causative factors a modest niche might be found for a kind of modified 'Mini-Lamarckism' as an explanation for some limited and rare evolutionary phenomena." Koestler is also very interested in Kammerer's obsession with coincidences. Kammerer kept for two decades a written record of his observations of coincidences, and in 1919 published *Das Gesetz der Serie* (The Law of Series) giving one hundred examples. What Kammerer called "seriality" is close to what Jung labeled "synchronicity." *Das Gesetz der Serie* expounds a theory of "a force of attraction comparable to universal gravity" that "correlates by affinity, regardless whether the likeness is one of substance, form or function, or refers to symbols." In this aspect of his thinking, Kammerer reinforces Koestler's own curiosity about phenomena with no apparent physical causes.

27   *The Roots of Coincidence: An Excursion into Parapsychology*. London: Hutchinson; New York: Random House, 1972.

"The ABC of ESP." Urges acceptance of parapsychology as a respectable area of study, acknowledging the hostility to it in many quarters but listing the illustrious scientists and other scholars who have served as presidents of the British Society for Psychical Research ("they include three Nobel laureates, ten Fellows of the Royal Society, one Prime Minister and a galaxy of professors, mostly physicists and philosophers"). Provides examples of interesting experiments, such as those conducted by the Rhines at Duke University and by the renowned classical scholar Gilbert Murray.

"The Perversity of Physics." Summarizes many of the puzzling phenomena revealed by quantum physics, with the general thesis that the acknowledged para-

doxes of contemporary science legitimize the study
of parapsychology. "The rapprochement between the
conceptual world of parapsychology and that of modern physics is an important step towards the demolition of the greatest superstition of our age--the
materialistic clockwork universe of early-nineteenth-
century physics."

"Seriality and Synchronicity." Reviews Kammerer's
study of what he called "seriality" (see *The Case of
the Midwife Toad*) to describe a non-physical force
at work in coincidences. Explains the way C.G. Jung,
aided by the physicist Wolfgang Pauli, arrived at a
similar hypothesis about "non-causal, non-physical
factors operating in nature," to which he gave the
name "synchronicity." "Kammerer confined himself to
analogies in naive physical terms, rejecting ESP and
mentalistic explanations. Jung went to the opposite
extreme and tried to explain all phenomena which
could not be accounted for in terms of physical
causality, as manifestations of the unconscious
mind." Judges Jung's conception of synchronicity
as obscure.

"Janus." Repeats in brief form his theory of
holons (see *The Ghost in the Machine*), and suggests
that acausal forces may contribute to the unity-in-
diversity found by many religious thinkers in the
creation. "Thus Synchronicity and Seriality are modern derivatives of the archetypal belief in the fundamental unity of all things, transcending mechanical causality."

"The Country of the Blind." Proposes that ESP
might be considered as "the highest manifestation
of the integrative potential of living matter," but
admits this is only a "speculative step." Suggests
an analogy between Lamarckism and ESP: just as almost all traces of acquired characteristics may be
filtered out in heredity, so may almost all traces
of extra-sensory communication be filtered out by
the organs of perception.

28   With Alister Hardy and Robert Harvie. *The Challenge
        of Chance: A Mass Experiment in Telepathy and Its
        Unexpected Outcome*. London: Hutchinson; New York:
        Random House, 1973.

        Koestler co-authored this book, with the individ-
        ual contributions as listed below in the table of
        contents.

PART ONE   /   *Telepathy or not--or what?*

  Introduction, *Alister Hardy*
  Planning the experiments, *Alister Hardy*
  Experimental results, *Alister Hardy & Robert Harvie*
  The control or mock "experiments," *Robert Harvie*
  General discussion, *Alister Hardy & Robert Harvie*

PART TWO   /   *Probability and serendipity*
  Robert Harvie

PART THREE   /   *Anecdotal cases*
  Arthur Koestler

PART FOUR   *Speculations on problems beyond our
  present understanding*
  Arthur Koestler

  Convergences and Clusterings

  Order from disorder

  The "hidden variables"

Appendix I
   *(a) Details of randomizing procedure adopted to
       produce the large control experiments*
   *(b) Further consideration of the adjacent coin-
       cidences*

Appendix II
   A note on the formula used in Part II

Appendix III
   *Catalog of responses at the Caxton Hall telepathy
   experiments*

The substance of this book is an account of an
experiment conducted at Caxton Hall, Westminster,
London, in 1967, involving 200 people meeting on
seven consecutive Monday nights for a series of
ESP tests. Koestler's contributions are the re-
counting of numerous anecdotes known to him and
speculations on ESP in the vein of his discussions
in *The Roots of Coincidence.*

29   *The Heel of Achilles: Essays 1968-1973.* London:
      Hutchinson; New York: Random House, 1974.

"The Urge to Self-Destruction." Notes that the
world since Hiroshima has been capable of complete
self-destruction, and that human behavior evinces
a flaw in biological evolution manifested in five
symptoms: (1) human sacrifice, a universal and paranoid ritual; (2) weak inhibitions against killing
one's own species; (3) war, "with its sub-varieties
of mass persecution and genocide"; (4) the split
between reason and emotion; (5) the failure of ethical behavior to keep up with technological progress.
Identifies five causes of man's predicament: (1) his
tripartite brain ("to put it crudely: evolution has
left a few screws loose somewhere between the neo-
cortex and the hypothalamus"); (2) the neonate's
long state of dependence, which leaves it vulnerable
later to authority figures; (3) the mutual dependence of the earliest carnivorous hominids, which
produced an excess of self-transcending tendencies
that lead to militant devotion to a group; (4) language, in that words are "man's most deadly weapon"
and in that languages create barriers; (5) man's
discovery of his mortality, which "saturated the
air with ghosts and demons."
      "Rebellion in a Vacuum." Defines the purpose of
education as "catalyzing the mind." Charges that the
education establishment the world over is dominated
by Reductionism, "Ratomorphism" (Behaviorism), and
doctrines of Randomness. Laments the "existential
vacuum" that characterizes so many young people and
intellectuals, and situates their rebelliousness in
a vacuum.
      "Can Psychiatrists Be Trusted?" Raises questions
about the objectivity of psychiatric diagnoses.
Asserts that psychology must grow out of its "obsession with rats in a maze" if it pretends to become a "real science of the human mind."
      "Life in 1980--The Rule of Mediocracy." Identifies
the main features of the "mediocrat" as "common
sense plus inertia." Worries about the 1980's as a
"Decade of the Demagogues." Foresees the endurance
of the institution of marriage, "but premarital and
extramarital affairs will be taken for granted."
      "Sins of Omission." Review of *While Six Million
Died* by Arthur D. Morse. Documents the various cynical ruses of England and the United States in refusing

to facilitate the emigration of Jews from Europe under Hitler.

"The Future, If Any." Review of *The Biological Time-Bomb* by Gordon Rattray Taylor. Evinces mild uneasiness about the possible blasphemies inherent in cloning, genetic engineering, etc.

"Going Down the Drain." Review of *The Doomsday Book* by Gordon Rattray Taylor. Expresses concern over the pollution of the earth's resources.

"Benighted Attitudes." Review of *The Biocrats* by Gerald Leach. Argues vigorously for liberal abortion and euthanasia laws.

"The Naked Touch." Review of *Intimate Behaviour* by Desmond Morris. Judges this a study of "the science of what is not worth knowing."

"Not By Hate Alone." Review of *Love and Hate* by Irenaus Eibl-Eibesfeldt. Recommends this book to anyone not convinced that humans have innate instincts or "a disposition for friendship and cooperation."

"Hypnotic Horizons." Review of *Mind and Body* by Stephen Black. Summarizes Black's work with hypnosis, endorsing its value as "a research tool to probe into the relations of mind and matter."

"Anatomy of a Canard." Review of *Rumour in Orléans* by Edgar Marin. Dismisses this study of the sociology of rumour.

"The Abishag Complex." Review of *The Greening of America* by Charles A. Reich. "One wonders how it came about that such a muddle-headed book has been at the top of the American best-seller list for several months."

"Prophet and Poseur." Review of *Antimemoirs* by André Malraux. "If we had a few Malrauxs in this country, intellectuals would perhaps be treated less condescendingly."

"Telepathy and Dialectics." Review of *Psychic Discoveries by the Russians* edited by Martin Ebon. Judges this work "a valuable source of information on a significant ideological development in Russia which to most Westerners will come as a surprise."

"Wittgensteinomania." Review of *Wittgenstein's Vienna* by Allan Janik and Stephen Toulmin. Applauds this interpretation of a man who set out "to circumcise logic" and all but succeeded "in castrating thought."

"In Memory of A.D. Peters." An obituary notice of his late friend and literary agent.

"Literature and the Law of Diminishing Returns."
Remarks of the old belief that science shows progress but art does not, that scientific progress is
not smooth and unbroken and that art does display
periods of technical progress. And "both seem to
move through cycles of revolution...."

"Science and Para-Science." Insists that the deterministic world-view is passé. Distinguishes two
connections between the collapse of determinism and
the rise that he perceives of "obscure mental con-
structs" with "quasi-mystical" implications: the
interest of physicists in parapsychology, and "the
mentalistic trend in biology and physics."

"Science and Reality." Defends his interest in
parapsychology, observing that "In 1969 the American Association for the Advancement of Science ap-
proved the application of the Parapsychological
Association to become an associate of that august
body."

"Solitary Confinement." A dialogue with Anthony
Grey, who spent time in solitary confinement in
China and wrote *Hostage in Peking*.

"The Faceless Continent." Offers his impressions
of the Australian national character: "Goodwill
devoid of grace, a down-to-earth pragmatism that
can be aesthetically offensive, a culture that is
deliberately, almost defiantly, suburban."

"Farewell to Gauguin." Laments the "coca-coloniza-
tion" of native cultures that he observed in a trip
around the world.

"Marrakech." Sketches the history of Marrakech
and its people.

"The Glorious and Bloody Game." Commentary on the
Fischer-Spassky world chess championship match in
Reykjavik in 1972.

"Mahatma Gandhi--Yogi and Commissar: A Re-Valuation."
Dismisses Gandhi's campaign for the universal use of
spinning wheels, and judges Gandhi's philosophy "self-
defeating." Agrees that independence would have come
much earlier without Gandhi. Concludes that what Gandhi gave to the Indian people were "the first stir-
rings of self-respect." "When all is said, the Mahatma, in his humble and heroic ways, was the greatest living anachronism of the twentieth century;
and one cannot help feeling, blasphemous though it
may sound, that India would be better off today and
healthier in mind, without the Gandhi heritage."

30   *The Thirteenth Tribe: The Khazar Empire and Its
        Heritage*. London: Hutchinson; New York: Random
        House, 1976.

        PART ONE: *Rise and Fall of the Khazars*
          I   Rise
         II   Conversion
        III   Decline
         IV   Fall

        PART TWO: *The Heritage*
          V   Exodus
         VI   Where From?
        VII   Cross-currents
       VIII   Race and Myth

        APPENDICES
          I   A Note on Spelling
         II   A Note on Sources
        III   The 'Khazar Correspondence'
         IV   Some Implications - Israel and the Diaspora

PART ONE. RISE

The Khazar Empire, made up of people of Turkish
stock, flourished from the seventh to the tenth
centuries, and in the eighth century dominated the
region between the Black Sea and the Caspian. Their
dominance in that area stopped the Arab advance into
eastern Europe in the eighth century, and they converted to Judaism about 740. Their empire collapsed
in the twelfth and thirteenth centuries, and the
evidence indicates that many of the Jewish Khazars
migrated to Eastern Europe--especially to Russia
and Poland. "This has led several historians to
conjecture that a substantial part, and perhaps the
majority of eastern Jews--and hence of world Jewry--
might be of Khazar, and not of Semitic origin."
Argues that "Should this turn out to be the case,
then the term 'anti-Semitism' would become void of
meaning, based on a misapprehension shared by both
the killers and their victims." Gives the complicated
history of the Khazars from their appearance in the
fifth century as "a later offspring of Attila's
horde." As Charles Martel's Franks saved Gaul and
western Europe, so the Khazars saved the eastern
approaches to the Volga, the Danube, and the East
Roman Empire itself. Pieces together the sketchy
reports of Khazar culture. Notes the double kingship

system--one divine, the other secular--apparently
adopted by the Khazars, and speculates that it may
have been somehow connected with the establishment
of Judaism. Points to Khazaria's reputation as a
"refugee haven," both before and after its conversion. Suggests that, caught between Muslims and
Christians, the Khazars may have been attracted to
the "neutrality" of Judaism. Considers it probable
that the Khazars converted in steps to a "rudiment-
ary form of Judaism, based on the Bible alone," much
like that of the fundamentalist Karaites of eighth-
century Persia. Stresses that the orthodox Jews of
the East were well aware of the Khazars, "but at
the same time the Khazars were regarded with certain
misgivings...." Comments on the "sad" belittlement
of Khazar history by the Soviet regime. Traces the
close relationship between the Khazars and the Mag-
yars in the ninth century, and the later decline of
the Khazars under the Rus.

PART TWO. THE HERITAGE
  Describes as "relatively well documented" the
Khazar heritage of the dominant Jews in medieval
Hungary. Cites the many place names in Poland and
the Ukraine that derive from "Khazar" or "Zhid"
(Jew), speculating that they may once have been in-
habited by Khazarian Jews. Notes that the Khazar
decline coincided in time (tenth century) with the
creation of "the nucleus of the Polish state."
Refers to various thirteenth-century documents that
indicate "considerable numbers" of Khazars in Poland
at the time; and says that the estimate of 500,000
Jews in the Polish-Lithuanian kingdom in the seven-
teenth century is reasonably consonant with the
"known facts about a protracted Khazar migration
via the Ukraine to Poland-Lithuania...." Argues
that some old Polish market towns "show a more
specific affinity with what we know--little though
it is--about the townships of Khazaria, which were
probably the prototypes of the Polish *shtetl*." Ad-
duces other parallels (e.g., in synagogue architec-
ture, clothing) that he considers possible evidence
of Khazarian influence on Jewish culture in Poland.
Outlines the known facts about Jewish migration
into Europe. Quotes the historian A. Vetulani: "in
earlier times, the main bulk of the Jewish population
originated from the Khazar country." Tries to show
"that the evidence from anthropology concurs with

history in refuting the popular belief in a Jewish race descended from the biblical tribe." Emphasizes that "The problem of the Khazar infusion a thousand years ago, however fascinating, is irrelevant to modern Israel," although "the lingering influence of Judaism's racial and historical message, though based on illusion, acts as a powerful emotional break by appealing to tribal loyalty."

31 *Janus: A Summing Up.* London: Hutchinson; New York: Random House, 1978.

A summing up of work from the previous twenty-five years. Hopes that the summary will add up to "a comprehensive system, which rejects materialism and throws some new light on the human condition."

"Prologue: The New Calendar." Dates the modern calendar from Hiroshima. Identifies the "outstanding pathological symptoms" of our species: (1) human sacrifice; (2) the killing of con-specifics; (3) the split between reason and emotion; (4) the disparity between technical progress and ethical behavior. Hypothesizes that man's destructive behavior originates in an evolutionary blunder separating "the deep ancestral structures of the brain, mainly concerned with instinctive and emotional behaviour, and the neocortex which endowed man with language, logic and symbolic thought." Includes as other destructive forces (1) the long dependent period of neonates, (2) language and its tendency to build "ethnic barriers," and (3) the fear of death.

I. "The Holarchy." Supports the doctrine of holism—that the whole is greater than the sum of its parts. Defines a "holon" as a sub-whole that is Janus-faced in that it looks upward to the larger unit of which it is a dependent part, and downward to the parts of which it is itself made up. Locates these holons in hierarchies, claiming that "hierarchic organization is a fundamental principle of living nature." Calls this hierarchic model an example of General Systems Theory, "whose purpose is to construct rhetorical models and discover general principles which are universally applicable to biological, social and symbolic systems of any kind...." Finds in hierarchic organization an argument against behaviorism and "the materialist *Zeitgeist*." Explains that "the term 'holon' may be applied to any structural or functional sub-system in a biological,

social or cognitive hierarchy, which manifests
rule-governed behaviour and/or structural *Gestalt*-
constancy." Elaborates the codes that govern the
structure and function of holons, assisted by "flexible strategies" derived from the environment. Distinguishes innate codes from learned ones.

II. "Beyond Eros and Thanatos." Attributes to all
holons both "an *integrative tendency* to function as
part of the larger whole, and a *self-assertive tendency* to preserve their individual autonomy." Diagrams the forms these polarities take on different
levels. Clears the way for his theory by attacking
Freud's conception of the primary drives of sexuality
(Eros) and the death-wish (Thanatos): "both are
based on biological novelties which appear only on
a relatively high level of evolution."

III. "The Three Dimensions of Emotion." Explains
his "three-dimensional conception of human emotions"
by a "homely analogy": "imagine your mental scenery
transformed into the saloon bar of a tavern, equipped
with a variety of taps, each serving a different
kind of brew; these are turned on and off as the
need arises. Then each tap would represent a different
drive, while the pleasure-unpleasure rating would
depend on the *rate of flow* through the tap....
Lastly, the ratio of self-assertive to self-
transcending impulses in emotive behaviour could be
represented by the *acid-alkaline scale*."

IV. "Ad Majorem Gloriam...." Points to the fact
that the self-transcending tendency in its devotion
to group ideals has caused infinitely more suffering
than the self-assertive tendency, which society controls quite effectively. Cites Stanley Milgram's
experiments at Yale, in which subjects were induced
to give "victims" electrical shocks (which they did
not know to be bogus) in the name of scientific
experiment.

V. "An Alternative to Despair." Urges a search for
a psychopharmacological alleviation of the split
between man's emotions and his reason, dissociating
himself from drug mystiques and documenting the
obvious truth that tinkering with nature is an
essential aspect of civilization.

VI. "Humour and Wit." Recapitulates the theory
detailed in *The Act of Creation*.

VII. "The Art of Discovery." Summarizes pertinent
passages from *The Act of Creation* and *The Sleepwalkers*.

VIII. "The Discoveries of Art." Condenses the
analysis of artistic creativity outlined in *The Act
of Creation*.

IX. "Crumbling Citadels." Attacks behaviorism and
Darwinism, which "base their explanations of biological and cultural evolution on essentially the
same model operating in two stages: the first step
ruled by blind chance, the second by selective re-
wards." Stresses that mutations do not spell evolution, and insists that Darwinism retains its position only because no convincing alternative has
appeared. States his belief in a "coordinating
activity" that guarantees genetic stability and
evolutionary modifications: *"The central problem
of evolutionary theory is how this vital coordinating activity is carried out."* Sympathizes with the
neo-Lamarckian view of evolution as a cumulative
process, "the outcome of the purposeful striving of
living organisms...," as opposed to the Darwinian
view of evolution as an accidental process.

XI. "Strategies and Purpose in Evolution." Cites
the existence in Australia of marsupial parallels
to placental mammals as evidence of "unitary laws
underlying evolutionary diversity, which permit virtually unlimited variations on a limited number of
themes." Defines as "biomorphic" the "purposeful
aspects inherent in the phenomena of life." Insists
that purposiveness is "a fundamental characteristic
of life which does not require the postulate of a
Purposer because it is inherent in the concept of
life itself." Sees in the innate drive of purposiveness another name for his concept of the integrative,
or self-transcending, tendency, which is present on
all levels. Summarizes: "For we have seen...that the
self-assertive tendency is indeed conservative, intent on preserving the individuality of the holon
in the here and now of existing conditions, whereas
the integrative tendency has the dual function of
co-ordinating the constituent parts of a system in
its existing state, *and* of generating new levels of
organization in evolving hierarchies--whether biological, social, or cognitive. Thus the self-
assertive tendency is oriented towards the present,
concerned with self-maintenance, whereas the integrative tendency may be said to work both for the
present and towards the future."

XII. "Free Will in a Hierarchic Context." Perceives in his hierarchy of holons an alternative to

mind-body dualism: self-consciousness diminishes
infinitely toward automatic behavior going down the
hierarchy, but increases infinitely going upward.
"Thus the mind-body dichotomy is not localized
along a single boundary or interface, as in classical dualism, but is present on every intermediary
level of the hierarchy." Compares this formulation
of the problem to the Principle of Complementarity
in physics that allows perceiving an event through
two different frames of reference at the same time.
Offers his own substitute for the maxim that to
know all is to forgive all: "understand all--forgive
yourself nothing."

XIII. "Physics and Metaphysics." A long discussion
of modern physics and its many puzzling phenomena,
the general burden of which is that if physics
merges into metaphysics, then parapsychology should
not be judged as disrespectable ("...if the parapsy-
chologist is out on a limb, the physicist is out on
a tightrope"). Suggests that just as there are various manifestations of energy (kinetic, potential,
thermal, electrical, nuclear, radiant), so may there
also be a common source of psychic phenomena: "in a
similar way, telepathy, clairvoyance, precognition,
psychokinesis and synchronicity are merely *different
manifestations under different conditions of the
same universal principle*--i.e., the integrative
tendency operating through both causal and acausal
agencies."

XIV. "A Glance Through the Keyhole." Concludes
with his agnostic's credo already expressed in *The
Invisible Writing*.

Appendix I. "Beyond Atomism and Holism--The Concept
of the Holon." Summarizes Chapters 1-4.

Appendix II. "An Experiment in Perception." Written with James J. Jenkins, this essay summarizes the
results of an experiment using a tachistoscope in an
undergraduate psychology class.

Appendix III. "Notes on the Autonomic Nervous
System." A very brief summary.

Appendix IV. "UFOs: A Festival of Absurdity."
Declares that "when we approach the borders of science, whether in ESP or quantum physics or ufology,
we must expect to encounter phenomena which seem to
us paradoxical or absurd."

31a   *Bricks to Babel. A Selection from 50 Years of His*
        Writings, Chosen and with New Commentary by the
        Author. London: Hutchinson; New York: Random
        House, 1980.

Explains that "this omnibus provides a guided tour,
with the author acting as guide, pointing out the
sights and deciding where to stop for a closer view."
The table of contents that follows provides an overview of the tour.

BOOK ONE: IN SEARCH OF UTOPIA
Part One: Promised Land
1   Arrow in the Blue
2   Kibbutz Life in the 'Twenties
3   The Horns of the Dilemma
4   The Poison of Holiness

Part Two: Land of Promise
5   Mount of Olives to Montparnasse
6   The Chinaman's Nod
7   Woe to the Shepherds
8   The Promethean Vision
9   The Expanding Universe
10 How to Fail as a Spy
11 A Blinkered Traveller
12 Prisoner in Spain
13 A Turning Point

Part Three: The God that Failed
14 The Gladiators
15 Darkness at Noon
16 Arrival and Departure

Part Four: Fighting the Cold War
17 Becoming Anglicised
18 The Yogi and the Commissar
19 The Right to Say "No"
20 The Good Samaritans
21 In Memory of George Orwell
22 The Age of Longing

Part Five: Birth of a Nation
23 Pompeii in Reverse
24 At the Crossroads
25 The Thirteenth Tribe

BOOK TWO: IN SEARCH OF A SYNTHESIS

E

CONTRIBUTIONS TO BOOKS

32   "A Sentimental Journey Through Palestine." In *Foreign
      Correspondent: Personal Adventures Abroad in Search
      of the News*. Ed. Wilfrid Hindle. London: George G.
      Harrap, 1939. Pp. 49-81.

      Recounts his trip to Palestine for the London *News
      Chronicle* in October, 1937. The big story was the
      deposition by the British of the Mufti of Jerusalem,
      spiritual leader of the Palestinian Moslems. The
      Mufti's whereabouts were a secret, but Koestler
      tracked him down in Beirut and got a statement from
      his assistant that provided Koestler with an import-
      ant scoop.

33   "The Intelligentsia." In *Little Review Anthology
      1945*. Ed. Denys Val Baker. London: Eyre and Spot-
      tiswood, 1945. Pp. 109-122.

      Annotated under *The Yogi and the Commissar*. See
      No. 106 for original publication source.

34   "What the Modern World Is Doing to the Soul of Man."
      In *The Challenge of Our Time*. London: Percival
      Marshall, 1948. Pp. 15-19.

      Annotated under *The Yogi and the Commissar* as
      "The Challenge of Our Time." See No. 109 for original
      publication source.

35   "The Candles of Truth." From the Foreword to *Stalin's
      Russia*, by Suzanne Labin. London: Gollancz, 1949.
      Pp. 7-10.

      Annotated under *The Trail of the Dinosaur*.

36   "Arthur Koestler." In *The God That Failed*. Ed.
        Richard Crossman and Howard Stafford. London:
        Hamish Hamilton, 1950. Pp. vii-xv.

37   "Eight Fallacies of the Left Babbitt." In *Verdict
        of Three Decades: From the Literature of Revolt
        Against Soviet Communism: 1917-1950*. Ed. Julien
        Steinberg. New York: Duell, Sloan and Pearce,
        1950. Pp. 512-520.

        Annotated under *The Trail of the Dinosaur* as "The
        Seven Deadly Fallacies." See No. 130 for original
        publication source.

38   "The War of Ideas: Appalling Alternatives." In
        America and the Mind of Europe. Ed. Lewis Galan-
        tiere. London: Hamish Hamilton, 1951. Pp. 47-61.

        Traces some of the issues in the cold war in
        Europe. Denounces the Left-Right choice in ideolo-
        gies as a "false dilemma." Concludes that "the
        Socialism-capitalist alternative has become void of
        meaning."

39   "Preface." In *Conspiracy of Silence* by Alex Weiss-
        berg. London: Hamish Hamilton, 1952. Pp. vii-xv.

        Alex Weissberg was an Austrian-born scientist and
        a member of the Communist Party who was arrested in
        1937 and accused of masterminding a Nazi plot to
        kill Stalin and scheming to commit sabotage in the
        Ukraine. Koestler says Weissberg had been chosen
        for a part in a "political melodrama."

39a   "Letter." In *The Golden Horizon*. Ed. Cyril Connolly.
        London: Weidenfeld and Nicolson, 1953. P. 71.

        Excoriates a reader who asked him by letter if his
        account of the massacre of Jews was "based on fact"
        or "artistic fiction." "As long as you don't feel,
        against reason and independently of reason, ashamed
        to be alive while others are put to death and guilty,
        sick, humiliated, because you were spared, you will
        remain what you are: an accomplice by omission."

40   "Mansklighetens kurvor"; "Andliga klimatskiften";
        "I jatteodlornasspar?" *Tro och moral. Inlagg I
        livsaskadningsfragor ov*. Stockholm: Albert
        Bonniers Forlag, 1955. Pp. 66-72.

41 Koestler and Albert Camus. *Réflections sur la peine capitale*. Paris: Calmann-Lévy, 1957.

Same introduction as in *Reflections on Hanging*.

42 "The European Cultural Community: Idea and Reality." In *Die Presse in Dienst der Einheit Europos*. Heft 7. Vienna: Wiener Schriften, 1959. Pp. 94-102.

43 "Einleitungsreferat der gerneinsame Nenner." In *Europa-Gesprach*. Vienna: Wiener Schriften, 1960. Pp. 19-29.

Annotated under *Drinkers of Infinity* as "Culture in Explosion." See No. 257 for original source.

44 An essay in *Rache ist Mein. Theorie und Praxis der Todesstrafe*. Stuttgart: Ernst Battenberg Verlag, 1961.

45 "Kepler and the Psychology of Discovery." In *The Logic of Personal Knowledge*. Ed. Marjorie Grene. London: Routledge and Kegan Paul, 1961. Pp. 49-57.

Passages from the Kepler section of *The Sleepwalkers*.

46 "Kultur in der Industriegesellschaft." In *Vienna Festival Wiener Schriften*. Heft 16. Vienna: Wiener Schriften, 1961. Pp. 156-157.

47 "Some Aspects of the Creative Process." In *Control of the Mind: A Symposium*. Eds. Seymour Farber and Roger Wilson. New York and London: McGraw-Hill, 1961. Pp. 188-208.

Condenses some of the major ideas in *The Act of Creation*.

48 "Anatomie des Snobismus." In *Uber den Snob*. Munich: R. Piper and Co., 1962. Pp. 50-58.

Annotated under *Trail of the Dinosaur* as "An Anatomy of Snobbery."

49 "The Polarity of Emotions." In *The Scientist Speculates: An Anthology of Partly-Baked Ideas*. Ed. I.J. Good. London: Heinemann, 1962. Pp. 107-111.

50   "Reflections on the Peninsula of Europe." In *Essays
        by Divers Hands: Being the Transactions of the
        Royal Society of Literature*. New Series (1962).

        Annotated under *Drinkers of Infinity* as "Reflec-
        tions on a Peninsula." See No. 256 for original
        source.

51   "The Intelligentsia." In *Partisan Review Anthology*.
        Ed. William Phillips and Philip Rahv. New York:
        Holt, Rinehart and Winston, 1962. Pp. 40-50.

        Annotated under *The Yogi and the Commissar*. See
        No. 106 for original source.

52   "The Crank." In *New Statesman Anthology*. Ed. Edward
        Hyams. London: Longmans, 1963. Pp. 180-181.

        Annotated under *The Yogi and the Commissar* as
        "The Great Crank." See No. 232 for original source.

53   "The Cosmic Mystery." In *The Structure of Prose*.
        Ed. James R. McConkey. New York: Harcourt Brace,
        1963. Pp. 294-311.

        Excerpts from *The Sleepwalkers*.

54   Participant in symposium *Maschine: Denkmaschine
        Staatsmaschine*. Hamburg-Berlin: Rv. Deckers Verlag,
        1963.

        A symposium on modern technology.

55   "The Boredom of Fantasy." In *Stages of Composition*.
        Ed. William Jones. Boston: D.C. Heath, 1964.
        Pp. 59-63.

        Annotated under *Trail of the Dinosaur*. See No. 251
        for original source.

56   "The Boredom of Fantasy." In *The Elements of the
        Essay*. Ed. Gerald Levin. New York: Harcourt Brace,
        1964. Pp. 194-199.

        Annotated under *Trail of the Dinosaur*. See No.
        251 for original source.

57 "A Conversation." In *Scaling the Wall: Talking to Eastern Europe, The Best of Radio Free Europe*. Ed. George Urban. Detroit: Wayne State University, 1964. Pp. 97-117.

Discusses with George Urban his decision to abandon political writing: "the clichés and labels of political thinking have really become very insignificant." In response to John Strachey in *The Strangled Cry*, explains that what he has rejected is "the arrogant and shallow optimism of the nineteenth century and particularly the utilitarian ethics of the nineteenth century." Reasserts his conviction about a subconscious element in scientific reasoning. Expresses doubt about "a spiritual revival within the framework of the established churches...." Condemns Marxist histories of science as "completely and utterly untrue." Remarks that "certainly it is true to say that people who have spent some time studying philosophy, history or the classics are much more likely to develop a sense of moral responsibility in the conduct of public affairs than are technicians." Calls C.P. Snow's "two cultures" controversy" "typically British."

58 "Reflections on the Peninsula of Europe." In *The Spoken Word* (Second Series). Ed. A.F. Scott. London and New York: St. Martin's Press, 1965. Pp. 55-66.

Annotated under *Drinkers of Infinity* as "Reflections on a Peninsula." See No. 256 for original source.

59 "Comedy." In *Comedy: Meaning and Form*. Ed. Robert W. Corrigan. San Francisco: Chandler, 1965. Pp. 214-216.

Excerpted from *Insight and Outlook*.

60 "Introduction: Behold the Lowly Worm." In *The Worm Re-Turns: from "Worm Runner's Digest."* Ed. James V. McConnell. Englewood Cliffs, New Jersey: Prentice-Hall, 1965. Pp. xvii-xxv.

Summarizes some of the interesting features of flatworm behavior and physiology.

61   "Motivation: A Biased Review." In *Stefanos: Studies
      in Psychology Presented to Cyril Burt*. Eds. Char-
      lotte Banks and P.L. Broadhurst. London: Univer-
      sity of London Press, 1965. Pp. 39-55·.

      Excerpt from *The Act of Creation*.

62   "Introduction." In *Mistress to Kafka: The Life and
      Death of Milena*. London: Secker and Warburg, 1966.
      Pp. 9-11.

      Milena Jesenska met Kafka when she was in her
      twenties, not long before he died at 41. She later
      worked in the Czech Resistance until she was cap-
      tured and sent to the concentration camp at Ravens-
      bruck, where she met Margarete Buber-Neumann. Milena
      Jesenska died in the camp in 1944.

63   "The Ubiquitous Presence." In *Ten Years After--A
      Commemoration of the Tenth Anniversary of the
      Hungarian Revolution*. Ed. Tamas Aczel. London:
      McGibbons and Kee, 1966. Pp. 204-206.

      Annotated under *Drinkers of Infinity*.

64   "Biological and Mental Evolution: An Exercise in
      Analogy." In *Knowledge Among Men: Eleven Essays
      on Science, Culture, and Society*. (Smithsonian
      Institution.) New York: Simon and Schuster, 1966.
      Pp. 93-107.

      Annotated under *Drinkers of Infinity*. See No. 182
      for original source.

64a   "Conversion." In *The Borzoi College Reader*. Ed.
      Charles Muscatine et al. New York: Knopf, 1971.
      Pp. 71-76.

      Excerpt from *The God That Failed*.

65   "The Act of Creation." In *Brain Function and Learn-
      ing: Proceedings of the Conference on Brain Func-
      tion*. Eds. Donald B. Lindsley and Arthur Lumsdaine.
      Berkeley: University of California Press, 1967.
      Pp. 338-343.

      Outlines two key aspects of his theory of crea-
      tion: bisociation and *reculer pour mieux sauter*.

66   "Johannes Kepler." In *The Encyclopedia of Philosophy*.
       New York: Macmillan Co. and The Free Press, 1967.
       Pp. 329-333.

       A brief summary of his evaluation of Kepler as
       written up in *The Sleepwalkers*.

67   "Reply." In *The Art of the Soluble* by P.B. Medawar.
       London: Methuen, 1967. Pp. 92-94.

       Replies to Medawar's review of *The Act of Creation*.
       See No. 175 for original source.

68   "Abstract and Picture Strip." In *The Pathology of
       Memory*. Eds. George A. Talland and Nancy C. Waugh.
       New York and London: Academic Press, 1969.
       Pp. 261-270.

       Defends his thesis in *The Act of Creation* that
       there are two kinds of memory: "abstractive" memory
       ("the dehydrated sediments of perceptions whose
       flavour has gone") and "picture-strip" memory ("the
       recall of scenes or details with almost hallucina-
       tory clarity"). Includes what became Appendix II in
       Janus: A Summing Up.

69   "Ethical Issues Involved in Influencing the Mind."
       In *The Ethics of Change: A Symposium*. Toronto:
       CBC Publications, 1969. Pp. 1-11.

       Calls the "ideal educator" a "catalyst," not an
       "influencing agent." Attacks the three R's of the
       educational system: Reductionism, Ratomorphism,
       and Randomness (as perceived in the random mutations
       commonly taught as part of the theory of evolution).
       See also No. 260.

70   "Rebellion in a Vacuum." In *The Place of Value in a
       World of Facts: Proceedings*. New York: Wiley Inter-
       science Division, 1970. Pp. 221-228.

       Annotated under *The Heel of Achilles*. See No. 204
       for original source.

71   "Rebellion in a Vacuum." In *Protest and Discontent*.
       Ed. Bernard Crick and William Robson. Harmonds-
       worth: Penguin, 1970.

       Annotated under *The Heel of Achilles*. *See No. 204.*

72   "Preface." In *Les Renards juneaux Paris 2010*. Paris:
        Calmann-Lévy, 1970. Pp. 7-9.

73   "The Urge to Self-Destruction." In *The Place of
        Value in a World of Facts: Proceedings*. New York:
        Wiley Interscience Division, 1970. Pp. 297-305.

        Annotated under *The Heel of Achilles*. See No. 198
        for original source.

73a   "La Pulsion vers l'autodestruction." *Revue de Medi-
        cine Functionelles* 1 (1969), n.p.

74   "Panel on Drugs and Society in the Year 2000." In
        *Psychotropic Drugs in the Year 2000: Use by Normal
        Humans*. Ed. Wayne O. Evans and Nathan S. Kline.
        Springfield, Illinois: Charles C. Thomas, 1976.
        Pp. 128-158.

        Repeats his thesis in *The Ghost in the Machine*
        "that there is in the native equipment of our species
        a built-in engineering error, a construction fault,
        which accounts for the paranoic streak running
        through our absurd and tortured history." Thus his
        hope for some alleviant from neuropsychopharmacology.

75   *Probleme in Gesprach. Rauschmittel und Suchtigkeit*.
        Bern and Frankfurt: Verlag Herbert Lang, 1971.

        A symposium on the drug culture, with Koestler as
        a participant.

76   "Beyond Atomism and Holism: The Concept of the Holon."
        In *The Rules of the Game: Cross-Disciplinary Essays
        on Models in Scholarly Thought*. Ed. Teodor Shanin.
        London: Tavistock; New York: Harper and Row, 1972.
        Pp. 233-248.

        Excerpt from *Beyond Reductionism: The Alpbach
        Symposium*. See No. 208 for original source.

77   "Preface." In *Experience et psychologie: la scolas-
        tique Freudienne*, by Pierre Debray-Ritzen. Paris:
        Fayard, 1972. Pp. I-IV.

78 "Introduction." In *The Inside Story of the World Chess Championship: Fischer vs. Spassky*. London: Times Newspapers Ltd., 1973. Pp. 7-15.

Summarizes the match, including the preliminary posturing. Speculates on chess as "a paradigm or symbol of the working of the human mind."

79 "The Tree and the Candle." In *Unity Through Diversity: A Festschrift for Ludwig von Beralanffy*. Ed. William Gray and Nicholas D. Rizzo. New York and London: Garden and Breach, 1973. Pp. 287-314.

"A slightly different version was first published in *Beyond Reductionism--The Alpbach Symposium*."

80 "The Limits of Man and His Predicament." In *The Limits of Human Nature: Essays Based on a Course of Lectures Given at the Institute of Contemporary Arts, London*. London: Allan Lane, 1973. Pp. 49-58.

Restates his thesis in *The Ghost in the Machine* that "evolution seems to have left a few screws loose somewhere between the neo-cortex and the brain-stem."

81 "Beyond Atomism and Holism." In *Beyond Chance and Necessity: A Critical Inquiry into Professor Jacques Monod's Chance and Necessity*. Ed. John Lewis. Atlantic Highlands, New Jersey: Humanities Press, 1974. Pp. 61-73.

An abridgement of "Beyond Atomism and Holism" in *Beyond Reductionism: The Alpbach Symposium*.

82 "Humor and Wit." In *Encyclopaedia Britannica*, 15th ed., 1974. Pp. 5-11.

Summary of ideas from *The Act of Creation*.

83 "Foreword." In *Born 1900: Memoirs* by Julius Hay. London: Hutchinson, 1974. Pp. 13-17.

Hay was an outstanding Hungarian dramatist and one of the figures behind the Hungarian Revolution in 1956. Koestler judges him "one of the outstanding dramatists of our time." See also No. 222.

84   "Postscript." In *New Directions in Parapsychology*.
      Ed. John Beloff. London: Elek Science, 1974.
      Pp. 165-169.

85   "Der innere Zensor und die West 36 Gerechten." In
      Radikal Touristen: Pilger aus dem Westen, Ver-
      bannte aus dem Osten. Munich: Verlag Herder, 1975.
      Pp. 140-153.

86   "Textes et inédits d'Arthur Koestler." In *Arthur*
      Koestler. Dirigé par Pierre Debray Ritzen. Paris:
      Editions de L'Herne, 1975.

      Includes: "Lectures de jeunesse," pp. 47-50.
                "Le temps heroiques," pp. 239-247. See
                   No. 131 for original source.
                "Preface à l'accusé d'Alexandre Weiss-
                   berg," pp. 248-257. See No. 39 for
                   annotation.
                "Lettre à Mamaine," pp. 340-341.
                "Histoire du Prix," pp. 356-358.
                "La Pulsion vers l'autodestruction,"
                   pp. 368-375. Annotated under *The Heel*
                   of Achilles.
                "Le Libre arbitre dans un contexte hiér-
                   archique," pp. 444-453. See No. 90 for
                   annotation.

87   "Whereof One Cannot Speak...?" In *Life After Death*.
      Ed. Arnold Toynbee, et al. London: Weidenfeld and
      Nicolson, 1976. Pp. 238-259.

      Traces some of the more puzzling phenomena identi-
      fied by modern physics. "It seems reasonable to assume
      that some of the basic insights gained by modern phy-
      sics are--*mutatis mutandis*--also applicable to the
      psychic field which is complementary to it, as mind
      is to body, corpuscle is to wave."

88   "The Chimeras." In *The Fully Automated Love Life of*
      Henry Keanridge and 12 Other Stories. Chicago:
      Playboy Press, 1976. Pp. 95-101.

      A short story. See No. 95 for original source.

89   "Introduction." In *Reunion* by Fred Ulman. New York:
      Farrar, Strauss and Giroux, 1977. Pp. i-iv.

      Praises this novella "about the age when corpses
      got melted into soap to keep the mother-race clean."

90   "Free Will in a Hierarchic Context." In *Mind and
        Nature: Essays on the Interface of Science and
        Philosophy*. Ed. John B. Cobb, Jr., and David
        Griffin. Washington, D.C.: University Press of
        America, 1977. Pp. 60-65.

        Summarizes his theories about "behavioural holons"
        as explained in *The Ghost in the Machine*. Reprinted
        in *Janus: A Summing Up*.

91   "Interview." In *The Author Speaks: Selected PW
        Interviews 1967-76*. New York: Bowker, 1977.

        See No. 246 for original source.

CONTRIBUTIONS TO PERIODICALS

Fiction

92   "Mixed Transport: An Episode from *Arrival and De-
      parture*." *Reader's Digest* 44 (February 6, 1944),
      132-136.

93   "Fatigue of the Synapses." *Partisan Review* 18 (Jan-
      uary 1951), 16-31.

      A chapter from *The Age of Longing*.

93a   "Interlude." *Harper's* 202 (February 1951), 48-54.

      Excerpt from *The Age of Longing*.

94   "Episode." *Encounter* 31 (December 1968), 35-38.

95   "The Chimeras." *Playboy* 16 (May 1969), 145, 235-6.

      See also No. 88.

Nonfiction

96   "Scum of the Earth: Epilogue." *New Statesman and
      Nation* 22 (September 13, 1941), 253-255.

      See *Scum of the Earth*, pp. 283-287.

97   "The Artist and Politics." *Saturday Review of Liter-
      ature* 25 (January 31, 1942), 3-4, 14-15.

98   "The Great Crank." *The Observer* (October 1942),
      13-14.

      Annotated under *The Yogi and the Commissar*.

99   "Anonymous Portraits." *New Statesman and Nation* 24
        (October 27, 1942), 255+

100   "Challenge to Knights in Rusty Armor." *New York Times
        Magazine* (February 14, 1953), 5-6.

        Annotated under *The Yogi and the Commissar* as
        "Knights in Rusty Armour."

101   "The Birth of a Myth." *Horizon* (London), April 1943.

        Annotated under *The Yogi and the Commissar* as "In
        Memory of Richard Hillary."

102   "We Need an Army of Pessimists." *New York Times Maga-
        zine* (November 7, 1943), 12-13.

        Annotated under *The Yogi and the Commissar* as "The
        Fraternity of Pessimists."

103   "The French 'Flu." *Tribune* (London), November 1943.

        Annotated under *The Yogi and the Commissar*.

104   "The Nightmare That Is a Reality." *New York Times
        Magazine* (January 1944).

        Annotated under *The Yogi and the Commissar* as "On
        Disbelieving Atrocities."

105   "A Farewell to Arms." *Canadian Forum* 23 (March 1944),
        273-274.

106   "The Intelligentsia." *Horizon* (London), March 1944.

        Annotated under *The Yogi and the Commissar*.

107   "Yogi, Commissar--or Humanist? Reply to Granville
        Hicks." *Antioch Review* 5 (June 1945), 298-299.

108   "Challenge to Russia: Lift the Iron Curtain!" *New
        York Times Magazine* (March 10, 1946), 7-8.

        Annotated under *Trail of the Dinosaur* as "A Way
        To Fight Suspicion."

109   "The Dilemma of Our Times." *Commentary* 1 (June 1946),
        1-3.

        Annotated under *The Trail of the Dinosaur*.

110   "Morals and Politics." *New Statesman* 32 (July 6, 1946), 9.

111   "The Great Dilemma That Is Palestine." *New York Times Magazine* (September 1, 1946), 5, 51-52.

112   "French Communists." *New Statesman and Nation* 33 (March 29, 1947), 216.

113   "Schöpferische Versuchung." *Die Wochenpost* 1, v (1946), 5-6.

114   "Koestler Finds a Trojan Horse in France." *New York Times Magazine* (January 5, 1947), 41-42.

      Wants Western Europe to organize against Communism.

115   "Letter to a Parent of a British Soldier in Palestine." *New Statesman and Nation* 34 (August 16, 1947), 126-127.

116   "London Letter." *Partisan Review* 14 (March-April 1947), 138-145.

      This "London Letter" and the two following are annotated under one entry in *Trail of the Dinosaur.*

116a "London Letter." *Partisan Review* 14 (July-August 1847), 341-345.

117   "London Letter." *Partisan Review* 15 (January 1948), 32-39.

118   "Auch England zwischen Ost und West." *Stuttgarter Rundschau* 2, xi (1947), 26-28.

119   "Alexander Stachanow macht Schule." *Rheinischer Merkur* 2, xxvi (1947), 14.

120   "Richard Hillary, Schriftsteller." *Merkur* 1, v (1947), 40-55.

121   "Die umgestulpte Pyramid." *Der Monat* 1, i (1948), 24-26.

122   "Brief aus Tel Aviv: Vom Ghetto zur Utopie." *Der Monat* 1, iii (1948), 94-98.

123   "Der Staat Israel." *WFZ; Wirtschafts--und Finanz-Zeitung* 2, xliii (1948), 2.

124   "Gestalt und Zukunft des Romans." *Universitas* 2 (1948), 1401-1404.

125   "Trugschlüsse der Linken." *Presse-Korrespondenze* Nr. 47 (1948), 9-11.

126   "Die Zukunft des Romans." *Europäische Rundschau* Heft 17 (1948), 805-806.

127   "Die Problematik unserer Zeit." *Umschau* 3 (1948), 279-282.

128   "De Gaulle und seine Bewegg." *Der Ruf* xv (1948), 6.

129   "Von acht politischen Täuschungen." *Neues Europa* Heft xi (1948), 15-20.

130   "Babbitts of the Left." *Life* 24 (May 3, 1948), 123-129.

       Annotated under *Trail of the Dinosaur* as "The Seven Deadly Fallacies."

131   "Les temps heroïques." *Occident* (1948).

       See also No. 86.

132   Translation of Jacob Weinshall's "Crank in Israel." *Horizon* 19 (June 1949), 399-410.

133   "The Novelist Deals with Character." *The Saturday Review of Literature* 32 (January 1, 1949), 7-8, 30-31.

134   "The Complex Issue of the Ex-Communist." *New York Times Magazine* (February 19, 1950), 10-11.

       Annotated under *Trail of the Dinosaur* as "Chambers, the Villain."

135   "For a European Legion of Liberty." *New York Times Magazine* (October 8, 1950), 9-10.

       Annotated under *Trail of the Dinosaur* as "The European Legion."

136   "Verlorene Illusionen Kommunismus." *Der Monat* 2, xx (1950), 133-139.

        Koestler's essay in *The God That Failed* in German translation.

137   "Das falsche Dilemma." *Der Monat* 2, xxii-xxiii (1950), 436-441.

138   "Die Pilgerfahrt eines Rebellen." *Der Monat* 2, xviii (1950), 563-565.

        Annotated under *Trail of the Dinosaur* as "A Rebel's Progress: To George Orwell's Death."

139   "Für eine europäische Freiheitslegion." *Der Monat* 3, xxvi (1950), 115-119.

        Annotated under *Trail of the Dinosaur* as "The European Legion." Not in the Danube edition.

140   "Der Versuchungen des Romanciers." *Welt und Wort* 5 (1950), 495-497.

141   "Appalling Alternatives." *The Saturday Review of Literature* 34 (January 13, 1951), 19-21, 94-95.

        Annotated under *Trail of the Dinosaur* as "The Right to Say 'No.'" See also No. 252.

143   "Freedom at Long Last." *Collier's* 128 (October 27, 1951), 32-33.

        Annotated under *Trail of the Dinosaur* as "The Shadow of a Tree."

144   "The Koestler Saga." *The New Yorker* 28 (July 26, 1952), 21-25.

        Reprint of a chapter from *Arrow in the Blue*.

145   "Der Druck der Umwelt. Gruppennachahnung ist eine Macht." *Die Kultur* 1, xii-xiii (1952-1953), 1.

146   "Ist die Intelligenze erkrankt? Eine Grundfrage an das Heute." *Die Kultur* 1, iv-v (1952-1953), 1.

147   "Politische Neurosen." *Der Monat* 5, lxii (1953), 227-237. See No. 16, "A Guide to Political Neuroses."

148   "Politcheskie nevrozy." Tr. Mikhail Leder. *Vremya i
       my* 23 (1977), 133-151.

       See also No. 147 and No. 153.

149   "Phantastische Langeweile. Science Fiction." *Der
       Monat* 5, lx (1953), 664-667.

150   "Einfühlung in die Welt des anderen. Gedanken über
       das Erkennen und Wiederkennen." *Die Kultur* 2,
       xxiv-xxv (1953-1954), 5.

151   "Bohemeleben in Tel Aviv." *Neue literarische Welt* 4,
       v (1953), 3.

152   "Gibt es politische Neurosen? Eine Diskussion um
       Arthur Koestlers Aufsatz." *Der Monat* 6, lxviii
       (1954), 150.

153   "Politiske neuroser." *Danske magasin* 2 (1954),
       102-116.

       See also No. 147 and No. 148.

154   "Vom Liebeswerben." *Mensch, Geschlecht, Gesellschaft*
       (1954), 97-104.

155   "The Trail of the Dinosaur." *Encounter* (May 1955),
       5-14.

       Annotated under *Trail of the Dinosaur*.

156   "Quand j'étais communiste." *Le Revue de Paris* 62
       (June 1955), 19-34.

       Excerpt from *The Invisible Writing*.

157   "Reply." *New Statesman and Nation* 52 (September 1,
       1956), 242.

       Replies to V.S. Pritchett's review of *Arthur
       Koestler* by John Atkins.

158   "Dawn of the Prefab Era." *The Saturday Review of
       Literature* 42 (November 14, 1959), 13-15.

159   "Last of the Saints." *Commentary* 29 (February 1960),
       120-122.
       Annotated under *The Lotus and the Robot* as Part I
       of "Four Contemporary Saints."

160   "Reflections on the Year 15 p.H." *New York Times
        Magazine* (March 20, 1960), 29, 87-88.

        Annotated under *Drinkers of Infinity* as "The Age
        of Discretion." Originally a BBC radio broadcast',
        February 25, 1960.

161   "Reply." *Isis* 51 (March 1960), 73-76.

        Replies to a review of *The Sleepwalkers* by Giorgio
        De Santillana and Stillman Drake.

162   "The Espresso Generation." *Mademoiselle* 50 (April
        1960), 120, 164-165.

163   "Trying to Talk with Other Planets." *Science Digest*
        47 (June 1960), 69-72.

164   "Love Affair with Norway." *Mademoiselle* 52 (February
        1961), 94-95, 139-140.

        Annotated under *Drinkers of Infinity.*

165   "Lotus and the Robot: Excerpt." *Horizon* 3 (March
        1961), 4-11.

        Annotated under *The Lotus and the Robot.*

166   "George Orwell." *Encounter* 17 (November 1961), 93.

        Replies to John Wain's review of Richard Rees's
        study of Orwell, *Fugitive from the Camp of Victory.*

167   "The Pressure of the Past." *Psychoanalysis and the
        Psychoanalytic Review* (Fall 1961), 25-39.

        Excerpt from *The Lotus and the Robot.*

168   "Der grösste Skandal Christenheit, Zum 400. Ger-
        burtstag von Galileo Galilei." *Weltwoche* (Zurich)
        32, Nr. 1598 (1964), 25.

169   "Japans Kurs liegt fest. Zum Goten oder Bösen."
        Die Zeit 19, xli (1964), 32.

170   "The Act of Creation, 1: The Dark Ages of Psychology."
        The Listener 71 (May 14, 1964), 785-791.

171   "The Act of Creation, 2: Games of the Underground."
       The Listener 71 (May 21, 1964), 825-828.

172   "The Act of Creation, 3: The Art of Discovery and
       the Discoveries of Art." *The Listener* 71 (May 28,
       1964), 861-864.

173   "The Act of Creation." *Spectator* 212 (June 5, 1964),
       755.

       Replies to D.R. Newth's review of *The Act of Cre-
       ation*.

174   "The Greatest Scandal in Christendom." *The Observer*
       (February, 1964).

       Annotated under *Drinkers of Infinity*.

175   "Reply to P.B. Medawar." *New Statesman* (June 19,
       1964), 950-952.

       See also No. 67.

176   "Eureka Process: Excerpt from *The Act of Creation*.
       Horizon 6 (Autumn 1964), 16-25.

178   "For Better or Worse Her Course is Set." *Life* 57
       (September 11, 1964), 63-79.

       A journalist's view of Japan. See also No. 169.

179   "The Greatest Scandal in Christendom." *Critic* 23
       (1964), 14-20.

       Annotated under *Drinkers of Infinity*. See also
       No. 174.

180   "Inversion Effects in the Tachistoscopic Perception
       of Number Sequences." *Psychon* 3 (1965), 75-76.

       Written with J. Jenkins. Annotated under *Janus: A
       Summing Up*.

181   "Aesthetics of Snobbery: Excerpts from *The Act of
       Creation*." *Horizon* 6 (Winter 1965), 50-53.

182   "Biological and Mental Evolution." *Nature* 208, No.
       5015 (November 12, 1965), 1033-1036.

       Annotated under *Drinkers of Infinity*.

183   "Evolution and Revolution in the History of Science."
        Encounter 25 (December 1965), 32-38.

        Annotated under *Drinkers of Infinity.*

184   "On Violence." *Adam: International Review* 5, No. 300
        (1965), 57-59.

        Summarizes his theory of the polarized self-
        assertive and self-transcending tendencies, a theory
        discussed at length in *The Ghost in the Machine.*

185   "Evolution and Revolution in the History of Science."
        The Advancement of Science (March 1966).

        Annotated under *Drinkers of Infinity.* See also
        No. 183.

186   "Of Geese and Men." *The Observer* (September 18,
        1966), 26.

        Annotated under *Drinkers of Infinity.*

187   "Dr. Moreau's Modern Islands." *New Statesman and
        Nation* 73 (May 26, 1967), 721.

        Annotated under *Drinkers of Infinity* as "The Patient
        as a Guinea Pig."

188   "Koestler on Svetlana." London *Sunday Times* (October
        1, 1967), 55-56.

        Annotated under *Drinkers of Infinity* as "Daughter
        to Stalin."

189   "Dissecting the Human Animal." *The Observer* (October
        15, 1967), 10-11.

        Annotated under *Drinkers of Infinity* as "Of Apes
        and Men."

190   "Man--One of Evolution's Mistakes." *New York Times
        Magazine* (October 19, 1969), 30-31, 108, 112-116.

        Annotated under *The Heel of Achilles* as "The Urge
        to Self-Destruction."

191   "Der Konstruktionsfehler." *Der Monat* 20 (1968), 33-37.

192   "What's Wrong with Us?" *The Observer* (April 28, 1968), 25-26.

       Annotated under *The Heel of Achilles* as "The Urge to Self-Destruction."

193   "Is Man's Brain an Evolutionary Mistake?" *Horizon* 10 (Spring 1968), 34-43.

       Excerpt from *The Ghost in the Machine*.

194   "Evolution of Man: What Went Wrong?" *Current* 69 (June 1968), 61-64.

       Repeats points made in *The Ghost in the Machine*.

195   "Farewell to Gauguin: A Joyless Traveler's Guide to the Fiji Islands." London *Sunday Times Magazine* (April 13, 1969), 76-79.

       Annotated under *The Heel of Achilles*.

196   "The Faceless Continent." London *Sunday Times Magazine* (May 25, 1969), 35.

       Annotated under *The Heel of Achilles*.

197   "Australia." *Atlantic* 223 (June 1969), 12-24.

       Annotated under *The Heel of Achilles* as "The Faceless Continent."

198   "The Urge to Self-Destruction." *The Observer* (September 28, 1969), 11-12.

       Annotated under *The Heel of Achilles*.

199   "Fiji." *Atlantic* 224 (October 1969), 18-25.

       Annotated under *The Heel of Achilles* as "Farewell to Gauguin."

200   "Mahatma Gandhi--The Yogi and the Commissar." *New York Times Magazine* (October 5, 1969), 27-29, 90-117.

       Annotated under *The Heel of Achilles*.

201   "The Mahatma Gandhi--The Yogi and the Commissar."
       London *Sunday Times Magazine* (October 5, 1969),
       20ff.

       Annotated under *The Heel of Achilles.*

202   "1980: The Rule of Mediocracy." London *Times* (Octo-
       ber 6, 1969), 10-12.

       Annotated under *The Heel of Achilles.*

203   "Man, One of Evolution's Mistakes?" *New York Times
       Magazine* (October 19, 1969), 28-30.

       Annotated under *The Heel of Achilles* as "The Urge
       to Self-Destruction."

204   "Rebellion in a Vacuum." *The Political Quarterly*
       40, No. 4 (October-December 1969), 374-382.

       Annotated under *The Heel of Achilles.*

205   "The Urge to Self-Destruction." *Chemistry in Britain*
       6 (1970), 165-166.

       Annotated under *The Heel of Achilles.*

206   "Can Psychiatrists Be Trusted?" *Encounter* 34 (March
       1970), 50-53.

       Annotated under *The Heel of Achilles.*

207   "Literature and the Law of Diminishing Returns."
       Encounter 34 (May 1970), 39-45.

       Annotated under *The Heel of Achilles.*

208   "Beyond Atomism and Holism--The Concept of the
       Holon." *Perspectives in Biology and Medicine* 13,
       No. 2 (Winter 1970), 131-154.

       Annotated under *Beyond Reductionism: The Alpbach
       Symposium.*

209   "The Case of the Midwife Toad." London *Sunday Times
       Magazine* (September 19, 1971), 20-21.

210   "Marrakech." *Atlantic* 228 (December 1971), 6-26.

       Annotated under *The Heel of Achilles*.

211   "The Chess Match of the Century." London *Sunday Times* (July 2, 1972), 33-34.

       Annotated under *The Heel of Achilles* as "The Glorious and Bloody Game."

212   "Echoes of the Mind." *Esquire* 78 (August 1972), 116-120, 156-158.

213   "Mechanics of the Supermind." London *Sunday Times Magazine* (September 3, 1972), 33-34.

       On the Spassky-Fischer chess match.

214   "Private Dubert's War, and Peace." London *Daily Telegraph Magazine* (August 17, 1973), 16-17.

215   "The Lion and the Ostrich: Ten Years On." *Encounter* (October 1973), 37-42.

       Excerpt from *Suicide of a Nation?*

216   "Beyond Our Understanding: Arthur Koestler Investigates the Mysterious World of the Inexplicable." London *Sunday Times Magazine* (November 25, 1973), 33-34.

217   "The Evidence of ESP." London *Daily Telegraph Magazine* (November 30, 1973), 20-21.

218   "Order from Disorder." *Harper's* 249 (July 1974), 54-64.

219   "Comment." *Impact of Science and Society* 24 (October 1974), 271-288.

       Adapted from *The Roots of Coincidence*.

220   "Less Equal Than Others?" *New Community* 3 (Spring-Winter 1974), 36-37.

221   "The Yogi and the Commissar Revisited." *Bulletin of
        the John Rylands Library* 57, No. 2 (Spring 1975),
        388-405.

222   "Introduction." In *Horizon* 17 (Winter 1975), 26-31.

        Annotated under No. 83. On Julius Hay.

Book Reviews

223   "Drinkers of Infinity." *Encounter* 9, No. 5 (November
        1957), 76-78.

        A review of Alexander Koyre's *From the Closed
        World to the Infinite Universe.*

224   "Of Dogs and Men." *The Observer* (October 1959).

        A review of William Sargant's *Battle for the Mind:
        A Physiology of Conversion and Brainwashing.* Anno-
        tated under *Drinkers of Infinity.*

225   "Of Geese and Men." *The Observer* (September 18, 1966).

        A review of Konrad Lorenz's *On Aggression.* Anno-
        tated under *Drinkers of Infinity.*

226   "Of Apes and Men." *The Observer* (October 15, 1967),
        10-11.

        A review of Desmond Morris's *The Naked Ape.* Anno-
        tated under *Drinkers of Infinity.*

227   "The Patient's Dilemma." *The Observer* (January 1,
        1964).

        A review of Brian Inglis's *Fringe Medicine.* Anno-
        tated under *Drinkers of Infinity.*

228   "The Patient as Guinea Pig." *The New Statesman* (May
        26, 1964).

        A review of M.H. Pappworth's *Human Guinea Pigs--
        Experimentation on Man.* Annotated under *Drinkers of
        Infinity.*

229   "Daughter to Stalin." London *Sunday Times* (January
        10, 1965).

        A review of Svetlana Alliluyeva's *Twenty Letters
        to a Friend*. Annotated under *Drinkers of Infinity*.

230   "Mistress to Picasso." *The Observer* (March 3, 1965).

        A review of Francois Gilot and Carlton Lake's
        Life with Picasso. Annotated under *Drinkers of In-
        finity*.

231   "Books of the Years?" *The Observer* (April 1, 1965).

        Annotated under *Drinkers of Infinity*.

Notes and Correspondence

232   "Anonymous Portraits: The Crank." *New Statesman and
        Nation* 24 (October 17, 1942), 255-256.

        Annotated under *The Yogi and the Commissar* as "The
        Great Crank."

233   "Morals and Politics." *New Statesman and Nation* 32
        (July 6, 1946), 9-10.

234   "French Communists." *New Statesman and Nation* 33
        (March 29, 1947), 216.

235   "Pritchett and Koestler." *New Statesman and Nation*
        52 (September 1, 1956), 242-243.

        See No. 157.

236   "Sleepwalkers and Vigilantes." *Isis* 51 (March 1960),
        73-79.

        See No. 161.

237   "Act of Creation." *Spectator* 212 (June 5, 1964),
        755.

G

INTERVIEWS

238   "A Visit with Arthur Koestler." *New York Times Book Review* (April 4, 1948), 4.

An interview with Harvey Breit.

239   "Talk with Arthur Koestler." *New York Times Book Review* (April 1, 1951), 24-25.

An interview with Harvey Breit.

240   "A Conversation." In *Scaling the Wall: Talking to Eastern Europe.* Ed. George Urban. Detroit: Wayne State University Press, 1964. Pp. 97-111.

Annotated under No. 57.

241   "Arthur Koestler Interview." *Quadrant* 14 (January-February 1969), 29-36.

Transcript of a lively interview on Melbourne television with Barry Jones. Talks about Jabotinsky, Palestine and Israel, the Utopian appeal of Communism, Willi Muenzenberg, Trotsky and Zinoviev as models for Rubashov, and his passage to England.

242   "A Conversation with Arthur Koestler: Man Is an Aberrant Species." *Psychology Today* 4, No. 1 (June 1970), 62-65, 78-84.

An interview with Elizabeth Hall. Topics: animal quarantine in England, Gandhi, Zen, drugs, *Darkness at Noon,* behaviorism, language learning, the mass media, the self-transcending tendency.

243   "Arthur Koestler at 65: A Fighter for Men's Minds
        Now Studies Their Brains." *New York Times Maga-*
        zine (August 30, 1970), 12-26.

        Reprinted from *L'Express*. Translated by Stanley
        Hoffman.

244   "Arthur Koestler." In *The Creative Experience*. Ed.
        Lawrence E. Abt and Stanley Rosen. New York:
        Grossman Publishers, 1970. Pp. 131-153.

        Topics: autistic thinking and scientific discovery,
        scientific creativity and artistic creativity, his
        childhood, Ernest Hemingway, writers who influenced
        him (Alfred Döblin, Thomas Mann, Hemingway, the
        early Thornton Wilder), theories of humor, Lysenkoism,
        integrity in writing.

245   "Science and Reality." An NBC broadcast interview.
        New York: September 1972.

        Annotated under *The Heel of Achilles*.

246   "*PW* Interviews Arthur Koestler." *Publishers Weekly*
        203 (April 30, 1973), 20-22.

        An interview with Peter Grosvenor.

247   "A Conversation with Arthur Koestler." *Saturday*
        Review 3 (March 6, 1976), 23-24.

        An interview with George Feifer.

248   "Arthur Koestler." In *L'Herne*. Ed. Pierre Debray-
        Ritzen. Paris: Editions de l'Herne, 1975.

        Special issue devoted to interviews with Koestler.
        Includes:
        "Naissance de la nevrose politique," pp. 30-31.
        "Premier utopie, première échec," pp. 34-35.
        "Dialogue avec Manes Sperber," pp. 72-79.
        "Les Fruits de l'utopie contemporaine," pp. 140-142.
        "Deuxième séjour à Paris (1933-1937)," pp. 159-160.
        "Irruption de la cruelle Espagne," pp. 169-170.
        "Le Dialogue avec la mort et l'écriture invisible,"
            pp. 174-178.
        "Libération," pp. 181-186.
        "Le zéro et l'infini," pp. 186-189.
        "Les Dernières batailles politiques," pp. 206-207.

248a "Appointment with Janus: A Profile of Arthur Koestler."
      The Observer Colour Supplement (February 26, 1978),
      16-20.

      An interview with John Heilpern.

248b "Arthur Koestler." *The Paris Review* (Summer 1984),
      183-201.

      An interview with Duncan Fallowell, the last inter-
      view given by Koestler before his death. Topics:
      his youth, Timothy Leary and drugs, his life in
      England, Indian saints, George Orwell.

H

SYMPOSIA, LECTURES, AND BROADCASTS

248c   "The Novelist's Temptations." Speech given at the
International Congress of the P.E.N. Club, September, 1941.

      Annotated under *The Yogi and the Commissar*.

249   "The Challenge of Our Time." BBC lecture, Spring, 1947.

      Annotated under *Trail of the Dinosaur*.

250   "The Future of the Novel." Part of a symposium in September, 1946.

      Annotated under *Trail of the Dinosaur*.

251   "The Boredom of Fantasy." BBC lecture, May, 1953.

      Annotated under *Trail of the Dinosaur*.

252   "The Right To Say 'No': An Outgrown Dilemma." Lecture given at the Congress of Cultural Freedom, June 25, 1950.

      Annotated under *Trail of the Dinosaur*.

253   "The Failure of Response." Lecture given at the Congress of Cultural Freedom, June 25, 1950.

      Annotated under *Trail of the Dinosaur* as "The Right To Say 'No': Four Contributions to the Congress for Cultural Freedom."

254   "Babbitts of the Left." Lectures given in U.S. in 1948.

      Annotated under *Trail of the Dinosaur* as "The Seven Deadly Fallacies."

255 "Artist on a Tightrope." Lecture given at the Symposium on "Belief and Literature," Calcutta, February, 1959.

Annotated under *Drinkers of Infinity*.

256 "Reflections on a Peninsula." Lecture given to the Royal Society of Literature, November 3, 1960.

Annotated under *Drinkers of Infinity*.

257 "Culture in Explosion." Lecture given at the International Symposium of "Art in Society," Vienna, 1960.

Annotated under *Drinkers of Infinity*.

258 Participant in a symposium on *Maschine: Denkmaschine Staatsmaschine*. Entwecklungstendenzen der modern industriegesellschaft. Hamburg-Berlin: Rv. Deckers Verlag, 1963.

259 "Gravity and the Holy Ghost." Lecture given at the Symposium on "The Scientific and Artistic Achievements of the Century of Enlightenment," at the Cinci Foundation, Venice, September, 1967.

Annotated under *Drinkers of Infinity*.

260 "Ethical Issues Involved in Influencing the Mind." In *The Ethics of Change: A Symposium*. Toronto: CBC Publishing, 1969. Pp. 1-11.

Annotated under No. 69.

261 "Rebellion in a Vacuum." In *The Place of Value in a World of Facts: Proceedings*. New York: Wiley Interscience Division, 1970. Pp. 221-228.

Annotated under *The Heel of Achilles*.

262 "Literature and the Law of Diminishing Returns." Lecture given at the Cheltenham Festival of Literature, November, 1969.

Annotated under *The Heel of Achilles*.

263   "The Urge to Self-Destruction." In *The Place of Value in a World of Facts: Proceedings*. New York: Wiley Interscience Division, 1970. Pp. 297-305.

       Annotated under *The Heel of Achilles*. This lecture, and No. 261, were given at the 14th Nobel Symposium, Stockholm, 1969.

263a   Participant in a symposium on "Going into Europe-- Again?" *Encounter* 36, No. 6 (June 1971), 8.

264   Participant in a panel on Drugs and Society in the Year 2000. Published in *Psychotropic Drugs in the Year 2000: Use by Normal Humans*. Ed. Wayne O. Evans. Springfield, Illinois: Charles C. Thomas, 1971. Pp. 128-158.

       Annotated under No. 74.

265   Participant in a symposium on *Probleme in Gespräch. Rauschmittel und Süchtigkeit*. Bern and Frankfurt: Verlag Herbert Lang, 1971.

266   "The Limits of Man and His Predicament." In *The Limits of Human Nature: Essays Based on a Course of Lectures Given at the Institute of Contemporary Arts, London*. London: Allan Lane, 1973. Pp. 49-58.

       Annotated under No. 80.

267   "The Lion and the Ostrich." The Eighth Annual Lecture under the "Thank-Offering to Britain Fund." Oxford: Oxford University Press, 1973.

       See introduction to *Suicide of a Nation?*

I

ADDENDA

268   "Mrak v polden." *Kontinent* 5 (1975), 251-272.

       French reaction to *Darkness at Noon*.

269   "T'ma v polden'." *Vremya i my* 1 (November 1975),
       7-114, and 2 (December 1975), 3-130.

270   "Tropa dinozvara." *Vremya i my* 10 (August 1976),
       90-113.

271   "Chelovek--oshibka Evoliutsy." *Vremya i my* 17 (May
       1977), 161-174.

272   "Iuda na pereput'e." *Vremya i my* 33 (September 1978),
       97-130.

273   "Sem' smertnykh grekhov." *Dvadtsat' dva* 3 (August
       1978), 210-214.

274   "Confrontation." London *Times* (November 18, 1978), 6.

275   "Confrontation." *Harper's* 257 (December 1978), 59-66.

276   "The Three Domains of Creativity." In *The Concept of
       Creativity in Science and Art*. Ed. Denis Dutton
       and Michael Krause. The Hague: Martinus Nijhoff
       Publishers, 1981. Pp. 1-17.

       Reprinted from *Challenges of Humanistic Psychology*.
       Ed. James F.T. Bugental. New York: McGraw-Hill, 1967.
       Condenses theory about creativity from *The Act of
       Creation*.

Secondary Sources

J

BOOKS AND COLLECTIONS OF ESSAYS

277   Atkins, John. *Arthur Koestler*. London: Neville
       Spearman, 1956.

       Treats Koestler's political ideas in a popular
       exposition without footnotes or bibliography.

278   Bishop, Reginald, and John Lewis. *The Philosophy of
       Betrayal. An Analysis of the Anti-Soviet Propaganda
       of Arthur Koestler and Others*. London: The Russia
       Today Society, 1945.

       Bilious Soviet apologetics.

279   Braatøy, Trygve. *Arthur Koestler og Psykoanalysen*.
       Oslo: J.W. Cappelens, 1947.

       Much of the discussion focuses on *Arrival and De-
       parture* and the Richard Hillary essay in *The Yogi and
       the Commissar*.

280   Calder, Jenni. *Chronicles of Conscience. A Study of
       George Orwell and Arthur Koestler*. London: Martin
       Secker and Warburg, 1968.

       Describes both Orwell and Koestler as propagandists
       first and novelists second. Although both men speak
       significantly for their times, Orwell is a better
       artist than Koestler and his works will survive
       longer.

281   Debray-Ritzen, Pierre, ed. *Arthur Koestler*. L'Herne
       Cahier No. 27. Paris: Editions de l'Herne, 1975.

           Koestler il y a vingt uns   Manes Sperber
           Portrait   Danielle Hunebell
           Un croisé sans croix: essai   Pierre Debray-Ritzen
             psychobiographique sur un
             contemporain capital

Lectures de jeunesse	Arthur Koestler
Arthur Koestler et le sionisme	Olivier Bourdet-Pléville
Un nationalism dangereux	Claude Bourdet
Un pionnier de grand coeur	Wolfgang von Weisl
Arthur Koestler et le communisme	Gérard Blum
Les temps héroïques	Arthur Koestler
Préface à L'Accusé d'Alexandre Weissberg	Arthur Koestler
Le bar du crépuscule	Robert Kanters
Arthur Koestler et les procès de Moscou	Pierre de Boisdeffre
Le dilemme de notre temps	Gérard Blum
Lettre à Mamaine	Arthur Koestler
(1947) Journal	Mamaine Koestler
Le combat contre la peine de mort	Jacques Léauté
L'histoire de *Vigil*	Cynthia Koestler
Histoire du Prix	Arthur Koestler
Arthur Koestler et le mystère en Asie	Max Olivier Lacamp
La pulsion vers l'autodestruction	Arthur Koestler
La cime et le ravin	Marcel H. Boisot
Arthur Koestler face à la connaissance	Quentin Debray
Trois entretiens sur Arthur Koestler avec: Rémy Chauvin, Louis Pauwels, Stan Ullam	Pierre Debray-Ritzen
La production littéraire d'Arthur Koestler depuis 1949	Cynthia Koestler
A propos de *Suicide d'une nation?*	Cynthia Koestler
Le libre arbitre dans un contexte hiérarchique	Arthur Koestler
Koestler et la pensée contemporaine	Alain de Benoit

282   Glagoleva, Emilia Nikolaevna. *Estetika antirazuma.*
       Moscow: Iskusstvo, 1972.

       Merrill and Frazier annotate this as follows:
       "Koestler is seen as a key figure in the literature
       of the irrational."

283   Goodman, Celia, ed. *Living with Koestler: Mamaine Koestler's Letters 1945-1951*. New York: St. Martin's Press, 1985.

Celia Goodman is Mamaine Paget Koestler's twin sister. She has here edited Mamaine's letters to her from the period when Mamaine lived with Koestler in Wales, in France, and in Pennsylvania. These lively letters reveal Koestler in many moods: drunk, happy, depressed, even physically abusive of Mamaine. Many glimpses of the great are provided, including Camus, Malraux, Sartre, John von Neumann, et al. Koestler appears in various settings--with his mother ("Typically, she handed K a cutting of a poem in which a woman tells her son that when she's dead he will realize how much he loved her"), and in trouble with the French police for drunk driving ("he socked the Commissaire"). On the night of their wedding, Koestler got drunk and Mamaine and Cynthia Jefferies ended up staying with Stephen Spender ("He said: I've always wanted to spend a night with you, it's too bad it was your wedding night"). A book of extraordinary interest to students of Koestler.

284   Hamilton, Iain. *Koestler: A Biography*. London: Macmillan, 1982.

Stresses the period in Koestler's life from 1940 through 1970, narrating events but offering little analysis. Sketches Koestler's political attitudes clearly, and summarizes Koestler's campaign to abolish capital punishment.

285   Harris, Harold, ed. *Astride the Two Cultures: Arthur Koestler at 70*. London: Hutchinson, 1975; New York: Random House, 1976.

Haynes, Renée. "Wrestling Jacob: Koestler and the Paranormal." Recapitulates Koestler's writings on parapsychology.

Nott, Kathleen. "The Trojan Horses: Koestler and the Behaviourists." Defends Koestler against the charge that he is beating a dead horse in his attacks on Behaviourism.

Koestler, Cynthia. "Twenty-Five Writing Years." Provides glimpses of Koestler at work.

Grigg, John. "The Do-Gooder from Seville Gaol."
Describes Koestler's good works: establishing the
Fund for Intellectual Freedom, campaigning against
capital punishment, providing awards for creative
work by prison inmates, and resisting the animal
quarantine laws in England.

Rees, Goronwy. "*Darkness at Noon* and the 'Grammatical Fiction.'" Summarizes Koestler's experiences
as a Communist, stressing their importance for the
ideas shaping *Darkness at Noon*. Emphasizes the significance of Rubashov's recognition that he has sup-
pressed the "grammatical fiction," the first person
singular, and maintains it is the guilt Rubashov
feels over this suppression that motivates him--as
much as anything--to confess. Points out that the
grammatical fiction involves a noticeable, though
perfectly justifiable, distortion of the historical
material on which Koestler based his novel. Concludes
that "Koestler's later writings have been very largely
an attempt to defend the claims of the 'grammatical
fiction' against those types of scientific thought
which regard it as no more than an unnecessary hypothesis and human beings as no more than a collection of
sense data."

Hamilton, Iain. "Wonderfully Living: Koestler the
Novelist." Defends Koestler's novels of "the real
world of telegrams and anger" against the Bloomsbury
variety of fiction stressing personal relations.

Beloff, John. "Koestler's Philosophy of Mind."
Characterizes Koestler as a "disenchanted humanist."
Summarizes fluently the mind-body arguments in contemporary thought and describes Koestler as an "emer-
gentist," for whom "every level of evolutionary development can give rise to new principles and new entities
that cannot be reduced to those that are to be found
at a lower level. Life may be one such emergent principle, mind would be another, perhaps the phenomenon
of language or rational thought would constitute yet
another." Koestler's interest in parapsychology suggests he may be a "cryptotranscendentalist," or at
least a Janus who presents the face of a mystic as
well as that of a sage.

Thorpe, W.H. "Koestler and Biological Thought." Maintains that Koestler's main views on science are confirmed by recent developments in scientific knowledge, especially as that knowledge counters the claims of reductionists. Good discussion of the issues involved in epiphenomenalism.

Barron, Frank. "Bisociates: Artist and Scientist in the Act of Creation." Summarizes the results of various studies of the personalities of scientists and creative artists, concluding that "science and art bisociate in the psychology of creativity."

Graubard, Mark. "*The Sleepwalkers*: Its Contribution and Impact." Thinks that Koestler is generally unfair to all but Pythagoras and Kepler in *The Sleepwalkers*, but praises the book and defends Koestler against the charges made by Giorgio de Santillana and Stillman Drake (see No. 583).

Webberley, Roy. "An Attempt at an Overview." Finds a continuity running through Koestler's works.

MacLean, Paul D. "The Imitative-Creative Interplay of Our Three Mentalities." Stresses the role of dissociation--isolation from the group--in true creative activity.

286   Huber, Peter Alfred. *Arthur Koestler: Das literarische Werk*. Zurich: Fretz & Wasmuth, 1962.

287   Kanapa, Jean. *Le traitre et le prolétaire; ou, L'entreprise Koestler and co. Ltd., suivi d'inédits sur le procès de Mathias Rakosi*. Paris: Editions Sociales, 1950.

Explains that during Rakosi's trial François Fejto gave *L'Esprit* a long psychological explanation of the traitor's confession much like the explanations given in *Darkness at Noon*.

288   Koestler, Cynthia. *Stranger on the Square*. Ed. Harold Harris. London: Hutchinson, 1984.

A joint memoir by the Koestlers, left unfinished at their deaths. Cynthia Koestler writes nine of the twelve essays and tells of her experience working for Koestler. Excellent personal glimpses.

289   Levene, Mark. *Arthur Koestler*. New York: Frederick
      Ungar, 1984.

      Gives an excellent introduction to Koestler's fic-
      tion. A detailed chronology of Koestler's life is fol-
      lowed by a biographical chapter and six chapters of
      brisk summary and criticism. Includes a helpful bib-
      liography.

290   Mays, Wolfe. *Arthur Koestler*. Guildford, England:
      Lutterworth Press, 1973.

      A clearly written fifty-page summary of Koestler's
      work through *The Case of the Midwife Toad*. Concludes
      that Koestler's "overall approach to philosophical
      problems is more in the continental tradition of
      Hegel, Marx and Kierkegaard."

291   Merrill, Reed, and Thomas Frazier. *Arthur Koestler:
      An International Bibliography*. Ann Arbor: Ardis,
      1979.

      Contains an introduction to Koestler's ideas; lists
      of all the appearances of Koestler's works through
      July 1978; a comprehensive secondary bibliography
      through the same period; and an appendix giving "Re-
      cent Science Literature Citing Works by Arthur Koest-
      ler." Many excellent photographs. Almost no annota-
      tions. An indispensable reference.

292   Mikes, George. *Arthur Koestler: The Story of a Friend-
      ship*. London: Andre Deutsch, 1983.

      Mikes is a Hungarian journalist who lives in London.
      He met Koestler in 1952 through their mutual interest
      in the Hungarian poet Endre Ady. They had a close
      friendship for over thirty years, sharing talk, com-
      pany, and Hungarian cuisine.

293   Nedava, J. *Arthur Koestler*. London: Robert Anscombe
      and Company, 1948.

      Defends Koestler's abilities as a novelist. Summar-
      izes with appreciative commentary the following books
      by Koestler: *Dialogue with Death, Darkness at Noon,
      The Yogi and the Commissar, Arrival and Departure*,
      and at length *Thieves in the Night*.

294   Pearson, Sidney A., Jr. *Arthur Koestler*. Boston:
       Twayne, 1978.

       Pearson emphasizes Koestler's rationalism and gives
       a balanced overview of his whole body of works. Offers
       a good introduction to all of Koestler's main ideas.
       Asserts that the diverse subjects of Koestler's books
       are connected by a fundamental unity of thought.

295   Sperber, Murray A. *Arthur Koestler: A Collection of
       Critical Essays*. Englewood Cliffs, N.J.: Prentice-
       Hall, 1977.

       Orwell, George. "Terror in Spain. Reviews *Spanish
       Testament*, judging the prison section to be "of the
       greatest psychological interest."

       Orwell, George. "Arthur Koestler." Believes that
       The Gladiators is in some ways "unsatisfactory,"
       finding that Koestler "falters" on *why* revolutions
       go wrong. Considers *Darkness at Noon* Koestler's
       masterpiece. Classifies *Arrival and Departure* as a
       "tract" with an "insufficient" political statement.
       Notes a "well-marked hedonistic strain" in Koestler's
       writings.

       Cowley, Malcolm. "Koestler the Disenchanted."
       Claims that *Dialogue with Death* is "no less moving
       today than it was when we still hoped for victory in
       Spain." Judges *Darkness at Noon* "not a safe guide to
       contemporary politics" but a valuable expression of
       "the everlasting conflict between the political uni-
       verse and the moral universe," as well as "a powerful
       work of fiction because it is, for its author, a
       ritual of sacrifice and atonement."

       Bellow, Saul. "A Revolutionist's Testament." Praises
       Koestler for attacking "the most difficult and troub-
       ling issues of private and political morality" in
       Arrival and Departure.

       Rosenberg, Harold. "The Case of the Baffled Radical."
       Criticizes Koestler's artistry in *Arrival and Depart-
       ure* as "quite thin" and regrets his "pervading glib-
       ness," but lauds his introduction into the novel of
       "political sophistication and a serious sense of the
       human drama of public events."

Matthiessen, F.O. "The Essays of Arthur Koestler."
Describes Koestler as "not an original, nor a particularly powerful, thinker" but "a man of acute feeling
who has suffered long and intensely." "Koestler is
most symptomatic of recent history in the degree to
which he has made politics a substitute for religion."

Wilson, Edmund. "Arthur Koestler in Palestine."
Decides that the neglect of the hero as a character
makes *Thieves in the Night* "rather unsatisfactory."
The first part of the novel is "rather implausible,"
but as a "series of dispatches" *Thieves in the Night*
is "satisfying as few such things are."

Rosenfeld, Isaac. "Palestinian Ice Age." Criticizes
Koestler's treatment of terrorism in *Thieves in the
Night,* and judges the novel most successful in its
dramatization of Palestinian politics between 1937
and 1939.

Pritchett, V.S. "The Best and the Worst, IV: Arthur
Koestler." Finds that "Guilt and self-pity have been
the price" of Koestler's restlessness, and that "the
neuroses of the journalist are exacerbated by his
special opportunities for seeing life." Regrets that
"not even in his own language, we feel, has he any
love of words or any sense of their precision and
grace." Concludes that *Darkness at Noon* is "a powerful
book, but not an imaginative work of the highest kind,"
and that in *Thieves in the Night* he is *very nearly*
prepared to justify violence." Admires Koestler's
fiction as "a stimulus, an incitement to others, an
imposing outline against the sky," that makes clear
"we have no novelist of the social or public conscience who has Koestler's scope or force--no journalist or reporter either."

Merleau-Ponty, Maurice. "Koestler's Dilemmas."
Calls Koestler a "mediocre" student of Marxism who in
Darkness at Noon misrepresents Marxist Communism,
which is "the manifestation of human values through
a process which might involve dialectical detours
but at least could not entirely ignore human purposes."
Rubashov is guilty because opposition to the Party is
not allowable at the time. Rubashov's error lies in
his inability to realize that "the only history we
are entitled to speak of is one whose image and future we ouselves construct by means of equally method-
ical and creative interpretations." Koestler errs in

seeing history as a "clockwork" for "Marxism is neither the negation of subjectivity and human action nor the scientific materialism with which Rubashov began."

West, Rebecca. "Roads to Communism and Back: Six Personal Histories." "Arthur Koestler's essay is one of the most handsome presents that has ever been given to future historians of our time," and *The God That Failed* is "a truly contemporary book."

Deutscher, Isaac. "The Ex-Communist's Conscience." Praises Koestler for giving in *The God That Failed* a "truthful and honest characterization of the type of ex-communist to which he himself belongs."

Spender, Stephen. "In Search of Penitence." Judges *The Invisible Writing* "so much better" than *Arrow in the Blue*. Perceives a double motive in *The Invisible Writing*: to represent himself as typical of his time, and "to assert his own identity." Admires the "immense range and variety" of *The Invisible Writing*. "At heart Koestler seems to me a religious man in search of penitence, homesick for a communion of saints. And in spite of his courageous self-examination, he does not seem to have discovered that his basic fault is pride."

Sperber, Murray A. "Looking Back on Koestler's Spanish War." Surveys the writings on Spain, finding significant revisions in *Dialogue with Death*. The intensity of Koestler's self-examinations makes his writings of the Spanish Civil War "a series of remarkable documents."

Newman, James R. "Arthur Koestler's *Insight and Outlook*: The Novelist Formulates a Philosophy with Circuit Diagrams." Dismisses *Insight and Outlook* as "invariably long-winded and turgid, often imprecise and superficial."

Ayer, A.J. "Mr. Koestler's New System." Concludes that the basic concepts (e.g., bisociation, self-asserting and self-transcending faculties) are overworked in *Insight and Outlook* and that Koestler is at his best when he treats specific points in psychology and aesthetics.

Hampshire, Stuart. "Science and the Higher Truth." Praises the "superbly sustained" narrative of *The Sleepwalkers*. Rejects Koestler's thesis that science and faith are fatally split, claiming that the "real difference" between the modern age and the medieval is that "the range of ascertained truth about the natural order has become too various, and too intricate, for any one man to grasp." Describes Koestler's treatment of Galileo as "unpredictably amazing." "There are five hundred pages of bold exposition of theories, with brilliant phrases, embarrassing phrases, philosophical reflections, laments about the modern world. All of it is intensely readable."

Empson, William. "A Full-Blown Lily." Comments wittily on Koestler's treatment of Zen and Yoga in *The Lotus and the Robot*, chiding him for giving aid and comfort to Christianity but admitting that "the exposure of Yoga was needed."

Steiner, George. "A Happy Few Leap Before Looking." Regrets the "gray, diffuse style" of *The Act of Creation*, which shows "little interest" in linguistics, modern logic, and the theory of mathematical inference. Perceives in Koestler's conclusions a "disarming banality" frequently, and judges the book as "*haute vulgarisation*."

Aiken, Henry David. "The Metaphysics of Arthur Koestler." Accuses Koestler of stretching his concepts too far, but praises *The Act of Creation* for its "fresh, exciting principles of orientation that suggest approaches to a *Weltanschauung* which I find exhilirating to contemplate." Koestler's principles are not scientifically verifiable, but the "vision" in *The Act of Creation* provides a "refreshment of the soul."

Fiedler, Leslie. "Toward the Freudian Pill." Reviews *The Ghost in the Machine*, regretting how Koestler keeps attacking such dead topics as "the limitations of orthodox Freudianism ... and Behavioural Psychology." Finds in Koestler "a scarcely concealed hatred and resentment of the young."

Toulmin, Stephen. "The Book of Arthur." Discerns in each of the works in Koestler's trilogy on creativity (*The Sleepwalkers, The Act of Creation,* and *The Ghost*

in the Machine) a book of "*truths* he is explaining"
and a book on the "Truth he is preaching." Judges
Koestler's refutation of Neo-Darwinism unconvincing.
Concludes of *The Ghost in the Machine* that there is
"no real connection between Koestler's prescription
for human folly and the 'scientific evidence' he offers in its support." Describes as "Manichaean"
Koestler's vision of the predicament bequeathed man
by evolution--caught between an urge to construction
and an urge to destruction. Thus, *The Ghost in the
Machine* is theology, not science.

ESSAYS AND REVIEW ARTICLES

296   Abel, Lionel. "The Koestler Pardon." *New Republic*
       191 (October 8, 1984), 28-32.

       Asserts that Koestler's relationship to his Jewish-
       ness is "hardly clear" either to him or to us. Judges
       Darkness at Noon his "greatest achievement." Concludes
       that the one serious charge against Koestler is that
       "in a world which required radical change" he "found
       no way of being radical." Accuses Koestler of a version
       of "Trotskyism" in his attention to ESP, Lamarckism,
       etc., but decides he cannot be condemned for lack of
       radical political action because such action is im-
       possible now.

297   Aiken, Henry David. "The Metaphysics of Arthur Koest-
       ler." *New York Review of Books* 3 (December 17, 1964),
       22-25.

       Annotated under No. 295.

298   "Alienation in Arthur Koestler's *Darkness at Noon*."
       In *Philosophy in Literature*. Berkeley: Fybate Lec-
       ure Notes, 1968. Pp. 35-41.

       Excellent summary of the opposed views of Koestler
       and Maurice Merleau-Ponty. Even if Merleau-Ponty is
       correct in arguing that Koestler misinterprets Marx
       in *Darkness at Noon*, Koestler is still right in saying
       that the show trials reveal what happens when Marxism
       is put into practice. Yet, Merleau-Ponty makes a good
       point in claiming that humanism and violence go to-
       gether in history: "Each humanitarian reform is ac-
       companied by violence and death."

298a   Axthelm, Peter M. "The Search for a Reconstructed
       Order: Koestler and Golding." In *The Modern Con-
       fessional Novel*. New Haven: Yale University Press,

1967. Pp. 97-127.

Summarizes *Darkness at Noon* at length and praises
its use of literary "doubles."

299   Ayer, A.J. "Mr. Koestler's New System." *New Statesman
      and Nation* 38 (July 30, 1949), 127-128.

Annotated under No. 295.

300   "Back Insurance." *Time* 61 (February 23, 1953), 39.

Recounts refusal of the actors in Mannheim, Germany,
to perform *Darkness at Noon* for fear of future occupation by the Russians.

301   Bantock, G.H. "Arthur Koestler." *Politics and Letters*
      1 (Summer 1948), 41-47.

Analyzes Koestler's first four novels (*The Gladiators, Darkness at Noon, Arrival and Departure,* and
Thieves in the Night), finding them all deficient in
feeling, mere "projection screens for his own prob-
lems--the related ones of integration and values."
Koestler fails as a novelist because (1) his aloofness
makes inevitable an "escape at the crucial moment"
and (2) he falls back on a "superimposed determinism
which avoids the necessity of a fully thought out
responsible solution."

302   Beadle, Gordon. "Anti-Totalitarian Fiction." *The
      English Record* 25 (Summer 1974), 30-33.

Summarizes *Darkness at Noon* among other anti-totalitarian novels.

303   Bellow, Saul. "A Revolutionist's Testament." *New York
      Times Book Review* (November 21, 1943), 1, 53.

Annotated under No. 295.

304   Benson, Frederick. *Writers in Arms: The Literary Im-
      pact of the Spanish Civil War*. New York: New York
      University Press, 1967.

Refers frequently to Koestler, summarizing his experiences.

305 Beum, Robert. "Epigraphs for Rubashov: Koestler's
     Darkness at Noon." *Dalhousie Review* 42 (Spring
     1962), 86-91.

     Judges *Darkness at Noon* as "immensely superior" to
     1984 and *Brave New World.* Defines "the structure of
     the novel as that of tragedy."

306 Boisdeffre, Pierre de. "De Victor Serge à Soljénitsyne:
     Une exploration et une explication de la terreur."
     Nouvelle Revue des Deux Mondes (November 1974),
     288-307.

     Includes Koestler with Victor Serge and Solzhenit-
     syn as reliable expositors of Stalin's reign of terror.

307 Burgess, Anthony. "Koestler's Danube." *Spectator* 215
     (October 1, 1965), 418-419.

     Remarks that the period of *The Gladiators, Thieves
     in the Night,* and *The Yogi and the Commissar* has "a
     strong smell of failure about it." *Thieves in the
     Night* is "a genuine novel smelling of a sharply ob-
     served Palestine," but *The Gladiators* is "not suffic-
     iently a work of the historical imagination." *Darkness
     at Noon* is a "magnificent" example of "a balance of
     the literary and the didactic." Koestler is "a light-
     bringer" who has done us "a lot of good."

308 Chaning-Pearce, Melville. "Yogi and Commissar: Con-
     templation and Action." *Friends Quarterly Examiner*
     80 (July 1946), 141-153.

     Agrees with Koestler's diagnosis in *The Yogi and
     the Commissar* of the ills of the age, and also with
     the needed treatment, but rejects the notion that
     man "can cure his own schizophrenia by 'taking thought.'"

309 Chiaromonte, Nicola. "Koestler, or Tragedy Made Fu-
     tile." *Politics* 2 (September 1945), 266-270.

     Dismisses *Darkness at Noon* and Arrival and Departure,
     calling them failures that result from Koestler's
     "pretentiousness, wanting to be the Dostoievsky of
     the fallen Left." Argues that Koestler misunderstood
     the attitude of the French people in 1940, misreading
     their puzzlement and falling prey to handy clichés
     about appeasement and the Hitler-Stalin pact. As a

consequence, "Koestler had chosen the worst: a middle-of-the-road path between despair and provisional hopes." Sneers at Koestler for "the typical futility of an intellectual who hasn't been able to face the facts." Charges Koestler in *The Yogi and the Commissar* with the same superficiality that he seems to think typifies most of his work.

310   Coates, J.B. *The Crisis of the Human Person. Some Personalist Interpretations.* London: Longmans, Green and Co., 1949. Pp. 176-190.

Summarizes Koestler's criticism of Marxism and scientism, finding nothing new but judging the exposition "brilliant and provocative." Interprets Koestler's disillusionment as "a cover for a conscious or unconscious hedonism."

311   Coltrera, Joseph T. "On the Creation of Beauty and Thought: The Unique as Vicissitude." *Journal of the American Psychoanalytical Association* 13 (July 1965), 634-703.

Refers frequently to *The Act of Creation* in an extremely wide-ranging discussion. Approves Koestler's view of the creative act not as epiphany but as a process that is "worked through to a permanent cognitive structure which organizes other ideas." Relates Koestler's notion of "radical novelty" to Thomas Kuhn's understanding of the effects of revolutionary scientific theories. Makes the interesting point that "Koestler's idea of learned skills strategically effected is but a poetic vision of the 'game theory' of his friend, the mathematician John von Neumann."

312   Cowley, Malcolm. "Koestler the Disenchanted." *New Republic* 107 (July 20, 1942), 89-90.

Annotated under No. 295.

313   Davis, Robert Gorham. "The Sharp Horns of Koestler's Dilemmas: Difficulties of Reconciling Ends and Means." *Antioch Review* 4 (December 1944), 503-517.

Summarizes the ends-means dilemma in *The Gladiators* ("The historic or political import of this parable is not clear"), *Darkness at Noon,* and *Arrival and*

Departure. "But in the rich interplay of multiple elements within the character that makes depth in great novels Koestler's work is deficient." Koestler prefers the "polarity of abstractions, of the mutually exclusive," to the use of reason. Concludes that in "his abnegation of reason at a moment when we need it most ... he is a harmful guide and teacher." (See Granville Hicks's response in No. 341.)

314 Deutscher, Isaac. "The Ex-Communist's Conscience." In *Russia in Transition and Other Essays.* London: Jonathan Cape, 1957. Pp. 203-216.

Annotated under No. 295.

315 Downing, Francis. "Koestler's Dialogue with Death." *Commonweal* 54 (June 1, 1951), 187-188.

Calls Koestler "our most brilliant exposer of the Soviet myth," but concludes that Koestler is inadequate in explaining the appeal of Communism.

316 Drucker, H.M. "Koestler's *Darkness at Noon.*" In *The Political Uses of Ideology.* London: London School of Economics and Political Science, 1974. Pp. 80-93.

Rebuts Irving Howe's charge (see No. 343) that *Darkness at Noon* is spoiled by an obsession with ideology: there can be "effective ideology and good fiction." Asserts that the novel is "the appropriate form of fiction for taking an ideological message to a literate middle-class audience."

317 Edman, Irwin. "Arthur Koestler als Philosoph." *Der Monat* 1 (June 1949), 151-153.

Unexamined.

318 Empson, William. "A Full-Blown Lily." *New Statesman* 61 (January 6, 1961), 21-22.

Annotated under No. 295.

318a Eucken-Erdsiek, Edith. "Labyrinth der Illusionen: Eine Auseinandersetzung mit Arthur Koestler." *Ordo: Jahrbuch für die Ordnung von Wirtschaft und Gesellschaft* 5 (1953), 267-286.

Discusses *Darkness at Noon, The God That Failed,*
and *The Yogi and the Commissar,* explicating the
"vier grossen Naivitäten": (1) the "weitverbreitete
Illusion" that it is possible to convince opponents
by reason; (2) that it is possible to reach opponents
on a human basis; (3) that there is any correspondence
between what a system claims to be and what it really
is; and (4) that there is a limit to what man can
endure.

319 Feifer, George. "Guru of the Western World." *The
      Daily Telegraph Magazine* (September 5, 1975),
      24-26, 29, 47, 51, 55-56.

      Stresses Koestler's detestation of the attention
      paid to his political writing ("I want to wipe off
      the label stuck to me by political partisans") and
      his annoyance at not being recognized as a seminal
      scientific thinker. A revealing interview in which
      Koestler discourses animatedly on a great many
      topics.

320 Fiedler, Leslie. "Toward the Freudian Pill." *New
      Statesman and Nation* 74 (October 27, 1967), 548-
      549.

      Annotated under No. 295.

321 Galligan, E.L. "The Usefulness of Arthur Koestler's
      Theory of Jokes." *South Atlantic Quarterly* 75
      (Spring 1976), 145-160.

      Judges Koestler's theory of humor very convincing.

322 Garaudy, Roger. "La mensonge à l'état pur: Arthur
      Koestler." In *Une littérature de fossoyeurs.* Paris:
      Editions sociales, 1947. Pp. 71-78.

      Describes as false the problem in *Darkness at Noon,*
      in which Koestler has doctored the text to make Ruba-
      shov's confession unintelligible.

323 Geering, R.G. "*Darkness at Noon* and *1984*--A Compara-
      tive Study." *Australian Quarterly* 30 (September
      1958), 90-96.

      "Koestler had illusions and lost them, Orwell had
      no illusions to lose."

324   Gibson, Arthur. "Visions of the Future." In *Humanism
      and Christianity*. Ed. Claude Geffré. London: Herder
      and Herder, 1973. Pp. 118-126.

      Discusses Koestler with Charles Reich and Alvin
      Toffler, basing his comments on *The Ghost in the
      Machine* and discovering "much pith" in Koestler's
      views on eugenics.

325   "Gibt es politische Neurosen? Eine Diskussion um
      Arthur Koestlers Aufsatz von Michael Freund, Leonard
      Woolf, Jules Monnerot, Alexander Mitscherlich,
      Theodor Adorno." *Der Monat* 6 (February 1954), 464-
      485.

      Prompted by Koestler's essay on political neuroses
      (see No. 147). Woolf thinks Koestler is mistaken in
      identifying a political neurosis, but judges him an
      original thinker. The discussion continues in No. 326.

326   "Gibt es politische Neurosen? Eine Diskussion um
      Arthur Koestlers Aufsatz von Richard Crossman,
      Bertrand de Jouvenel, Hans Kohn, u.a." *Der Monat* 6
      (May 1954), 140-150.

      Continues the discussion begun in No. 325. Crossman
      rejects the view that wrong opinions reveal a political
      neurosis. In an epilogue, Koestler replies to Michael
      Freund that if a fool acts foolishly, he is foolish,
      but if an intelligent man acts foolishly, he is neu-
      rotic. Koestler concludes that Richard Crossman,
      Bertrand de Jouvenel, and Leonard Woolf are more on
      his side than not.

327   Gilbert, Arthur N. "Pills and the Perfectability of
      Man." *Virginia Quarterly Review* 45 (Spring 1969),
      315-328.

      Rejects Koestler's proposal for a drug that would
      mitigate man's urge to violence, partly on the
      grounds that violent behavior originates in "societal
      conditions" as well as in human nature.

328   Giniewski, Paul. "Arthur Koestler: un antisemita
      ebreo?" *Rassegne Meusile di Israel* 41 (1975),
      181-183.

      Discusses Koestler's attitude toward Zionism as

seen by Claude Bourdet, Olivier Bourdet-Pleville,
and Wolfgang von Weisl in their essays included in
No. 281.

329   Glicksberg, Charles I. "Arthur Koestler and Communism."
       Queen's Quarterly 53 (Winter 1946-1947), 418-429.

       Summarizes Koestler's work admiringly, praising him
       for "wresting a tragic intensity out of the contemp-
       orary crisis of alienation."

330   Gollwitzer, H. "Der Mensch und die Dinosaurier: Eine
       Antwort an Arthur Koestler." *Der Monat* 83 (August
       1955), 475-479.

       Continues the discussion begun in No. 359. Finds
       Koestler influenced too much by a model of life
       drawn from the Middle Ages.

331   Gray, James. "We Walk in Anguish." In *On Second
       Thought*. Minneapolis: University of Minnesota,
       1946. Pp. 237-240.

       Calls *Arrival and Departure* "one of the most im-
       portant novels of our time."

332   "Grösse ohne Heimat." *Christ und Welt* 2 (October 13,
       1949), 9.

       Comments on Koestler's career through *Insight and
       Outlook*. "Man kann nur wünschen, dass sich Koestler
       wieder mit Kraft dorthin wendet, wo seine grosse
       Begabung und Ursprünglichkeit liegt."

333   Haerdter, Richard. "Der Mensch ohne Mythos und Illus-
       ionen: Bemerkungen zum Fall Arthur Koestler." *Die
       Gegenwart* 4 (July 1, 1949), 13-16.

       Unexamined.

334   Hampshire, Stuart. "Science and the Higher Truth."
       New Statesman and Nation 57 (January 31, 1949),
       159-160.

       Annotated under No. 295.

335 Handlin, Oscar. "The Worlds of Arthur Koestler."
    Atlantic 222 (December 1968), 92-96.

Identifies three constant themes in Koestler's
work: "the consequences of man's will to transform
society; the nature of his place in the world; and
his capacity for rational understanding and action."

336 Harrington, Michael. "The Political Novel Today."
    Commonweal 63 (October 28, 1955), 79-82.

"Arthur Koestler as a novelist and political propa-
gandist is a first-rate second-rater."

337 Harrington, Michael. "The Unpolitical Political:
    Koestler Suspended in Mid-Air." *Anvil* 7 (Winter
    1956), 6-8.

Places Koestler in "mid-air" because his disillusionment with Stalinism has never been replaced with a
genuine conviction. Attributes Koestler's ambiguity
to his disjunctive mind set, seeing everything in
the light of either the Yogi or the Commissar: "This
fundamental division is repeated over and over throughout Koestler's work." Even in *Darkness at Noon* "he is
stating another one of his insoluble philosophic
dilemmas and not engaging in political analysis."

338 Hausman, Carl Ransdell. "Understanding and the Act
    of Creation." *Review of Metaphysics* 20 (September
    1966), 88-112.

Finds "certain mechanistic aims" in *The Act of Creation* in that Koestler explains mental phenomena by
"antecedent biological, emotional, and environmental
causes"--thus creating a "tension which threatens
the development of a coherent theory." Identifies
four ways in which Koestler's theory is limited: (1)
no "consistent characterization" of originality, (2)
ambiguity about the role of determinism, (3) the im-
plied teleology is "left unexamined," and (4) issues
are not pursued far enough. Yet *The Act of Creation*
is "rich in suggestiveness."

339 Hayman, Ronald. "The Hero as Revolutionary: Koestler's
    Novels." *London Magazine* 12 (December 1955), 56-68.

Defends Koestler's novels as *novels*.

340   "Der Heilige und der Revolutionar." *Sonntagsblatt* 1,
       No. 23 (1948), 3-4.

       Unexamined.

341   Hicks, Granville. "Arthur Koestler and the Future of
       the Left." *Antioch Review* 5 (Summer 1945), 212-223.

       Replies to Davis's criticism in No. 313. Tries to
       calm the liberals who call Koestler "irresponsible."
       Koestler approaches "the problem of values in the
       modern world" in a "tentative experimental spirit."
       A generally sympathetic essay.

342   Hoffman, Frederick J. "*Darkness at Noon*: The Conse-
       quences of Secular Grace." *Georgia Review* 13 (Fall
       1959), 331-345.

       Says of *Darkness at Noon* that "its outlines are a
       secular parallel of the theological passion of Thomas
       à Becket in Eliot's *Murder in the Cathedral*."

343   Howe, Irving. "Malraux, Silone, Koestler: The Twenti-
       eth Century." In *Politics and the Novel*. New York:
       Meridian Books, 1957. Pp. 203-234.

       Praises *Darkness at Noon* for its account of the
       arrest of Rubashov, but maintains that "the novel is
       crucially flawed, and Rubashov thinned into abstract-
       ness, by Koestler's simple and often crude theorizing
       about the moral premises which, he claims, were the
       basis of the Old Bolshevik capitulation to Stalin."
       Criticizes the either/or dilemma in *Darkness at Noon*
       and concludes that the novel does not "yield a cred-
       ible portrait of man thinking."

344   Joad, C.E.M. *Decadence: A Philosophical Inquiry*.
       London: Faber and Faber, 1948. Pp. 220-226.

       Calls *The Yogi and the Commissar* a "brilliant"
       book. "Koestler is, I think, one of the outstanding
       minds of the age." Criticizes Koestler for "undue
       concentration upon personal experience." Laments
       his asking of determinism not Is it true? but From
       what need does it spring? "Koestler's mode of treat-
       ment is typical of much of the thinking which is in-
       spired by modern psychology."

345   Kahn, Lothar. "Arthur Koestler and the Jews." *The
       Chicago Jewish Forum*. 18 (Summer 1960), 341-346.

       Excellent analysis of Koestler's attitudes toward
       Jews and Zionism. Discerns in Koestler's barren
       childhood the roots of his later "obvious need for
       belonging in some larger and impersonal groups."
       Points to the coexistence in Koestler of a cold
       rationalist and an "inveterate romanticist." Docu-
       ments the ambivalence in Koestler's attitude toward
       Jews: a revulsion for Jewish ethnocentrism balanced
       by a fierce championing of the rights of Jews. Sees in
       Koestler's support for Zionism the conviction that a
       return to the soil would purge Ghetto Jews of their
       "habitual over-smugness." "The story of Koestler is
       that of an incomplete Jew who, though he leaned over
       backward to develop one phase of Jewishness, was too
       deficient in others ever to achieve fullness."

346   Klingopulos, G.D. "Arthur Koestler." *Scrutiny* 16
       (June 1949), 82-92.

       Judges Koestler as a more serious writer than Or-
       well, with an unquestionable "literary gift." "But
       Mr. Koestler's intensity is so unrelieved and so in-
       sistent that it seems often not to emerge from the
       situation in a novel but rather to satisfy some need
       in the author." Sums up Koestler as "something of a
       disappointed commissar." *Twilight Bar* is "without
       value." Criticizes *Thieves in the Night* for "its
       attempt to provoke intense feelings against the Arabs,"
       but praises it for "the intelligent analyses of the
       problems facing the new colonists" in Palestine.
       Condemns the "justification for terrorism" in *Thieves
       in the Night* ("the indulgence of animosity against
       the Arabs is gross"). "As a propagandist he is thor-
       oughly unscrupulous. His sardonic tone of the man who
       has suffered seems at times a form of conceit."

347   Kneller, George F. *The Art and Science of Creativity*.
       New York: Holt, Rinehart and Winston, 1966. Pp. 41-
       46.

       Praises *The Act of Creation* as "the most embracing
       synthesis of recent years." It has "accomplished the
       twofold task of any great synthesis: to open a host
       of avenues for detailed research and to describe the
       entire field within which this research may proceed."

348   Knopfelmacher, Frank. "Koestler at 70." *Quadrant* 104
          (1976), 41-46.

          Explains "the Doctrine of the Unsullied Intentions:
          the proposition that the old bolsheviks, and to a
          lesser extent even No. 1 himself, were men whose im-
          petus to action was morally praiseworthy and who were
          entrapped by the unintended consequences of empirically
          false premises within their philosophies." Points out
          the evidence against this doctrine in *The Gulag Archi-*
          pelago. Produces, "in fairness to the dead generations
          of Rubashovs," a defense of their acts based on their
          conviction that World War I revealed the corruption
          of capitalism and the need to change the system at
          any cost.

349   "Koestler: Die grosse Illusion." *Der Spiegel* 7 (March
          11, 1953), 27-31.

          A sympathetic, appreciative overview of Koestler's
          life and work.

350   Lasky, Melvin J. "Arthur Koestler." *Colloquium* 3,
          No. 4 (1949), 11-13.

          Discusses *Darkness at Noon, Thieves in the Night,*
          and *Arrival and Departure*, stressing Koestler's dis-
          illusionment with Communism. In German.

351   Lea, F.A. "Arthur Koestler." In *Voices in the Wilder-*
          ness: From Poetry to Prophecy in Britain. London:
          Brentham Press, 1975. Pp. 101-215.

          Surveys Koestler's career admiringly, approving
          especially of the attacks on behaviorism and the
          hypothesis of the Janus-faced holon.

352   Lentz, Serge. "Arthur Koestler, le poisson pilote:
          Vie et oeuvre de l'écrivain Arthur Koestler, anal-
          yste passioné des problèmes de notre civilisation."
          Realités No. 350 (March 1975), 58-63.

          A popular survey of Koestler's work, praising his
          accomplishments in his books on science.

353   Levene, Mark. "Arthur Koestler: Of Messiahs and Muta-
          tions." *Modernist Studies: Literature and Culture*
          1920-1940 2 (1976), 37-48.

Connects Koestler's political novels to the works
on science through their intense quest for an over-
riding faith: he is "the purest, certainly the most
tenacious, ideologue of faith in our time." Regrets
Koestler's relinquishment of his literary power in
the interest of his "personal messianism." Praises
The Gladiators and *Darkness at Noon*. Finds Koestler
unconcerned with theoretical systems; instead he
ultimately measures every structure for its secular
redemptive value. Calls *Thieves in the Night* "morally
disquieting" but also Koestler's "most relaxed work
of fiction." *The Age of Longing* is "a prolonged rite
of exorcism and revenge." A broad survey with per-
ceptive commentary.

354   Lewis, Wyndham. "Essays." In *The Writer and the Ab-
       solute*. London: Methuen, 1952. Pp. 180-184.

Contends that Orwell learned much from Koestler,
with *Darkness at Noon* helping him to write *1984*.
But whereas they agreed on the bad end of the Russian
Revolution, Orwell would not, like Koestler, condemn
the aftermath of all revolutions.

355   Ling, T.O. "The Yogi and the Commissar Revisited."
       John Rylands Library Bulletin 57 (Spring 1975),
       388-405.

Fills in the middle of the spectrum between the
Yogi and the Commissar. Not much concerned specifically with Koestler.

356   Martin, E.W. "Arthur Koestler and the Time-Spirit."
       The Irish Ecclesiastical Record 71 (May 1979),
       416-425.

Stresses the need to read Koestler's work chrono-
logically because in the series of initiations through
which he has progressed Koestler reflects his own
"close communion with the time-spirit, or the spirit
of the European community on the intellectual plane."
Explains the "two inner compulsions" of the early
Koestler: "the awakening of the social conscience"
and an understanding of the need for people to be
"interested and enthusiastic, faithful and believing."

357   Matthiessen, F.O. "The Essays of Arthur Koestler."
       New York Times Book Review (May 27, 1945), 1, 21.

       Annotated under No. 295.

358   Maulnier, Thierry. "To, czego nawet Koestler nie
       przewidziat." *Kultura* Nr. 16-17 (February-March
       1949), 167-175.

       Analyzes the show trial of Jozsef Cardinal Mind-
       szenty, comparing his behavior to Rubashov's. But
       since Mindszenty neither believed that the end justi-
       fies the means nor swore loyalty to the Communist
       Party, his patently false confession is inexplicable
       in terms of the psychology dramatized in *Darkness at
       Noon*.

359   "Der Mensch und der Dinosaurier." *Der Monat* 82
       (July 1955), 370-379.

       A discussion of *The Trail of the Dinosaur* by Joachim
       Günther, Erich Kuby, Erwin Reisner, Otto Heinrich v.d.
       Gablentz, and Rudolph Hartung. Günther finds Koestler
       too pessimistic and Kuby cautions that Communism cannot
       be blamed for everything that is wrong in the world.
       Reisner thinks that Koestler depicts the vicissitudes
       of humanity with clear vision. The discussion contin-
       ues in No. 330.

360   Merleau-Ponty, Maurice. "Koestler's Dilemmas." In
       Humanism and Terror. Boston: Beacon Press, 1969.
       Pp. 1-24.

       Annotated under No. 295.

361   Merleau-Ponty, Maurice. "The Yogi and the Proletarian."
       In *Humanism and Terror*. Boston: Beacon Press, 1969.
       Pp. 149-177.

       Argues that Koestler should not have blamed Marxism
       for the "suffocating philosophy of the Commissar."
       "For fear of having to forgive, he pretends not to
       understand." Koestler's humanism reveals a "vicious
       side" in politics--he does not progress. Asserts that
       "if one applies Koestler's principles without com-
       promise, they condemn Anglo-Saxon and Societ politics
       alike." Calls the debate between the Western democ-
       racies and Communism a debate between "one Commissar
       and another."

362   Meyerhoff, Hans. "Farewell to Politics." *Commentary*
      21 (June 1956), 596-598.

      The essays in *The Trail of the Dinosaur* are
      "timely" but do not probe beneath the surface.

363   Miles, John A., Jr. "Retrospective: Arthur Koestler."
      Zygon 9 (December 1974), 339-351.

      "Koestler's attitude toward institutional religion
      is one of considerable sensitivity but little enthus-
      iasm." Continued in No. 364.

364   Miles, John A., Jr. "Retrospective: Arthur Koestler,
      II." *Zygon* 10 (June 1975), 191-211.

      Summarizes Koestler's religious thought at length.
      Except in his discussions of Freud and Bergson in
      Insight and Outlook, Koestler speaks "not as a phil-
      osopher to philosophical issues but as a scientific
      journalist of artistic temperament to perceived per-
      sonal and cultural urgencies." Describes *The Sleep-
      walkers* as a combination of Thomas Kuhn's "sociologi-
      cal sensitivity" and Herbert Butterfield's "historical
      erudition."

365   Moloney, Michael Francis. "Koestler's Dilemma."
      America 92 (November 13, 1954), 186-187.

      Gives a generally favorable summary of most of
      Koestler's works, finding him to be an author
      struggling with his past.

366   Morse, J. Mitchell. "Social Relevance, Literary
      Judgment, and the New Right; or The Inadvertent
      Confessions of William Styron." *College English*
      30 (May 1969), 605-616.

      Of *Darkness at Noon*: "It is no diamond, it is a
      bag of mush. As a work of art, it doesn't exist."

367   Mortimer, Raymond. "The Art of Arthur Koestler."
      Cornhill 146 (Winter 1946), 213-222.

      Finds that Koestler is "not English; he is not a
      novelist; and how far is he, as a writer, even lika-
      ble?" His English lacks "personal flavor," but *The
      Gladiators* is "a brilliant essay." "He treats

ordinary peaceable enjoyment as trivial or even dis-
creditable," and "feels impelled, predestined to
guerrilla loneliness, a mixture of Don Quixote and
a rogue elephant." Furthermore, "Not even Swift is
more lacking in geniality." But the writings are
"immensely impressive" even though the endorsement
of violence in *Thieves in the Night* must be condemned.

368   Moseley, Edwin M. "Christ as Marxist Variant: Koest-
       ler's *Darkness at Noon*." In *Pseudonyms of Christ
       in the Modern Novel*. Pittsburgh: University of
       Pittsburgh, 1962. P. 189.

       "Perhaps the contemporary intellectual is not far
       enough away from identification with Rubashov to
       answer the question about himself: Antichrist or
       Christ?"

369   Newman, James R. "Arthur Koestler's *Insight and Out-
       look*: The Novelist Formulates a Philosophy with
       Circuit Diagrams." *Scientific American* 180 (March
       1949), 56-59.

       Annotated under No. 295.

370   Nott, Kathleen. "Koestler and His Critics." *Encounter*
       30 (February 1968), 76-81.

       Defends Koestler against the reviewers who attacked
       The Ghost in the Machine.

371   Orwell, George. "Arthur Koestler." *Focus 2*. London:
       D. Dobson, 1946. Pp. 27-38.

       Annotated under No. 295.

372   Orwell, George. "Catastrophic Gradualism." *Common
       Wealth Review* 2 (November 1945), 12, 14.

       Scorns the theory of "Catastrophic Gradualism"
       (well defined by the banality that you cannot make
       an omelet without breaking eggs), and defends Koest-
       ler against those who reproach him for ignoring the
       omelet cooked by Stalin. (In this argument Orwell
       pre-empts the criticism of Koestler by Merleau-Ponty
       two years later in *Humanisme et terreur*. See No. 360.)
       Places Koestler closer to the Commissar than to the
       Yogi. Asserts that things would have been about the

same in Russia if either Lenin or Trotsky had been
in power instead of Stalin.

373   Orwell, George. "Terror in Spain." *Time and Tide* 18
      (February 5, 1938), 177.

      Annotated under No. 295.

374   Paechter, Heinz. "Reporter des Nichts." *Wort und
      Wahrheit* 8 (April 1953), 314-316.

      Praises Koestler for being an intelligent popular-
      izer of philosophy and a good reporter. Stresses the
      nihilism and scepticism in Koestler's thought.

375   Paetel, Karl O. "Arthur Koestler und die Fragwürdig-
      keit der Idealogien." *Ruf* 2 (May 1, 1947), 5-6, 12.

      Surveys Koestler's work appreciatively.

376   Paetel, Karl O. "Ignazio Silone und Arthur Koestler
      als Zeugen europäischer Selbstbehauptung."
      Deutsche Rundschau 77 (February 1951), 117-127.

      Unexamined.

377   Prescott, Orville. "The Political Novel: Warren,
      Orwell, Koestler." In *In My Opinion: An Inquiry
      into the Contemporary Novel*. Indianapolis: Bobbs-
      Merrill, 1952. Pp. 22-39.

      Describes Koestler's novels as "primarily propa-
      ganda pamphlets." Calls *Darkness at Noon* the most
      effective totalitarian novel of our time," but *The
      Gladiators* is an artfully indirect apology for Com-
      munism." *Arrival and Departure* is a "deeply felt
      political parable" but "inept and clumsy." *Thieves
      in the Night* reveals that Palestine "confused his
      moral vision," but *Promise and Fulfillment* is "clear
      and judicious." *The Age of Longing* is "gruesomely
      interesting, intellectually disturbing," but "quite
      mediocre as a work of art."

378   Pritchett, V.S. "The Best and the Worst, IV: Arthur
      Koestler." *Horizon* 15 (May 1947), 233-47.

      Annotated under No. 295.

379   Rahv, Philip. "Testament of a Homeless Radical."
       Partisan Review 12 (Summer 1945), 398-402.

       Reviews *The Yogi and the Commissar*, admiring "the
       sense of contemporaneity" in Koestler's work. Praises
       Koestler's "epigrammatic brilliance" but deplores
       the "startling effects" and "element of the mere-
       tricious" in his style. Disagrees with Koestler's
       imputation of neuroticism to the intelligentsia as
       a group. Minimizes Koestler's stress on the importance
       for creative writers of knowledge of the social and
       natural sciences. Endorses Koestler's description of
       the Soviet economy as State-capitalism rather than
       Socialism.

380   Redman, Ben Ray. "Arthur Koestler: Radical's Progress."
       College English 13 (December 1951), 131-136.

       Summarizes the early life and the novels. "But
       Koestler himself is a more interesting character
       than any he has created, for, as his books reveal
       him to us, he is a fascinating figure--at once highly
       individual and typically representative--in the great
       novel of our times."

381   Reitz, Hellmuth. "Arthur Koestler." *Welt und Wort* 4
       (January 1949), 13-16.

       Discusses Koestler's work favorably, concentrating
       on *Arrival and Departure* and *The Yogi and the Com-
       missar*.

382   Rivett, Kenneth. "In Defence of Arthur Koestler."
       The Australian Quarterly 19 (September 1947),
       90-94.

       Summarizes Koestler's work and defends him against
       Australian critics. Perceives in Koestler an identifi-
       cation with a "freemasonry of suffering" derived from
       his experiences among those intellectuals who have
       "paid with their own bodies the price of their con-
       victions." Suspects Koestler may have underestimated
       the strength of the "English tradition of gradual re-
       form." Defends Koestler's support of the Jewish min-
       ority in *Thieves in the Night*, pointing to a Freudian
       "repetition-compulsion" in him on behalf of "small
       violent minoroties," but admits Koestler has not
       understood the British view on Palestine.

383 Roche, John P. "Koestler at the Crossroads." *New Republic* 134 (February 13, 1956), 19.

Admits that he is "perpetually disappointed" with the essays in *The Trail of the Dinosaur*. Decides that Cassandra as "lay analyst, cultural anthropologist, or cosmologist" becomes "trivial, or merely dull." But Koestler remains "surely one of the great political analysts of our time."

384 Roland, Albert. "Christian Implications in Anti-Stalinist Novels." *Religion in Life* 22 (Summer 1953), 400-412.

Discovers an "effective dramatic power" in *Darkness at Noon* and identifies an "exquisitely Christian connection between sin and death" in Koestler's criticism of Stalinism. Perceives an "essentially Christian" position in *Arrival and Departure*.

385 Rosenberg, Harold. "The Case of the Baffled Radical." *Partisan Review* 11 (Winter 1944), 100-103.

Annotated under No. 295.

386 Rosenfeld, Isaac. "Palestinian Ice Age." *New Republic* 115 (November 4, 1946), 592-593.

Annotated under No. 295.

387 Scott-James, Rolfe Arnold. *Fifty Years of English Literature, 1900-1950*. London: Longmans, Green, 1951. Pp. 174-176.

Judges that Koestler succeeds with "brain-stuff in fiction." "He is writing novels which illuminate the major problems of the contemporary world without deviating from the way of the imagination."

388 Slumstrup, Finn. "Arthur Koestlers anden halvleg." *Dansk Udsyn* 53, No. 1 (1973), 29-44.

Broad discussion of Koestler's science writing.

389 Smith, R.D. "Detours and Oases: A Note on Koestler." *Orion* 2. London: Nicholson and Watson, 1945. Pp. 55-62.

Examines the first three novels, *Spanish Testament*, and *Scum of the Earth*.

390 Spender, Stephen. "In Search of Penitence." *New York Times Book Review* (September 21, 1952), 4-5, 36.

     Annotated under No. 295.

391 Sperber, Murray A. "Looking Back on Koestler's Spanish War." *Dalhousie Review* 57 (Spring 1977), 107-118.

     Annotated under No. 295.

392 Stanford, Derek. "Arthur Koestler." In *Writers of Today*. Ed. Denys Val Baker. London: Sidgwick and Jackson, 1946. Pp. 85-95.

     Discusses Koestler's work through *The Yogi and the Commissar*.

393 Steele, Peter. "*Darkness at Noon*." *The Critical Review* 12 (1969), 73-82.

     Defends *Darkness at Noon* as a work of art. Stresses the meaning of the prison as a microcosm of the world and views the book "at least as much in the perspective of tragedy as in the perspective of some kind of thesis or of illustrative document." Analyzes the tensions between "a dark inside and a dark outside, between part and future, and ... between absolute collusion and absolute acquiescence."

394 Steiner, George. "A Happy Few Leap Before Looking." *Book Week* 2 (October 25, 1964), 4, 10.

     Annotated under No. 295.

395 Strachey, John. *The Strangled Cry*. New York: William Sloane Associates, 1962.

     Evaluates the Russian Revolution--and Stalinist oppression--as a natural outgrowth of the Enlightenment, and identifies *Darkness at Noon* as "the starting point of the literature of reaction" to rationalism. "The book reaches but does not develop what was to become the main theme of that literature, namely the retreat from rationalism." Adds an interesting note on the novel's title: "Koestler told me that the title had actually been thought of by Daphne Hardy and that he didn't quite know what it meant but that it seemed to have the right ring to it." Offers his own sense of the title's meaning: "an eclipse of human reason, just when the enlightenment should have reached its noontide, in the coming to power of the first government to be consciously based on rationalism."

396 Swingewood, Alan. "The Revolution Betrayed: Koestler and Serge." In *The Novel and Revolution*. London: Macmillan, 1975. Pp. 169-189.

Gives useful summary of the events preceding the Moscow trials. Compares *Darkness at Noon* with Victor Serge's *The Case of Comrade Tulayev* (1945).

397 Toulmin, Stephen. "Arthur Koestler's Theodicy." *Encounter* 41 (February 1979), 46-57.

Enumerates the "three positions on which Koestler concentrates his destructive fire": behaviourist psychology, neo-Darwinist evolution theory, and the belief in historical coincidences. Criticizes Koestler for misrepresenting J.B. Watson and for devoting too much firepower to popular works like B.F. Skinner's *Beyond Freedom and Dignity*. Finds the concept of the holon to be useful, but more so in popular treatments of science than in professional journals. Deplores Koestler's "tendency to prefer sloppy phrase-making to exactitude." Concludes that Koestler is wrong in his hypothesis that an "evolutionary mistake" occurred in the development of the human brain. Judges that "the dogmatism that Koestler attributes to 'the scientific establishment' is, in fact, a rhetorical fiction." Identifies randomness as the focus of Koestler's strongest objections. Explains that all events in evolution may be *caused*, but that they do not seem directed toward betterment, and that (contrary to Koestler's argument) these events are "quite capable of producing, by Darwinian means, results indistinguishable at first sight from those of Lamarckian inheritance." Attributes Koestler's abhorrence of randomness to his need to believe in a world governed in its workings by sufficient reason—hence the theodicy that Koestler has constructed in his works. Compares Koestler to Leibniz in that Leibniz rejected a contingent creation because the period he lived in demanded a "rational reconciliation" of contending religious factions. Thus, Leibniz's theodicy had an

underlying "ideological programme." As a product of
a similarly fragmented civilization, Koestler also
has conceived a theodicy out of ideological motives.
But the pharmacological solution proposed by Koestler
is misguided.

398   Toulmin, Stephen. "The Book of Arthur." *New York
       Review of Books* 10 (April 11, 1968), 16-21.

       Annotated under No. 295.

399   Toulmin, Stephen. "Koestler's *Act of Creation*: Vision,
       Theory, Romance." *Encounter* 23 (July 1964), 58-70.

       Calls *The Act of Creation* "scarcely the kind of
       book one can summarise." Finds that "much of Koestler's
       long and careful discussion of contemporary psycho-
       logical theory is valuable and pertinent," but criti-
       cizes the last section for not taking into account
       the insights into linguistics of contemporary analyt-
       ical philosophy. In general, there is too much at-
       tempt to be "all-embracing" and "his fundamental
       concepts will not stand up to the strain he puts
       upon them." The two halves of the book are not suf-
       ficiently related to one another. The main argument
       of the book is more a "philosophical vision of nature"
       than a scientific theory--"an essentially *romantic*
       vision of nature."

400   Viereck, Peter. "*Darkness at Noon* Revisited." Fore-
       word to *Darkness at Noon*. New York: New American
       Library, 1961. Pp. vii-xiv.

       Asserts that its "artistic vision" and "mystical
       insight" make *Darkness at Noon* more than mere polit-
       ical history. Finds a moral equation in the novel:
       "that idealists of self-righteous ruthlessness are
       destroyed by the non-ideal consequences of their own
       inner flaw." Identifies Rubashov as an "amalgam of
       Alex and Eva Weissberg, the Moscow trial role of
       Bukharin, the personality and pince-nez of Trotsky,
       the physique of Radek, and perhaps a darker side of
       Koestler himself." Points to Dostoevsky as the main
       literary influence on *Darkness at Noon,* citing es-
       pecially Pyotr Verkhovensky in *The Possessed* as a
       forerunner of Stalinism.

401 Weintraub, Stanley. "The Adopted Englishman." In
*The Last Great Cause: The Intellectuals and the
Spanish Civil War*. New York: Weybright and Talley,
1968. Pp. ˆ20-143.

Summarizes Koestler's experiences in Spain.

402 West, Rebecca. "Roads to Communism and Back: Six
Personal Histories." *New York Times Book Review*
(January 8, 1950), 3, 27.

Annotated under No. 295.

403 Wilson, Edmund. "Arthur Koestler in Palestine."
The New Yorker 22 (November 16, 1946), 109-114.

Annotated under No. 295.

404 Wimsatt, William K., Jr., and Cleanth Brooks.
"Tragedy and Comedy: The Internal Focus." In
Literary History: A Short History. New York: Ran-
dom House, 1957. Pp. 575-580.

Call the criticism of Freud's theory of the comic
in Koestler's *Insight and Outlook* "competent and informed." Summarize Koestler's theorizing in *Insight
and Outlook* and describe it as "an attractive scheme."

405 Woodcock, George. "Five Who Fear the Future." *New
Republic* 134 (April 16, 1956), 17-19.

Includes Koestler with George Orwell, H.G. Wells,
George Bernard Shaw, and Aldous Huxley as anti-
Utopians.

406 Woodcock, George. *The Writer and Politics*. London:
Porcupine Press, 1948. Pp. 175-196.

Finds that Koestler lacks Silone's "emotional
identity with the lives of the poor," and that this
lack leads to the "shifting, expatriate character
of Koestler's work." Koestler's fiction is "shallow
on the physical, emotional and spiritual levels."
In *Darkness at Noon* Koestler is a "brilliant journalist" rather than a "constructive artist." *Arrival and
Departure* is "unconvincing," but *The Yogi and the
Commissar* is "a very valuable book." Notes the support of terrorists in *Thieves in the Night*.

REVIEWS OF WORKS BY KOESTLER

407   Davis, Elmer. "A Proletarian Messiah." *Saturday
        Review of Literature* 20 (July 15, 1939), 7.

        The Gladiators is "effective" for its picture of
        history but the characters are not strongly drawn.
        There is "a good deal of meat" in the novel.

408   "Gladiators Uprising." *TLS* (March 11, 1939), 147.

        Calls *The Gladiators* an "eloquent and absorbing"
        story, and praises its "vision of human society."

409   Mitchison, Naomi. "Marxist Rome." *New Statesman and
        Nation* 17 (March 18, 1939), 436.

        Describes *The Gladiators* as "the first Marxist
        historical novel" in a favorable review.

410   Pritchett, V.S. "*The Gladiators*." *Christian Science
        Monitor* (April 15, 1939), 10.

        Praises *The Gladiators*.

411   Reid, Forrest. "*The Gladiators*." *Spectator* 162
        (March 24, 1939), 502.

        Reviews *The Gladiators* favorably.

412   Young, Stanley. "On the Man-Eating Pattern of His-
        ory." *New York Times Book Review* (July 16, 1939),
        6.

        Finds a "cynical joyousness" in *The Gladiators*--
        an "Olympian book."

413   "Brightest in Dungeons." *Time* 37 (May 26, 1941),
       98-102.

       Praises *Darkness at Noon.*

414   Cowley, Malcolm. "Punishment and Crime." *New Repub-
       lic* 104 (June 2, 1941), 766-767.

       Judges that *Darkness at Noon* is "not particularly
       impressive" as a "political document." "His novel is
       best when it is moral and personal rather than pol-
       itical."

415   Dobrée, Bonamy. "*Darkness at Noon.*" *Spectator* 166
       (January 3, 1941), 20.

       A favorable notice.

416   Fischer, Max. "Trials." *Commonweal* 34 (June 13,
       1941), 186.

       Dislikes *Darkness at Noon* for its "materialistic
       and atheistic atmosphere."

417   Littell, Robert. "*Darkness at Noon* by Arthur Koest-
       ler." *Yale Review* 30 (Summer 1941), xii.

       Brief praise for the novel's dramatization of
       ideology.

418   Marriott, Charles. "New Novels." *Manchester Guard-
       ian* (January 3, 1941), 7.

       Says of *Darkness at Noon*, "The moral of the book
       might be if you elect to live by logic, by logic
       you will be damned."

419   Marsh, Gwen. "*Darkness at Noon.*" *Horizon* 3 (March
       1941), 223-224.

       Koestler conveys "with great psychological accur-
       acy the mentality of the Communist Party" in this
       "very fine novel."

420   Martin, Kingsley. "Bourgeois Ethics." *New Statesman
       and Nation* 21 (February 8, 1941), 130-132.

       Unexamined.

421   McHugh, Vincent. "*Darkness at Noon.*" *The New Yorker*
      17 (May 31), 1941), 69.

      Favorable notice.

422   Orwell, George. "*Darkness at Noon.*" *New Statesman
      and Nation* 21 (January 4, 1941), 15-16.

      "The Moscow trials were a horrible spectacle, but
      if one remembered what the history of the Old Bol-
      sheviks had been it was difficult to be sorry for
      them as individuals." *Darkness at Noon* is "most val-
      able as an interpretation of the Moscow 'confessions'
      by someone with an inner knowledge of totalitarian
      methods."

423   Rothman, N.L. "Three Stages of the Soviet Mind."
      Saturday Review of Literature 24 (May 24, 1941), 7.

      The characters in *Darkness at Noon* are "less per-
      sonalities than voices expressing ... their party
      factions and points of view." Does not admire Ruba-
      shov.

424   Salomon, Louis B. "Moscow Purge." *Nation* 152 (May 24,
      1941), 620.

      Calls *Darkness at Noon* "a compelling narrative."
      "The most amazing thing about the book, in fact, is
      the austere economy with which Mr. Koestler has
      compressed one of the most crucial dilemmas of to-
      talitarian political philosophy into a compact,
      meaty novel of less than 270 pages, presenting at
      once a vividly conceived personal tragedy and an
      ideological conflict of the first magnitude."

425   Seaver, Edwin. "*Darkness at Noon* by Arthur Koestler."
      Direction 4 (Summer 1941), 41.

      Brief notice.

426   Strauss, Harold. "The Riddle of Moscow's Trial."
      New York Times Book Review (May 25, 1941), 1, 18.

      Judges *Darkness at Noon* a "splendid" novel that
      gives "an effective explanation of the Moscow
      treason trials."

427   "Tragedy of Logic." *TLS* (December 21, 1940), 641.

       Gives a favorable notice of *Darkness at Noon.*

428   "Zu Arthur Koestlers Buch *Darkness at Noon.*"
       Abendland 2, No. 4 (1947), 122.

       Unexamined.

429   Brown, John Mason. "The Iron Transparency." *Saturday
       Review of Literature* 34 (February 3, 1951), 22-24.

       Reviews the stage version of *Darkness at Noon* and
       chides the liberals who pretend the story is laid
       in "Cuckoo-Borough-on-Clouds. It is, alas, anchored
       in reality and its truth is part of its power."

430   Clurman, Harold. "*Darkness at Noon.*" *New Republic*
       124 (February 5, 1951), 22-23.

       Describes the play as "a sort of *Reader's Digest*
       melodrama."

431   Dupee, F.W. "Literature on Broadway." *Partisan
       Review* 18 (May 1951), 331.

       Darkness at Noon "makes a fairly effective play."

432   Marshall, Margaret. "*Darkness at Noon.*" *Nation* 172
       (January 27, 1951), 92-93.

       Praises the play for its "dramatic and telling"
       episodes. "The production is worth seeing for the
       setting and its extraordinary manipulation."

433   Moore, Charles Werner. "Pilgrim's Lament."
       Theatre Arts 35 (September 1951), 41, 82-83.

       Darkness at Noon doesn't reach tragedy on the
       stage because it is a "drama of idea" and because
       of its directing and acting.

434   Comfort, Alec. "The Desire for Martyrdom." *Life and
       Letters Today* 40 (January 1944), 55-62.

       Stresses the "psychiatric claims" of *Arrival and
       Departure*, interpreting it as coming close to a
       psychoanalysis of Koestler himself and praising the

accuracy of Koestler's insights. Finds Koestler's work full of "unconscious desmophiliac and odynophiliac fantasies."

435   Cowley, Malcolm. "Port of Refuge." *New Republic* 109 (November 22, 1943), 721-722.

Some of the scenes in *Arrival and Departure* are "brilliant or deeply moving" but Peter Slavek, the hero, is unconvincing.

436   Fuerst, Rudolph A. "*Arrival and Departure* by Arthur Koestler." *Psychoanalytic Review* 33 (January 1946), 102-107.

Calls Koestler's identification of neurosis as the source of political action "a generalization without scientific basis."

437   "The Idealist." *TLS* (November 13, 1943), 545.

Describes *Arrival and Departure* as a "striving, impassioned and at times profound novel" and praises the "dramatic symbol and introspective discovery," but notes "some confusion of imaginative motive."

438   Lasky, Melvin. "Dialog mit der Geschichte." *Der Monat* 1 (1949), 93-95.

Reviews *Arrival and Departure.* "Er gleicht Zarathustra, der von seinem Bege herabkommt, um zu verkünden, dass Gott gestorben sei."

439   Orwell, George. "Freud or Marx." *Manchester Evening News* (December 9, 1943), 2.

Judges *Arrival and Departure* not a good novel, but a "valuable" fable of the times. "The moral, if any, is that the struggle is bigger than the individual."

440   Phillips, William. "Koestler and the Political Novel." *The Nation* 159 (August 26, 1944), 241-242.

Discerns in *Arrival and Departure* a "remarkable feeling for the dilemmas of the political intelligence." Finds in Peter Slavek "a self-portrait as politically agile and aware as Koestler himself."

441   Rahv, Philip. "Lost Illusions." *Kenyon Review* 6
        (Spring 1944), 288-292.

        Admires the writing in *Arrival and Departure* but
        finds the novel unimpressive as fiction. Rejects
        Koestler's attribution of neurotic motives to polit-
        ical action, and criticizes the resolution of the
        political problem as weak. "In Koestler's work
        the phrase always goes beyond the content: that is
        the price he pays for his facile brilliance."

442   Rees, David. "The Revolutionary." *Spectator* 217
        (November 25, 1966), 697-698.

        Classifies *Arrival and Departure* as "an enduring
        minor classic." Observes that Koestler explains in
        a Postscript to this new edition that Peter Slavek
        "was modelled on the young Hungarian poet, Endre
        Havas, who, though disillusioned with the party,
        rejoined it, and returned to Hungary in 1945."

443   Reinhold, H.A. "*Arrival and Departure* by Arthur
        Koestler." *Commonweal* 39 (December 24, 1943),
        255-256.

        Calls *Arrival and Departure* "a very great book."

444   Spender, Stephen. "Anatomy of a Hero." *Time and Tide*
        25 (January 1, 1944), 12-13.

        Protests the dominance of Koestler's "blind faith
        in the analytic method." Koestler and the hero of
        Arrival and Departure are "quite lost in this awful
        machine of a world."

445   Toynbee, Philip. "*Arrival and Departure*." *New
        Statesman and Nation* 26 (December 4, 1943), 371-
        372.

        Maintains that Koestler is "probably the cleverest
        novelist writing in English today." Rejects the
        charge that Koestler is too cerebral, and praises
        Arrival and Departure highly.

446   Trilling, Diana. "Revolution and Neurosis." *The
        Nation* 157 (December 4, 1943), 672-673.

        Arrival and Departure is as "tricky and unconvinc-
        ing as it is brilliant." Rejects the "foregone--

mistaken--conclusion that psychoanalysis is at odds with revolutionary activity."

447 "*Diebe in der Nacht*: Arthur Koestler--seine Geschichte und Bedeutung." *Sie* 2 (March 23, 1947), 7.

Surveys Koestler's career, summarizes *Thieves in the Night,* and praises Koestler for the impartiality of his novel about Palestine ("Niemals ist Koestler einseitig").

448 Glazer, Nathan. "The Parlor Terrorists." *Commentary* 3 (January 1947), 55-58.

Rejects the support for terrorism he perceives in *Thieves in the Night* and rejects Rahv's claim (see No. 453) that the real issue in the novel is a political one. Concludes that "for the Jews themselves this book can be as harmful as it is frivolous."

449 Glazer, Nathan. "The Parlor Terrorists." *Commentary* 3 (March 1947), 285-287.

A discussion made up of replies to Glazer's review of *Thieves in the Night* (see No. 448).

450 Greenberg, Clement. "Koestler's New Novel, *Thieves in the Night.*" *Partisan Review* 13 (November-December 1946), 580-582.

Disagrees with Koestler's depiction of European Jews, sneers at his "newfound Anglophilia," and judges *Thieves in the Night* "negligible" as art.

451 Howarth, Herbert. "Koestlers Palästina-Chronik." *Jüdische Rundschau* (March 1947), 39-41.

Reviews *Thieves in the Night* favorably.

452 Lerner, Max. "Koestler on Terrorism." In *Actions and Passions: Notes on the Multiple Revolutions of Our Times*. New York: Simon and Schuster, 1949. Pp. 51-53.

Surprised by Koestler's reversal of his position on ends and means in accepting terrorism. Finds *Thieves in the Night* "not a particularly good novel."

453   Rahv, Philip. "Jews of the Ice Age." *Commentary* 2
        (December 1946), 591-593.

        Thieves in the Night is good reporting but a bad
        novel even though it is "the best book on the situ-
        ation of the Jews in Palestine available in English."
        Defends Koestler's stance on terrorism and calls
        Isaac Rosenfeld (see No. 386) "unfair."

454   Trilling, Diana. "*Thieves in the Night* by Arthur
        Koestler." *The Nation* (November 9, 1946), 530-
        534.

        Praises the historical depiction in *Thieves in
        the Night* but criticizes the defense of terrorism.

455   "Without a Shadow." *TLS* (October 26, 1946), 517.

        Describes *Thieves in the Night* as "an impassioned
        and arresting piece of work" but "not the best that
        Mr. Koestler can do." Accuses Koestler of being
        "almost over-anxious to concede familiar psycho-
        logical observations about Jews," but finds the
        book "a very intelligent if imperfectly resolved
        novel."

456   Aaron, Daniel. "*The Age of Longing* by Arthur Koest-
        ler." *Hudson Review* 4 (Summer 1951), 314-316.

        Traces a formula for anti-Communist novels and
        jeers at Koestler's "pseudo-scientific theorizing."
        Calls *The Age of Longing* Koestler's "farthest
        retreat from reality."

457   Charques, R.D. "*The Age of Longing*." *Spectator* 186
        (April 20, 1951), 534.

        Unexamined.

458   Crossman, R.H.S. "Darkness at Night." *New Statesman
        and Nation* 41 (April 28, 1951), 482, 484.

        The Age of Longing lacks unity and is "a politi-
        cian's *Point Counter Point*."

459   Fischer, Max. "Koestler's Longing and Despair."
       Commonweal 53 (March 9, 1951), 546-547.

       Reviews *The Age of Longing*. "He is distracted by
       picayune interests, by mischievousness, by bed
       stories of poor taste and he forgets much tto easily
       that he is writing a story of paramount spiritual
       struggle."

460   Frederiksen, Emil. "Arthur Koestlers Dommedags-
       praediken." *Dansk magasin* 45 (May 1951), 245-248.

       Reviews *The Age of Longing*.

461   "Hoffnung auf Amnestie." *Der Spiegel* 5 (April 4,
       1951), 37-39.

       Reviews *The Age of Longing* favorably.

462   Irvine, Gerard. "World Without Grace." *Time and
       Tide* 32 (April 21, 1951), 350.

       Praises the "genuinely funny satirical writing"
       mocking Left-wing intellectuals in *The Age of Long-
       ing*. Judges the portrait of Leontiev to be as effec-
       tive as that of Rubashov. Perceives that the novel
       is in a way a "resetting" of Dostoevsky's legend of
       the Grand Inquisitor: "What men of the age long for
       is the certainty and the authority of faith to save
       them from the intolerable burden of freedom."

463   J.G.W. "*The Age of Longing* by Arthur Koestler."
       Twentieth Century 149 (June 1941), 441-443.

       The Age of Longing is, "indeed, a pathetic book,
       but extremely interesting in its badness." Koestler
       "enormously exaggerates the decadence of the West,"
       and the "perfunctory" treatment of French intellect-
       uals is "shocking and vulgar." "But anyone who takes
       evil seriously is worth reading."

464   Jungk, Robert. "Arthur Koestlers verzweifelte Gott-
       suche." *Weltwoche* 19 (March 16, 1951), 9.

       Summarizes *The Age of Longing*.

465   Mann, Golo. "Was uns nicht helfen Kann." *Neue
       Schweizer Rundschau* 19 (July 1951), 183-187.

       Notes the lack of hope in *The Age of Longing*.

466   Miller, Perry. "Koestler as Pedagogue." *The Nation*
       172 (March 3, 1951), 207.

       Disparages *The Age of Longing* for being "conven-
       tional and often tedious." "If the best that Koest-
       ler can preach in his literal tract is faith in a
       faith not yet disclosed, perhaps this accounts for
       the artificiality."

467   Montesi, Gotthard. "Die Einsamen Wölfe." *Wort und
       Wahrheit* 6 (July 1951), 552-555.

       Describes the characters in *The Age of Longing*
       as types set in a tragedy of European intellectu-
       alism.

468   Rovere, Richard. "When the Will to Resist is Gone."
       New York Times Book Review (February 25, 1951),
       1, 29.

       Judges *The Age of Longing* "the most moving thing
       he has done since *Darkness at Noon*" despite "appal-
       lingly maladroit" passages. Praises Koestler's in-
       telligence, but he is "not a writer of great warmth
       or compassion."

469   Thiebaut, M. "Koestler, Lothar, Soldati." *Revue de
       Paris* 58 (October 1951), 157-158.

       Mentions *The Age of Longing* in a review with two
       other novels.

470   "War of Nerves." *TLS* (April 20, 1951), 244.

       Summarizes the early novels and finds "clumsy"
       and "threadbare" passages in *The Age of Longing*.

471   West, Anthony. "Some Conceptions of Man." *The New
       Yorker* 27 (March 17, 1951), 121-122.

       Koestler cannot "break the hold Communism has on
       his mind" because he is "divided by an unbridgeable
       gulf from the conception of the individual developed
       in the West since the Renaissance." Koestler's ideas
       coincide with those of Dostoevsky's Grand Inquisitor
       since the main theme of *The Age of Longing* is the
       death of God that left man in spiritual pain, "since
       there is a primal necessity for a recognizable

authority to supply the world with justice and
meaning." Koestler apparently thinks the Inquisitor
has the "right of the argument" in chastising Christ
for having rejected a worldly kingdom. "About real
Westerners, for whom the intolerable thing is not
to be free, he has nothing to say."

472   Wolfe, Bertram. "The Shadow Before." *Partisan Re-
       view* 18 (July-August 1951), 471-473.

       Characterizes *The Age of Longing* as "a monologue
       of the despairing Koestler without the responses of
       the fighting Koestler." The novel gets its impact
       from its "unity of mood, a unity of lack of hope
       and lack of will."

473   Broyard, Anatole. "Cosmos Without Characters."
       New York Times (April 3, 1973), 41.

       Describes *The Call Girls* as a "poor imitation"
       of Aldous Huxley's novels.

474   Fuller, Roy. "Survival." *The Listener* 88 (October
       26, 1972), 556.

       "A novel of ideas quite staggeringly up-to-date
       and comprehensive."

475   "Irresistible Satire." *Economist* 245 (October 25,
       1972), 65-66.

       Judges *The Call Girls* pleasant satire, but not
       lasting.

476   Jones, Mervyn. "A Joke Perhaps?" *New Statesman* 84
       (October 27, 1972), 608.

       Concludes that *The Call Girls* is either "a very
       bad book" or "a trap." Maybe "the intellectual
       hollowness of *The Call Girls* is as deliberate as
       the unflattering portraits of the characters."

477   Lomas, Herbert. "Going Off the Motorway." *London
       Magazine* 12 (December 1972), 155-156.

       "*The Call Girls* is a readable and witty exercise
       in the Peacock-Huxley genre."

478   "Mental Models." *TLS* (October 27, 1972), 1274.

        Dismisses *The Call Girls* as "rather condescending,"
        but acknowledges its "vivid review of the state of
        mental engineering."

479   "Extinction as Farce." *TLS* (December 15, 1945), 597.

        Twilight Bar is "more crude than lively."

480   "Correspondents in Spain." *TLS* (January 1, 1938), 4.

        Thinks that Koestler's account of his confinement
        in *Spanish Testament* is very good, but laments the
        "mainly Republican propaganda" of the long preface.

481   Marks, John P. "*Spanish Testament*." *Spectator* 160
        (January 21, 1938), 96.

        Includes *Spanish Testament* in a discussion of
        several books on the Spanish Civil War.

482   Peers, E.A. "*Spanish Testament*." *Bulletin of His-
        panic Studies* 15 (April 1938), 118-119.

        Although the first part has some "appallingly bad
        propagandist argument," *Spanish Testament* is "a fine
        and moving piece of writing."

483   Peeters, Jozef. "*Ein Spanisches Testament*." *De
        Vlaamsche Gids* 27 (October 1938), 46.

        Brief notice of the publication of *Spanish Testa-
        ment* in Zurich.

484   Warner, Sylvia Townsend. "We Are Gentlemen." *Left
        Review* 3 (January 12, 1938), 745-747.

        Spanish Testament is an "excellent book."

485   L.S. "*Dialogue with Death*." *Life and Letters Today*
        34 (August 1942), 150.

        Calls *Dialogue with Death* "one of the classics"
        of the Spanish Civil War.

486   Cowley, Malcolm. "Decline and Fall." *New Republic* 105 (December 8, 1941), 768-769.

    Praises Koestler's "instinctive vitality" and sense of humor in *Scum of the Earth*.

487   Dobrée, Bonamy. "*Scum of the Earth*." *Horizon* 4 (September 1941), 209-211.

    Not as good as *Darkness at Noon*, which was "completely successful," but *Scum of the Earth* is a "brilliant and moving narrative, executed with superlative honesty."

488   "Exiles in France." *TLS* (September 20, 1941), 466.

    Summarizes *Scum of the Earth*.

489   Lania, Leo. "Zero-Point of Infamy." *Saturday Review of Literature* 24 (October 18, 1941), 12.

    Scum of the Earth is "a deeply moving analysis of our entire time" and deserves "a permanent place in the ranks of the spiritual documents of our epoch."

490   Martin, Kingsley. "*Scum of the Earth*." *New Statesman and Nation* 22 (October 11, 1941), 339.

    Scum of the Earth is a "a fine piece of straight reporting."

491   Read, Herbert. "A Moral Climate." *Spectator* 167 (September 26, 1941), 312.

    Admires *Scum of the Earth*.

492   Strauss, Harold. "A Searing Story of Concentration Camps." *New York Times Book Review* (October 5, 1941), 3.

    Scum of the Earth is "a personal narrative of intense power and poignancy."

493   Aron, Raymond. "Fidelité des apostats." *Le Table Ronde* 30 (June 1950), 52-65.

    Reviews *The God That Failed*. Claims that *Darkness at Noon* confirmed many Communists in their faith and revived in many of them a nostalgia for the lost community.

494   Hatch, Robert. "Studies in the Permanent Crisis."
       New Republic 122 (March 13, 1950), 19.

       The God That Failed is "compelling evidence that
       when a Communist is cured, he is cured permanently."

495   Miller, Merle. "How They Became Communists and How
       They Changed Their Minds." *New York Herald Tribune
       Book Review* (January 8, 1950), 7.

       Favorable notice of *The God That Failed*.

496   Niebuhr, Reinhold. "To Moscow and Back." *The Nation*
       170 (January 28, 1950), 88-90.

       Offers only one complaint about *The God That
       Failed*: "None of the authors speculate very pro-
       foundly of the reasons which persuade modern men
       to seek a Utopia or why their dreams turn into
       nightmares."

497   Pritchett, V.S. "Books in General." *New Statesman
       and Nation* 39 (January 21, 1950), 68.

       Speaks of Koestler's "brilliant and wounded mock-
       ery of the jargon of Communism" in *The God That
       Failed*." "We feel that Koestler's restless, acquis-
       itive and drama-seeking temperament lost little in
       his conversion." Judges Silone's and Wright's ac-
       counts "by far the best."

498   Rapp, Af Antonius. "Arthur Koestlers veje til og
       fra kommunismen." *Dansk magasin* 44 (July-August
       1950), 367-374.

       Reviews *The God That Failed*.

499   Schlesinger, Arthur M., Jr. "Dim Views of the Red
       Star." *Saturday Review of Literature* 33 (January 7,
       1950), 11.

       The God That Failed is a "book of great power,
       fascination, and significance." Koestler is "witty
       and penetrating."

500   "Two-Way Rebellion." *TLS* (February 3, 1950), 67.

       The God That Failed is "well conceived, well writ-
       ten, well produced, well timed and well out of the
       ordinary."

501 Ashe, Geoffrey. "Koestler and the Infinite." *Commonweal* 56 (September 26, 1952), 609-612.

Summarizes *Arrow in the Blue* and wishes Koestler would give his views on the Catholic Church.

502 Brown, Spencer. "Arthur Koestler, the Mellow Machine Gun." *American Mercury* 75 (October 1952), 99-103.

Likes *Arrow in the Blue*. Remarks that Koestler's inability to enjoy either love or friendship is his "fundamental defect."

503 "A Diversity of Occupations." *TLS* (October 31, 1952), 706.

Summarizes *Arrow in the Blue* and expresses pleasure at looking ahead to the next volume of autobiography.

504 Dowling, Allan. "In the First Person." *Partisan Review* 20 (January-February 1953), 122-125.

Observes of *Arrow in the Blue* that Koestler is "more interested in *causes* than in human beings." Koestler is "an enthusiast whose ardors often peter out rather quickly."

505 Geismar, Maxwell. "From a Westward Europe." *Saturday Review of Literature* 35 (September 27, 1952), 10-11.

Describes Koestler's attitude toward Zionism as "ambivalent." Koestler has "the knowledge of sophistication, not of truth." Complains that the "human world" of *Arrow in the Blue* is "self-enclosed, abstract, sterile."

506 Lowenthal, Marvin. "Arthur Koestler, the Man of Many Causes, Begins a Self-Portrait." *New York Herald Tribune Book Review* (September 21, 1952), 5.

Admiring notice of *Arrow in the Blue*.

507 Mayberry, George. "Quiet Flows the Danube." *New Republic* 127 (September 22, 1952), 26.

Reviews *Arrow in the Blue*, finding "an infinite melancholy that plays over these precisely written pages."

508   Pritchett, V.S. "Books in General." *New Statesman
        and Nation* 44 (November 8, 1952), 550-551.

        Koestler's "egotism has enabled him to write the
        headlines of our public conscience." Koestler's
        being "governed" by things in "sets of two" makes
        for good "didactic journalism." *Arrow in the Blue*
        is "a mellower and far wiser book than any he has
        yet written." Judges the chapters on Vienna and
        Palestine the best.

509   Schlesinger, Arthur, Jr. "Cassandra Revisited."
        Vogue 156 (August 15, 1970), 40.

        Sums up the personality revealed in *Arrow in the
        Blue* and *The Invisible Writing*: "For all the occas-
        ional posturing, self-dramatization, conceit, and
        cheapness of metaphor and argument, here is the
        testament of a brave, bright, prickly, reckless,
        impatient, witty, hostile, man."

510   Spender, Stephen. "Koestler's Story of His Fervent
        Quest for a Utopia." *New York Times Book Review*
        (September 21, 1952), 4-5, 36.

        Describes Koestler as "a new kind of writer--very
        significant for our time--who has tried to make art
        out of the events which are generally thought of as
        the material of journalism." The weakness of *Arrow
        in the Blue* lies in Koestler's tendency to "regard
        ruthless analytic honesty as the supreme virtue."
        Observes that what Koestler lacks is "simply the
        element of love." *Arrow in the Blue* suffers from
        being "theory-ridden." "To Mr. Koestler, though,
        the pattern is everything, and when he has explained
        it away the essence has evaporated."

511   Weightman, John G. "A Child of the Century." *Twenti-
        eth Century* 153 (January 1953), 72-75.

        Arrow in the Blue is "a wry commentary on the
        messiness and tragedy of life."

512   West, Anthony. "Turns for the Worse." *The New Yorker*
        28 (November 1, 1952), 113-117.

        Arrow in the Blue is "often very funny, on the
        anecdotal level," but Koestler is "not only a
        lightweight but something of a bore."

513   West, Rebecca. "*Arrow in the Blue*." *Time and Tide*
       (November 1, 1952), 1265-1266.

       Appreciates the picture in *Arrow in the Blue* of
       "a nervous, jerky, arrogant, contentious bantam-
       weight" who was unmatched in the "physical or moral
       courage with which he went out and got the facts
       about the new world." Praises the book for being
       "delightfully and morally impressive" and "beauti-
       fully clean of self-pity." Complains only of Koest-
       ler's assertion that conversion to Communism in the
       1930s was "a spontaneous expression of an optimism
       born of despair," describing it instead as "simply
       a new game for the bourgeoisie."

514   "Arthur Koestler: Spiritual Odyssey." *TLS* (July 2,
       1954), 419.

       Appreciative summaries of *Dialogue with Death*
       and *The Invisible Writing*.

515   De La Bedoyere, Michael. "Arthur Koestler." *Catholic
       World* 179 (September 1954), 460-463.

       Says that *The Invisible Writing* "has nothing
       whatever to offer to the reader except rather
       hysterical denunciations of current political ap-
       peasement."

516   Geismar, Maxwell. "Search for a Soul." *Saturday
       Review of Literature* 37 (October 31, 1954), 18.

       Calls *The Invisible Writing* "highly interesting"
       and describes Koestler as "a master of the half-
       insight."

517   "Huldigung an einen Spion." *Der Spiegel* 8 (July 21,
       1954), 32.

       Summarizes incidents from *The Invisible Writing*.

518   Kuic, Vukan. "Red Days and Invisible Ink." *Chicago
       Review* 9 (Spring 1955), 122-127.

       Summarizes much of *The Invisible Writing* and
       endorses Orwell's judgment that "The chink in
       Koestler's armour is his hedonism."

519   "Last Train to Nowhere." *New Statesman and Nation*
        48 (July 3, 1954), 9-10.

        Describes the case history in *The Invisible
        Writing* "'typical' only in being extreme," and
        finds it "perhaps the most remarkable autobiography
        since the *Confessions* of Rousseau." Cautions that
        Koestler's new judgments on England are not likely
        to be any more reliable than his old ones on Russia.
        "Koestler would like us to see in him the fanatic
        of anti-Communism, the martyr in search of a stake;
        and we do our best. But he preaches with such gusto,
        describes his sufferings with such gaiety, that we
        pay him the greatest of compliments. We refuse to
        take him seriously. He has qualified as an honorary
        member of the Pickwick Club."

520   Leonard, John. "Teaching the 20th Century." *New
        York Times* (June 23, 1970), 41.

        Remarks apropos of *Arrow in the Blue* and *The In-
        visible Writing* that Koestler is "the West's pre-
        eminent journalist."

521   Litvinoff, Emanuel. "*The Invisible Writing* by
        Arthur Koestler." *Spectator* 193 (July 2, 1954),
        26-28.

        The Invisible Writing is valuable for "its analy-
        sis of the mind and soul of a neurasthenic idealist
        during a seven years' journey through the closed
        system of Communist dialectics."

522   Lowenthal, Marvin. "World of Double-Think and
        Double-Cross." *New York Herald Tribune Book Re-
        view* (October 10, 1954), 4.

        The "ultimate significance" of *The Invisible
        Writing* lies in the extent to which the self-revela-
        tions are typical.

523   Niebuhr, Reinhold. "The God that Failed." *New Re-
        public* 131 (October 25, 1954), 19.

        Koestler is "never boring" in *The Invisible
        Writing*. Wonders how Koestler could "stick to his
        Communist creed for seven years." The autobiography
        is valuable for the "new light on various facets
        of totalitarianism."

524   Paeschke, Heinz. "Chronik eines intellektuellen
          Revolutionars." *Merkur* 9 (November 1955),
          1080-1083.

          Praises *The Invisible Writing* as "eine der auf-
          schlussreichsten unserer Tage."

525   Pfaff, William. "Survivor's Debt." *Commonweal* 61
          (January 21, 1955), 431-433.

          Names *The Invisible Writing* as "one of an honour-
          able company of books which assimilated the advent-
          ures of our time."

526   Ropp, Theodore. "*The Invisible Writing* by Arthur
          Koestler." *South Atlantic Quarterly* 54 (April
          1955), 286-288.

          Whereas *Arrow in the Blue* was "both ponderous and
          pretentious," *The Invisible Writing* "contains some
          excellent reporting."

527   .T.T. "Koestler afslutter Selvbiografien." *Danske
          magasin* 2 (1954), 431-433.

          Summarizes *The Invisible Writing*.

528   Weales, Gerald. "Up to Date on Arthur." *Hudson
          Review* 8 (Spring 1955), 155-160.

          Refers to Koestler's "**immense** pomposity" in *The
          Invisible Writing* but admits that he is "a good
          reporter when he wants to be." "This cocky little
          man, over-impressed with his own virtues and his
          own vices, happened to be intimately connected
          with a great many of the major events of recent
          history."

529   Arendt, Hannah. "The Too Ambitious Reporter."
          Commentary 1 (January 1946), 94-95.

          Concludes that the wit in *Twilight Bar* "makes the
          play much more enjoyable than Koestler's tremendously
          'serious' novels." Praises *The Yogi and the Commissar*
          but finds that Koestler's "arbitrary polarities" re-
          veal an "innocent emptiness" that is "particularly
          shocking" in the opposite extremes of the Yogi and
          the Commissar.

530   Bentley, Eric Russell. "Les Marxistes d'antan."
        Sewanee Review 54 (Winter 1946), 165-169.

        Attacks Koestler sharply in a review of *The Yogi
        and the Commissar*. "Mr. Arthur Koestler is not an
        important writer. He is a self-important writer.
        He is not a creative artist. He is an actor. He is
        not a critic. He is an opinion-monger. He is not a
        philosopher. He is a manufacturer of slogans. He is
        not a thinker. He is a juggler with metaphors. He
        is not a man but--as Nietzsche said of Wagner--a
        disease. He is a highbrow Walter Winchell, a Franz
        Werfel of the Left."

531   Birkenfeld, Günther. "Die Deutschen und Arthur
        Koestler." *Der Monat* 1 (January 1949), 99-101.

        Reviews *The Yogi and the Commissar* favorably.

532   Borkenau, Franz. *"The Yogi and the Commissar."*
        London Tribune (May 11, 1945), 15.

        Accuses Koestler of looking backward too much in
        his appraisal of socialism. Although Koestler is
        not an "objective sociologist," he is a "first-rate
        humanitarian."

533   Brogan, Denis. "The Claims of Candour." *Spectator*
        174 (May 4, 1945), 412.

        Favorable notice of *The Yogi and the Commissar*.

534   Haerdter, Robert. "Der Mensch ohne Mythos und
        Illusionen." *Die Gegenwort* 4 (July 1, 1949),
        13-16.

        Praises Koestler's insight in the essays in *The
        Yogi and the Commissar*.

535   Knox, Israel. "Koestler's Confession." *The Menorah
        Journal* 33 (October 1945), 230-236.

        Praises the "weighty essays" on Communist Russia
        in *The Yogi and the Commissar*. Discerns "a note of
        nebulous mysticism in these essays," a vague sym-
        pathy for "the philosophy of the Far East."

536   Laski, Harold J. "Mr. Koestler." *Manchester
        Guardian* (May 9, 1945), 3.

        Attributes Koestler's bitterness toward the Left
        in *The Yogi and the Commissar* to a "fatigue of life."
        Charges Koestler with being satisfied only by "in-
        vective and denunciation." Koestler "has now become
        the unconscious instrument of the very reaction he
        was so anxious once to destroy."

537   Martin, Kingsley. "*The Yogi and the Commissar*."
        New Statesman and Nation 30 (September 22, 1945),
        197-198.

        Accuses Koestler of being "much less than just"
        with the Left in *The Yogi and the Commissar,* and
        not always accurate (e.g., his damaging statements
        about Vercors have since been proven false). Claims
        the picture of Russia is not balanced.

538   Mayberry, George. "Ex-Communist Manifesto." *New
        Republic* 112 (June 4, 1945), 794-795.

        Charges Koestler with raising more problems than
        he settles in *The Yogi and the Commissar.*

539   Phillips, William. "A Tract for Our Times." *Kenyon
        Review* 7 (Autumn 1945), 705-709.

        Describes the three essays on Soviet Russia in
        The Yogi and the Commissar as "brilliant analyses
        of the Soviet myth." Criticizes Koestler's harsh
        judgment of Gide. Attributes Koestler's distinction
        to his "ability to *epigrammatize* the confusions of
        the times." Koestler "combines informed and sophisti-
        cated historic sensibilities with a weakness for
        facile and tricky formulations."

540   Slonim, Marc. "*The Yogi and the Commissar and Other
        Essays* by Arthur Koestler." *Yale Review* 35 (Autumn
        1945), 179-181.

        Praises Koestler's analysis of the Soviet mind
        and Soviet society.

541   Toynbee, Philip. "*The Yogi and the Commissar*."
        Horizon 12 (July 1945), 69-72.

        Reviews *The Yogi and the Commissar* favorably.

542   Woolf, Leonard. "Disillusion." *New Statesman and
       Nation* (May 19, 1945), 324.

       Judges *The Yogi and the Commissar* "a disturbing
       book" in which Koestler's bitterness sometimes
       defeats his purpose.

543   "A Wounded Idealist." *TLS* (May 12, 1945), 219.

       Sneers at *The Yogi and the Commissar* for its
       "ephemeral critical stuff" that is "assembled here
       to doubtful advantage." Finds Koestler "frequently
       both evasive and a little cheap." His "sincere
       enough rage of disappointed political idealism
       tends to deprive him of both judgment and practical
       direction." Criticizes the failure to give a "balanced
       picture" of Russia.

544   "All-In Psychology." *TLS* (August 19, 1949), 539.

       Summarizes the arguments in *Insight and Outlook*
       but remaining sceptical and noting "the vagueness
       of the fundamental concepts" expressed in a style
       "infected with psychological jargon."

545   Deutsch, Babette. "Clumsification of Ratiocination."
       The Survey 85 (March 1949), 176-177.

       Finds Koestler "moving in the right direction"
       in *Insight and Outlook*, but faults him for "awk-
       wardness" of presentation, pretentiousness, and
       failing to realize how much of what he presents
       could already be found in such writers as Coleridge
       and Alfred North Whitehead.

546   Geismar, Maxwell. "Bisociation--A Philosophical
       System." *Saturday Review of Literature* 32
       (February 19, 1949), 13-14.

       Judges the literary sections of *Insight and Out-
       look* "particularly good."

547   Horst, Karl-August. "Arthur Koestler: Psychoanal-
       ytiker und Romancier." *Merkur* 4 (December 1950),
       1333-1337.

       Summarizes the arguments in *Insight and Outlook*.

548   *"Insight and Outlook* by Arthur Koestler." *Dublin Magazine* 25 (January-March 1950), 50-51.

"The general effect is stimulating; but with a large measure of over-simplification, of definitions too commodious."

549   Kecskemeti, Paul. "Koestler as System-Maker." *Partisan Review* 16 (May 1949), 536-539.

Objects that Koestler's convergence between "physiological and psychological lines of explanation" in *Insight and Outlook* is "more verbal than real." The book is "buoyant and confident on the surface and so defeatist deep inside." Concludes that "In its decisive aspects, it shows the full impact of the de-humanizing trend of our era."

550   L.M.P., Jr. *"Insight and Outlook* by Arthur Koestler." *Theatre Arts Monthly* 33 (May 1949), 7.

Disparages the "jargon-packed pages" and the "baffling array of charts and diagrams." Maintains that the "whole-hearted espousal of the opaque scientific medium seriously mars his presentation."

551   McGary, John Keith. "Koestler--Inside and Out." *Antioch Review* 10 (March 1950), 151-156.

Summarizes *Insight and Outlook*, criticizing the use of insect societies in discussing human society. Remarks on "the inadequacy of his understanding of human nature." Judges *Insight and Outlook* "richly suggestive and acutely disappointing."

552   Oakeshott, Michael. "Creative Activity--A Formula." *Spectator* 183 (July 1, 1949), 20, 22.

Despite its "long-windedness" and over-elaborateness, *Insight and Outlook* is an exciting book.

553   Rolo, Charles. "Art, Life, and Science." *Atlantic* 182 (December 1948), 111-116.

Summarizes *Insight and Outlook* and calls it "an exceedingly difficult book."

554   Rosenfeld, Isaac. "Aesthetics without Experience."
        Kenyon Review 11 (Spring 1949), 321-325.

        Decides that the theory underlying *Insight and
        Outlook* lacks "the amplitude the subject matter
        requires."

555   Welsh, Paul. "*Insight and Outlook* by Arthur Koest-
        ler." *South Atlantic Quarterly* 48 (July 1949),
        483-485.

        The theory of self-transcendence in *Insight and
        Outlook* is held together only by ambiguity.

556   Arnold, G.L. "A Prophet Abroad." *Nineteenth
        Century and After* 146 (October 1949), 225-232.

        A severe and detailed criticism of *Promise and
        Fulfillment*. Praises only the passages in which
        the observant eye of the journalist is revealed.
        Finds the tone offensive to Jews, Arabs, and the
        British alike. Notes a number of factual "blunders
        of an elementary kind." Appreciates the "sulphurous
        chapter on "John Bull's Other Ireland." Denounces
        Koestler's treatment of the middle class in Arab
        Palestine and his "uncritical acceptance of polit-
        ical myths, whether Arab or Jewish." Maintains that
        Koestler's "impassioned advocacy" of the Zionist
        cause is unconvincing. Describes the defence of
        pure nationalism as a "piece of sophistry." Judges
        the analysis of Zionist leadership as "among the
        least satisfactory" passages. "To the genuine
        Zionist ... Mr. Koestler's championship of his
        cause can scarcely be anything but an embarrass-
        ment."

557   Feinsilver, Lillian Mermin. "A Note on Arthur
        Koestler." *Chicago Jewish Forum* 9 (Winter 1950-
        1951), 125-129.

        Criticizes Koestler sharply for arguing in
        Promise and Fulfillment that orthodox Jews "must
        either follow the imperative of their religion,
        the return to the Promised Land--or recognize
        that the faith is no longer theirs." Judges
        Koestler's position as "incredibly naive" and
        "based on the false premise that there is an im-
        mediate choice to be made, that allegiance must be
        declared one way or another between Israel's flag
        or the red-white-and blue."

558   Fiedler, Leslie. "Koestler and Israel." *Partisan
       Review* 17 (January 17, 1950), 92-96.

       In *Promise and Fulfillment* Koestler reports "with
       astonishing impact the senseless and ultimately
       brutal policy of the British in Palestine." Koestler
       overestimates Jabotinsky. Questions Koestler's con-
       fidence in the ability of Western Jews to assimilate.

559   Hodgkin, Edward. "Envoi to Zion." *Spectator* 183
       (September 23, 1949), 394, 396.

       Judges *Promise and Fulfillment* "a work of uneven
       merit" with too much "hack-work" propaganda. The
       historical section is the least valuable, for
       Koestler does not always get his facts right.

560   "The Jews in Palestine." *TLS* (October 28, 1949),
       691.

       Promise and Fulfillment is "one of the best books
       that has yet appeared on Jewish Palestine," and is
       "excellent" in its treatment of terrorism.

561   Lichtheim, George. "The End of Jewish History."
       Commentary 8 (November 1949), 502-504.

       Finds that its "extreme lack of organization"
       makes *Promise and Fulfillment* "unsatisfactory."
       Even though it attempts too much, it is worth
       reading, "but it tells one more about the author
       than about his subject."

562   Reynolds, Quentin. "The Palestine Story: Past and
       Future." *New York Times Book Review* (October 23,
       1949), 3, 44.

       Finds the political and economic forces behind
       the conflict to be analyzed "brilliantly and
       thoroughly" in *Promise and Fulfillment*. The book
       has "much that is new" and it is hard "to dismiss
       anything" in it.

563   Syrkin, Marie. "Koestler on Palestine." *The Nation*
       169 (October 22, 1949), 398-401.

       Condemns *Promise and Fulfillment* as "so pervasively
       partisan that it becomes primarily a political
       tract." Except for his "championship of the

Revisionists and the Irgun," Koestler always
speaks "from both sides of his mouth."

564   Woolf, Leonard. "The Promised Land." *New Statesman
        and Nation* 38 (October 29, 1949), 490, 492.

        Promise and Fulfillment is "both a moving and a
        brilliant book" which is "scrupulously fair to
        and so critical of all sides." Praises the last
        part of the book especially.

565   Barrett, William. "Yogi versus Commissar." *New
        York Times Book Review* (December 4, 1955), 28.

        Argues that if in *The Trail of the Dinosaur*
        Koestler writes "like a man already dead, it is
        because he is one of those crying for rebirth."

566   Harrington, Michael. "The Recurring Dilemma."
        Commonweal 63 (January 6, 1956), 359.

        Koestler's answers in *The Trail of the Dinosaur*
        come to "a tremendous void, an aching, a hope
        without an object."

567   Roche, John P. "Koestler at the Crossroads."
        New Republic 134 (February 13, 1956), 19.

        Reports that he was "perpetually disappointed"
        in *The Trail of the Dinosaur,* in which "Cassandra
        becomes trivial, or merely dull." Disputes Koest-
        ler's contention in the essay "Judah at the Cross-
        roads" that Jews should either settle in Israel or
        give up their Judaic identity.

568   Schlesinger, Arthur M., Jr. "The Logic of Mortality."
        Saturday Review 39 (January 7, 1956), 62.

        Reviews *The Trail of the Dinosaur*: "while one
        regrets his farewell to politics, one can only
        admire the integrity which produced the decision."

569   Walsh, Chad. "The Cold, Clear-Headed Realism of a
        Philosophical Ex-Communist." *New York Herald
        Tribune Book Review* (December 4, 1955), 3.

        Calls Koestler's "clear-headed realism" in *The
        Trail of the Dinosaur* a "precious asset."

570   "Warning for the Lukewarm." *New York Times Book Review* (December 4, 1955), 28.

       Review of *The Trail of the Dinosaur*.

571   Ehrmann, H.B. "*Reflections on Hanging*." *Annals of the American Academy of Political and Social Sciences* 314 (November 1957), 2-3-204.

       Reflections on Hanging is "a powerful book" which gives a "devastating exposure of the utter imbecility of the highest English judges when they discuss the death penalty."

572   Gilmour, Jan. "The Death Penalty." *Spectator* 196 (April 13, 1956), 502-503.

       Reflections on Hanging presents "a concise and accurate survey of capital punishment in this country." The chapter on free will is "unconvincing and irrelevant," but otherwise the book is "dazzling."

573   Hatch, Robert. "The Tenacity of the Gallows." *The Nation* 185 (August 3, 1954), 54.

       Praises *Reflections on Hanging* except for the discussion of free will.

574   "A Life for a Life." *TLS Supplement* (April 30, 1956), 239.

       Unexamined.

575   Niebuhr, Reinhold. "Justice and the Death Penalty." *New Republic* 137 (August 26, 1957), 18-19.

       Judges *Reflections on Hanging* an "excellent" book except for its discussion of free will.

576   Rovere, Richard. "Matter of Life and Death." *The New Yorker* 33 (September 14, 1957), 164-170.

       Describes *Reflections on Hanging* as a "notable work of the humane intelligence." Observes that Koestler's "passion has a transcendental base."

577 Tannenbaum, Frank. "After a Murder, a Rope." *New York Times Book Review* (June 30, 1957), 6, 18.

Summarizes the arguments in *Reflections on Hanging*

578 Agassi, Joseph. "On Explaining the Trial of Galileo." *Organon* 8 (1971), 137-166.

A substantial critique of *The Sleepwalkers*. "Though Koestler is no scholar, his work is of value." Praises the "very vivid picture" Koestler gives of Galileo's trial, but finds the attack on Galileo the scientist far too severe. Admits that Koestler has raised many problems for Galileo's supporters and destroyed the "old idealized picture" of Galileo. Rejects Koestler's portrait of a rigid Galileo who was drawn into conflict by irascibility rather than by absorption in the truth, contending that after 1613 Galileo might well have been sincere in his struggle with Bellarmine. Defends Bruno: "Koestler's dismissal of the thesis that Bruno was a martyr of science is unworthy of criticism." Cites specific points on which Koestler errs: (1) in claiming that Galileo raised opposition unnecessarily to *Discourse on Floating Bodies*; (2) in asserting that Galileo "demolished" his opponents; (3) in beginning with the assumption that Galileo and Urban VIII were both "irresponsible rascals"; (4) in characterizing Simplicio in the *Dialogue* as "the clown who is kicked in the pants"; (5) in following Catholic scholars in doubting Galileo's good faith throughout the events surrounding the dialogue and the trial; (6) in missing Galileo's "great idea" to explain the tides by "existing mechanisms plus a hypothesis concerning initial conditions"; and (7) in failing to appreciate the greatness and novelty of the various ideas promoted by Galileo, and of ideas invented much later, including the idea of tentativity in science.

579 Aury, Dominique. "Les Somnambules." *La Nouvelle revue française* 8 (November 1960), 909-913.

Praises *The Sleepwalkers* as "un livre considérable, solidement."

580   Barraclough, Geoffrey. "Aimless Weather."
        Spectator 202 (January 23, 1959), 125.

        Generally favorable review of *The Sleepwalkers*.
        "The story deserves telling for its intrinsic
        interest."

581   Brome, Vincent. "Mr. Koestler's Compendium."
        Time and Tide 40 (February 14, 1959), 187-188.

        States that *The Sleepwalkers* "fills a very im-
        portant gap in those compendiums ... which enable
        the average intelligent reader to grasp the general
        outline of intellectual development." Expresses
        scepticism about Koestler's sense of a need for a
        "synthesis of ancient religion with modern science."

582   Cohen, I. Bernard. "Koestler on Kepler and the
        History of Man's Picture of the Universe."
        Scientific American 200 (June 1959), 187-192.

        Judges *The Sleepwalkers* "a solid job of research"
        that succeeds best with the treatment of Kepler.
        Rejects Koestler's condemnation of modern science
        as a "modern version of scholasticism." "When all
        is said and done, Koestler's eloquence in describing
        just how disorderly and illogical the progress of
        science can be may even outweigh his deficiencies
        as a historian."

583   De Santillana, Giorgio, and Stillman Drake. "Arthur
        Koestler and His Sleepwalkers." *Isis* 50 (Septem-
        ber 1959), 255-260.

        Severe criticism of Koestler's treatment of
        Galileo in *The Sleepwalkers*.

584   Diogenes. "Beware the Orthodox!" *Time and Tide*
        March 7, 1959), 268.

        Refers to *The Sleepwalkers* as "an absolute 'must'
        for all who would understand the present chronic
        schizophrenia of the world of things and the world
        of thought." *The Sleepwalkers* leaves an impression
        of the human mind's "deep unreceptivity."

585   Frankel, Charles. "The Road to Discovery Is in
         Itself a Thing of Wonder." *New York Times Book
         Review* (May 24, 1959), 6, 30.

         Describes *The Sleepwalkers* as "an unusually
         lively and informative book."

586   Gasteyer, Charles. "*The Sleepwalkers*." *Sky and
         Telescope* 18 (August 1959), 577.

         Corrects a few errors and omissions, and recom-
         mends *The Sleepwalkers* "enthusiastically" for its
         "sound scholarship and original interpretation."

587   Goodfield, J. "*The Sleepwalkers*." *Discovery* 20
         (June 1959), 266-268.

         Praises the discussions of men but criticizes
         the treatment of science and ideas. Finds Koestler
         especially weak in problems of dynamics. Reproves
         him for dismissing and patronizing other scholars'
         works.

588   Graubard, Mark. "*The Watershed*." *Science* 133
         (May 12, 1961), 1472-1473.

         This reprint of the Kepler section from *The
         Sleepwalkers* is "the liveliest, most scholarly,
         and best part of that excellent work."

589   Hall, A.R. "The Psychopathology of Science."
         Nature 183 (May 23, 1959), 1419-1420.

         The Sleepwalkers gives a "vivid account" of the
         shift from the medieval to the modern cosmology.
         Claims that Koestler under-rates Ptolemy and that
         his views on Galileo and Kepler are "highly per-
         sonal." Concludes that "the brilliance of the book
         lies in the literary use of historiography."

590   Krutch, Joseph Wood. "Bold, Exciting Look at the
         Wayward Road of Science." *New York Herald Tribune
         Book Review* (July 19, 1959), 1.

         Says of *The Sleepwalkers* that "any reader would
         have to be very well informed indeed not to learn
         something from it and very averse to bold specu-
         lation not to find the speculative parts highly
         stimulating."

591   "Man and the Universe." *TLS* (January 30, 1959),
      55.

      Charges Koestler with being "unjust" in condemn-
      ing Plato in *The Sleepwalkers*. Disputes Koestler's
      harsh treatment of Galileo for being "too tender
      to the obscurantism of the Inquisition."

592   Munitz, Milton K. "*The Sleepwalkers*." *Science* 130
      (August 7, 1959), 326-328.

      Praises the Kepler section but says that "Koest-
      ler's indictment of modern science lacks convincing-
      ness."

593   Rowland, John. "*The Sleepwalkers*." *Hibbert Journal*
      57 (April 1959), 299-301.

      Calls *The Sleepwalkers* "an important book."

594   Toulmin, Stephen. "*The Sleepwalkers*." *Journal of
      Philosophy* 59 (August 30, 1962), 500-503.

      Summarizes much of *The Sleepwalkers* in a favor-
      able review.

595   "The World of Science." *TLS* (June 1, 1962), 417.

      Brief notice of *The Watershed*.

596   Bowers, Faubion. "Dyspeptic Pilgrim." *The Nation*
      192 (March 11, 1961), 217-219.

      Koestler's "devastatingly negative" view of
      India and Japan in *The Lotus and the Robot* makes
      him "the Ugly American." Judges Koestler's book
      a "personal diatribe" that does a disservice to
      both East and West.

597   "Brief Encounter." *TLS* (January 6, 1961), 14.

      The Lotus and the Robot is too "tendentious"
      and reveals an "inadequate and superficial know-
      ledge of the East." "Time and time again he throws
      the baby out with the bath water."

598   Conze, Edward. "Dr. Koestler and the Wisdom of the
       East." *Hibbert Journal* 59 (January 1961), 178-
       181.

       Asserts that Koestler's "blindness to the men-
       tality of Eastern sages is here almost complete"
       in *The Lotus and the Robot*.

599   Enright, D.J. "The Yogi and Mr. Koestler."
       Spectator 205 (November 4, 1960), 695-696.

       Judges that *The Lotus and the Robot* is "light,
       very readable, sometimes too casual, and enter-
       taining." Disagrees that India and Japan are
       "spiritually sicker than the West." Koestler has
       perhaps over-reacted, but his "sharp book" has a
       "special deflatory value."

600   Greenberg, Martin. "Part of the Truth." *Reporter*
       24 (March 30, 1961), 53-55.

       The Lotus and the Robot is "a little spoiled by
       its touches of vulgarity, by the glib antitheses
       and slick metaphorical characterizations of culture
       and history." Suspects that Koestler has done the
       East "less than justice."

601   Hicks, Granville. "No Mecca in Mysticism." *Saturday
       Review* 44 (March 24, 1961), 17.

       Believes that Koestler's conclusions in *The
       Lotus and the Robot* are sound.

602   Hook, Sidney. "But There Was No Light." *New York
       Times Book Review* (March 5, 1961), 7, 26.

       Reviews *The Lotus and the Robot* appreciatively.

603   Kennedy, Ludovic. "Legal Barbarians." *Spectator*
       207 (September 15, 1961), 343-345.

       Supports very strongly the conclusions in
       Hanged by the Neck.

604   "Britain the Ostrich." *TLS* (December 5, 1963), 1003.

       Declares that *Suicide of a Nation?* is unnecessar-
       ily alarmist.

605   Carstairs, G.M. "Suicidal Gesture." *Spectator*
       211 (July 19, 1963), 85.

       Suicide of a Nation? offers "a lively farrago"
       of essays.

606   Hobsbawn, Eric. "Koestler's England." *New York
       Review of Books* 2 (April 2, 1964), 13-14.

       Reviews *Suicide of a Nation?*

607   "Really?" *Economist* 209 (December 28, 1963),
       1343-1344.

       Finds *Suicide of a Nation?* to be "an earnest
       and radical-minded attack on the self-satisfied
       and dull." "Most of what is said is true; but it
       is not the whole truth."

608   De Mott, Benjamin. "Koestler's Kit." *Harper's*
       (January 1965), 92-94.

       Cites lapses in taste and style in *The Act of
       Creation*, which buries the sense of wonder under
       abstractions.

609   Eiseley, Loren. "The Genesis of Genius." *New York
       Times Book Review* (October 18, 1964), 3, 40-41.

       The Act of Creation is a a "big and untidy"
       book in which Koestler reveals "occasional gul-
       libility about the historical data he handles."
       Decides it is a useful book to sample and return
       to.

610   Eysenck, J.J. "*The Act of Creation*." *Annals of
       the American Academy of Political and Social
       Sciences* 360 (July 1965), 198-199.

       The Act of Creation is not really adequate as a
       work to popularize science, for Koestler is not
       well informed about the scholarship on creativity.
       What Koestler says about behaviorism is "largely
       irrelevant and untrue," and the book "illustrates
       the dangers of unskilled labor."

611   Haynes, Renée. "Spheres in Collision." *The Month*
       32 (1964), 261-266.

       Summarizes much of *The Act of Creation* with
       praise, but finds that "the interaction of Mr.
       Koestler's ideas with those of religion is however
       curiously discontinuous." "The dominant impression,
       first and last, produced by this book is one of
       inexhaustible intellectual vitality."

612   Hilgard, Ernest R. "Creativity: The Juxtaposition
       and Integration of Disparate Categories."
       Science 147 (January 1, 1965), 37-38.

       Book One of *The Act of Creation* is much better
       than Book Two. The book is "a rich experience"
       even though it has no "strong pattern of organiza-
       tion" and is "a little pretentious as a work of
       science."

613   Hoffman, Frederick J. "Arthur Koestler: A Long
       Way to Creation." *Sewanee Review* 73 (October-
       December 1965), 726-731.

       Believes that *The Act of Creation* "will remain
       as Koestler's major statement," but it "stops
       short of greatness."

614   "Invention." *TLS* (July 2, 1964), 561-562.

       Summarizes *The Act of Creation* at length and
       judges that Koestler overdoes his attack on be-
       haviorism. Gives a restrained review but admits
       the richness of ideas in the book.

615   Janeway, Elizabeth. "Man and His Strange Imagin-
       ings." *Saturday Review* 47 (October 17, 1964),
       35-36.

       Calls *The Act of Creation* Koestler's "magnum
       opus" in which he has tied together C.P. Snow's
       two cultures. Agrees with other reviewers that a
       great deal of interesting information is overworked
       by theories.

616   Kadt, J. "Arthur in Wonderland: Koestler's *The
       Act of Creation*." *Tirade* 8 (October 1964),
       615-641.

       In Dutch.

617   Mays, Wolfe. "Koestler on the Nature of Scientific
       Creativity." *Journal of the British Society for
       Phenomenology* 4 (October 1973), 248-255.

       Defends Koestler against the reviews of *The Act
       of Creation* by Miller (see No. 619) and Medawar
       (see No. 618), but is not entirely convinced of
       the accuracy of Koestler's theory of bisociation.

618   Medawar, P.B. "*The Act of Creation.*" In *The Art
       of the Soluble.* London: Methuen, 1967. Pp. 85-
       98.

       This chapter includes Medawar's review of *The
       Act of Creation* printed originally in *New States-
       man* 67 (June 19, 1964), 950-952, along with Koest-
       ler's response to the review and Medawar's final
       rejoinder to Koestler.
       Charges Koestler with "amateurishness," an over-
       blown style, and having "no grasp of how scientists
       go about their work." Finds nothing of value in
       Koestler's theories. (See No. 617.)

619   Miller, George A. "Arthur Koestler's View of the
       Creative Process." *Scientific American* 211
       (November 1964), 145-149.

       Charges Koestler with ignoring too much recent
       work on creativity. Assigns Koestler to the "psy-
       chodynamic" school of thinkers on creativity.
       Notes Koestler's distrust of logic. Finds it hard
       to understand the difference between Koestler's
       bisociation and just plain association. Dislikes
       Koestler's "genius for analogy." "A scientist
       who reads the book as a scientific treatise will
       find it an irritating and pretentious performance."

620   "Moments of Truth." *American Behavioral Scientist*
       8 (June 1965), 36-37.

       "Who can be harmed by such a work?"

621   Moray, Neville. "Outside the Cave." *The Listener*
       71 (June 25, 1964), 1028-1029.

       Attacks sharply Koestler's animadversions on
       the "ratomorphic" school of modern psychology,
       retorting that it is entirely untrue that young

scientists are forced to adopt the jargon of rat psychology to advance their careers. Accuses Koestler of drawing a factually false picture of modern psychology not because he is ignorant of its accomplishments but because "he dislikes the idea of a science of human behaviour so much that he cannot help being unfair to it even where it has been moderately successful and indeed where it has helped him." Attributes much of Koestler's wrongheadedness to confusion over Behaviourism as a philosophy ("that was long ago") and behaviourism as a method used by psychologists of all persuasions and dispositions.

622   Newth, D.R. "Koestler's System." *Spectator* 212 (May 29, 1964), 728.

Admits that Koestler has found an "important phenomenon" in bisociation but doubts that he has captured or tamed it. Says Koestler has "played fairly with the biological material." Complains of too much exposition of other thinkers, but praises the clarity of the explanations.

623   Nott, Kathleen. "The Bloom and the Buzz." *Commentary* 38 (November 1964), 84, 86, 88.

Judges *The Act of Creation* an "immense and splendid work" and applauds the assault on behaviorism.

624   Schwartz, Gary E., and David Shapiro, eds. *Consciousness and Self-Regulation: Advances in Research*. New York and London: Plenum Press, 1976. Pp. 362-363.

Discuss *The Act of Creation* briefly.

625   Simpson, George Gaylord. "*The Act of Creation*." *Isis* 57 (1966), 126-127.

"Indeed Koestler is wandering through well-charted lands without a map. It is possible to share his untutored zest, but that does not qualify him as a guide."

626 Smith, John Maynard. "Theories and Connections."
The Listener 71 (May 28, 1964), 881-882.

Contends that Koestler's "illuminating" idea
"has become fundamentally misleading when blown
up into a system of thought." Rejects Koestler's
claim for the fundamental importance of the bisociative act: "as the whole truth it is nonsense."
Stresses the importance of Popper's thesis that
scientific ideas have to be susceptible in principle to falsification by observation, and remarks
that "Koestler, with his interest in the genesis
of ideas, is complementary rather than antagonistic
to Popper." Dismisses Koestler's arguments because
he presents no over-arching scientific theory of
originality: "it is magnificent, but it is not
science."

627 Wieser, Wolfgang. "Schöpferische Akt und schöpferische Gestaltung." *Merkur* 21 (April 1967),
376-382.

Summarizes *The Act of Creation* and expresses
reservations about Koestler's main ideas.

628 Alston, William P. *"The Ghost in the Machine."*
Philosophy Forum 9 (June 1971), 349-355.

Unexamined.

629 Hawkins, David. "A Difficult Pill to Swallow."
Natural History 77 (May 1968), 64.

"What I miss is the sense and sensitivity cul-
tivated in a long tradition of concern for the
nurture of human development." Thinks that Koestler errs in *The Ghost in the Machine* in not recognizing how many of our problems come from cultural
not biological evolution.

630 Hicks, Granville. "A Prescription for Social Ills."
Saturday Review 51 (February 24, 1968), 39-40, 52.

Calls Koestler "a master of exposition" in *The
Ghost in the Machine*. "For myself, I hope that
the drug is discovered in time."

631   "Homo Sapientior." *TLS* (November 2, 1967), 1028.

     "Perhaps the most important thing about *The
Ghost in the Machine* is simply the view it affords
of an original and restless mind seeking to enlarge
the survival chances of some kind of rational hu-
manism--if not against the risk of final self-
immolation, then at least through and beyond the
noisy idolatry of the ratomorphs."

632   Jones, W.T. "*The Ghost in the Machine*." *Journal
of Value Inquiry* 5 (Spring 1971), 148-151.

     Unexamined.

633   Karp, Walter. "Seeking a Koestlerian Revolution."
Book World 2 (February 25, 1968), 4.

     Brief notice of *The Ghost in the Machine*.

633a   Kretch, David. "Assault on the Citadel." *Science*
160 (May 10, 1968), 649-650.

     Describes the attack on behaviorism in *The Ghost
in the Machine* as embarrassing. Even though it is
"an unfair and unscholarly job" with a very narrow
approach to psychology, the book has no boring
chapters.

634   Lear, John. "A Pill That Elides Evolution."
Saturday Review 51 (February 24, 1968), 39,
48-49.

     Remains sceptical of Koestler's proposal in *The
Ghost in the Machine* of a pill to improve human
nature, but sees Koestler's purpose as "to woo
people from reliance on metaphysical authority
to enforce peace among men."

635   Lifton, Robert Jay. "Man as Mistake." *New York
Times* (April 17, 1968), 3, 41.

     Reviews *The Ghost in the Machine*. Reprinted in
his *History and Human Survival* (New York: Random
House, 1970) as "Deceptions of War and Peace."

636   Mudrick, Marvin. "Prometheus at Work and Play."
         Hudson Review 21 (Summer 1968), 391-398.

         A very hostile review of *The Ghost in the
         Machine*. "Koestler begins to sound more and more
         unambiguously like a retired political hack and
         second-rate novelist."

637   "An Outsider's View." *The Lancet* No. 7526 (Novem-
         ber 11, 1967), 1050.

         Charges Koestler with unfairness to behaviorism
         in *The Ghost in the Machine*. Koestler's "hypothet-
         ical pill" is a "curiously defeatist remedy for a
         champion of free will."

638   Rycroft, Charles. "Holons and Hierarchies." *New
         Society* 10 (October 19, 1967), 559-560.

         Sympathizes with Koestler's attempt in *The
         Ghost in the Machine* to rescue man from the mech-
         anism of behaviorism, but derides Koestler's
         theory of "schizophysiology" as nonsense. "He
         forces the pieces together and imposes coherence
         where as yet there is none."

639   Sargant, William. "Into Orbit." *Spectator* 219
         (October 27, 1967), 505.

         The Ghost in the Machine is "science fiction
         gone into orbit."

640   Fyvel, T.R. "*Drinkers of Infinity.*" *New Statesman*
         77 (January 3, 1969), 19-20.

         Reviews Jenni Calder's *Chronicles of Conscience*
         (No. 280) along with *Drinkers of Infinity*. Says
         Calder is right to link Orwell and Koestler.
         Finds the essays in *Drinkers of Infinity* to be
         stimulating "conversation pieces."

641   "Ideas-Man." *TLS* (October 24, 1968), 1203.

         Offers only general remarks on *Drinkers of
         Infinity*. "Mr. Koestler's brilliance lies in his
         power to process ideas."

642   Manuel, Frank. "*Drinkers of Infinity.*" *Saturday
        Review* 52 (November 15, 1969), 36.

        "A writer of parts should perhaps leave the
        task of collecting his occasional pieces to
        posterity, if it is so minded."

643   Rowley, Peter. "*Drinkers of Infinity.*" *New York
        Times Book Review* (November 30, 1969), 70.

        A brief notice.

644   "The Organicist Backlash." *TLS* (November 20, 1969),
        1341.

        Beyond Reductionism is "rich in suggestiveness"
        but many questions are ignored.

645   Steiner, George. "Life-Lines." *The New Yorker* 47
        (March 6, 1971), 98-116.

        The papers in *Beyond Reductionism* are "pro-
        foundly interesting and controversial." A long,
        informative essay.

646   Witonski, P.P. "*Beyond Reductionism: The Alpbach
        Symposium.*" *National Review* 22 (June 30, 1970),
        691.

        Refers in passing to *The Sleepwalkers* as "an
        intellectual disaster." Calls *Beyond Reductionism*
        a "mixed bag" with enough worthwhile essays to
        justify buying it.

647   Young, Robert. "The Naked Marx." *New Statesman*
        78 (November 7, 1969), 666-667.

        Mentions *Beyond Reductionism* briefly in a broad
        survey of issues in evolution.

648   Carlson, Elof Axel. "*The Case of the Midwife Toad.*"
        Quarterly Review of Biology 47 (September 1972),
        322-324.

        Concludes that "the book fails in its objec-
        tives." It is historically inaccurate. It does
        not prove Kammerer's innocence. It adds no new
        support for Lamarckism. Suggests that Koestler

does not understand the role of mutation in neo-Darwinism and attacks a neo-Darwinism "of his own creation."

649   Claiborne, Robert. "Can Genes Learn? Arthur Koest-ler Thinks So." *New York Times Book Review* (April 2, 1972), 17-18.

Summarizes *The Case of the Midwife Toad* without judgment.

650   Coleman, William. "*The Case of the Midwife Toad.*" *Journal of the History of Medicine and Allied Sciences* 28 (January 1973), 61-63.

Calls writing Kammerer's story "a valuable ser-vice" but criticizes Koestler's account as "not a serious study in biology." Koestler has written "neither science nor history" in a book "replete with misapprehensions" resulting partly from his "perverse" understanding of evolutionary biology between 1900 and 1925.

651   Edelson, Edward. "Playing Dice with the World." *Book World* 6 (April 2, 1972), 5.

Brief notice of *The Case of the Midwife Toad.*

652   Gould, Stephen Jay. "Zealous Advocates." *Science* 176 (May 12, 1972), 623.

Sympathizes with Koestler's revision of the "common reading" of Kammerer's story, but thinks *The Case of the Midwife Toad* fails to convince because of Koestler's overdoing of his argument. Remarks that in Kammerer's time Lamarckism was a "majority opinion." Koestler's understanding of modern evolutionary theory is "misinformed." Gould accepts Kammerer's experiments, but "they constitute no case of Lamarckian inheritance." Notes that Koestler ignores Kammerer's "ardent" socialism, which led Kammerer to an a priori "vision of the perfectibility of man."

653   "Individual Paradigms and Population Paradigms." *TLS* (October 22, 1971), 1309-1310.

Summarizes the issues in *The Case of the Midwife Toad,* calling the book "fascinating reading."

654   Lear, John. "Nuptial Pads and a Question of In-
         heritance." *Saturday Review* 55 (April 1, 1972),
         63-65.

         Summarizes *The Case of the Midwife Toad* and
         lauds Koestler for reviving the subject.

655   Lenihan, John. "*The Case of the Midwife Toad.*"
         The Philosophical Journal 10 (January 1973),
         83-87.

         Admits that Koestler tells Kammerer's story
         well, but is sceptical of Koestler's conclusion
         that someone else may have tampered with Kammer-
         er's controversial specimen in order to discredit
         him.

656   Maloff, Saul. "Kröteküsser." *New Republic* 166
         (April 15, 1972), 24-26.

         Summarizes the arguments in *The Case of the
         Midwife Toad,* calling it "a masterly learned and
         elegant brief."

657   Morison, Robert S. "The Strange Case of Paul Kam-
         merer." *Natural History* 81 (June 1972), 90-94.

         Appreciates Koestler's reconstruction of the
         spirit of Viennese culture in *The Case of the
         Midwife Toad.*

658   Newth, D.R. "Green Fingers and Black Ink." *New
         Statesman* 82 (October 1, 1971), 442-443.

         Thinks that Koestler is wrong to express sym-
         pathy for Lamarckism in *The Case of the Midwife
         Toad.*

659   Taylor, John. "A Warning to Scientists." *The
         Listener* 86 (October 7, 1971), 483-484.

         Praises the "excellent piece of detective work"
         in *The Case of the Midwife Toad.* "All scientists
         should read Koestler as a salutary account of
         what may befall them if they don't look out."

660 Werskey, Paul Gary. "Kammerer Redivivus."
    Nature 234 (December 24, 1971), 489-490.

    Decides that Koestler has proved Kammerer's
    innocence in *The Case of the Midwife Toad*, but
    accuses Koestler of being unfair to the early
    neo-Darwinians. Explains that in Kammerer's day
    liberals like Kammerer tended to be environment-
    alists and conservatives leaned toward hereditar-
    ianism. "Koestler has viewed his materials through
    the wrong end of the microscope."

661 Wolff, Etienne. "Les amphibiens a l'honneur: à
    propos du livre d'Arthur Koestler." *Nouvelle
    Revue des Deux Mondes* 1 (May 1972), 305-314.

    "Le livre de Koestler n'apporte rien de nouveau
    à cet égard et ne doit pas nous donner d'illusions."

662 Gardner, Martin. "Arthur Koestler: Neoplatonism
    Rides Again." *World* 1 (August 1, 1972), 67-69.

    Rejects all of Koestler's arguments in *The
    Roots of Coincidence* for the respectability of
    parapsychology.

663 Herbert, Hugh. "*The Roots of Coincidence*." *Man-
    chester Guardian* (February 7, 1972), 8.

    On Koestler: "He has been the paradigm of the
    pan-European intellectual of the 'tween-war
    years: a man with one foot in politics and one
    in the arts, five fingers in science and the
    others round a glass, self-searching, committed,
    and somewhat vain."

664 Joravsky, David. "The Head on Jung's Pillow."
    New York Review of Books 19 (September 21,
    1972), 23-24.

    Criticizes Koestler for propagating "mythic
    biology" in *The Case of the Midwife Toad*. Points
    out that whereas Koestler cites C.H. Waddington's
    1957 book giving a hint of support to Lamarckism,
    Waddington himself repudiated all Lamarckism on
    the basis of modern biochemistry. Very dismissive
    of both *The Case of the Midwife Toad* and *The
    Roots of Coincidence*.

665   Lehmann-Haupt, Christopher. "Arthur Koestler in
         Wonderland." *New York Times* (August 11, 1972),
         27.

         Thinks that Koestler carries his ideas on ESP
         too far in *The Roots of Coincidence*.

666   Lomas, Herbert. "A Penchant for Lesbians, and
         Others." *London Magazine* 12 (June-July 1972),
         149-154.

         Mentions *The Roots of Coincidence* briefly in a
         review of several books.

667   Maddox, John. "Holons." *The Listener* 87 (February
         10, 1972), 187-188.

         Dismisses Koestler's claims for parapsychology
         in *The Roots of Coincidence*. Maintains that Koest-
         ler misconceives physics in his insistence that
         determinism and causality are no longer intellectu-
         ally respectable. Challenges Koestler to show why
         the tendencies toward autonomy revealed by separate
         organs ("holons") cannot be expected to yield their
         secrets to biology.

668   Mays, Wolfe. "*The Roots of Coincidence*." *Journal
         of the British Society for Phenomenology* 4
         (May 1973), 188-189.

         The Roots of Coincidence is "stimulating read-
         ing." Koestler can make difficult things seem
         "extremely simple--perhaps too simple."

669   "Psi in the Sky?" *TLS* (May 19, 1972), 659.

         Koestler's arguments in *The Roots of Coincidence*
         falter when he tries to bend physics and psychology
         toward each other. Disparages the book in general
         but lauds the introduction to the theories of
         Adrian Dobbs.

670   Robertson, Anthony. "Sleepwalker." *Nature* 237
         (June 16, 1972), 411.

         Dismisses *The Roots of Coincidence* as "too
         light and derivative to be worth considering at
         length."

671   Rycroft, Charles. "Unthinkable." *New Statesman*
       83 (February 11, 1972), 180.

       Remains sceptical of Koestler's arguments in
       The Roots of Coincidence.

672   Brophy, Brigid. "A Classic Non-Contibution to
       Knowledge." *The Listener* 89 (January 3, 1974),
       22-23.

       Reviews *The Challenge of Chance*, with her
       sentiments expressed in the title of the review.

673   "*The Challenge of Chance*." *Contemporary Psychol-
       ogy* 21 (December 1976), 890.

       A brief comment on *The Challenge of Chance*.

674   Inglis, Brian. "It So Happened." *Guardian* 109
       (November 17, 1973), 23.

       A notice of *The Challenge of Chance*.

675   Krippner, Stanley. "Theories of Parasychology."
       Psychology Today 8 (November 1974), 26-28.

       Calls *The Challenge of Chance* "worthwhile
       because Koestler's intriguing speculations just
       may be right."

676   Rush, Joseph. "*The Challenge of Chance*." *Journal
       of the American Society for Psychical Research*
       69 (April 1975), 174-177.

       Expresses doubts about the validity of the
       experiments described in *The Challenge of Chance*.

677   Thouless, R.H. "*The Challenge of Chance*." *Journal
       of Parapsychology* 38 (December 1974), 423-427.

       Finds the evidence for ESP in *The Challenge of
       Chance* "impressive, both in quality and amount."

678   "Through Time and Space." *Economist* 249 (December
       15, 1973), 115.

       Says of *The Challenge of Chance* that nobody
       will be converted to belief in ESP, but that
       the book is "intellectually honest."

679   Toynbee, Philip. "A Sponge in the Post." *The
       Observer* (November 4, 1973), 39.

       Reviews *The Challenge of Chance.* Describes the
       way Koestler assumes a teleological process at
       work in the universe, and admits the idea is ac-
       ceptable to him.

680   Boyers, Robert. "Sanity and Limitation." *New
       Republic* 172 (February 1, 1975), 25-27.

       The Heel of Achilles is not a "formidable
       contribution" to modern thought.

681   E.H. "*The Heel of Achilles.*" *Psychology Today* 8
       (February 1975), 115.

       Brief notice of *The Heel of Achilles.*

682   "*The Heel of Achilles.*" *Christian Century* 92
       (February 26, 1975), 206.

       Very brief notice ("worth reading").

683   "*The Heel of Achilles.*" *Contemporary Review* 224
       (June 1974), 334.

       Short notice.

684   Medawar, P.B. "Getting It Right, and Wrong."
       Spectator 232 (April 27, 1974), 515.

       Finds *The Heel of Achilles* "compulsively read-
       able." Rejects Koestler's claim of an innate flaw
       in human "genetic programmes."

685   Ryan, Alan. "Finding the Thread." *The Listener*
       91 (May 9, 1974), 605.

       "*The Heel of Achilles* is unashamedly odds and
       ends, and very good some of those odds and ends
       are."

686   Toynbee, Philip. "Occasional Koestler." *The
       Observer* (April 21, 1974), 36.

       Thinks Koestler underestimates Gandhi. Praises
       Koestler's "cheerful, urchin irreverence" in *The
       Heel of Achilles.* Calls him an "original thinker."

687   Wilson, David. "Paper Tigers." *New Statesman* 87
       (May 17, 1974), 698-699.

       Reviews *The Heel of Achilles*. "He fails to
       persuade only when he strays into the murky
       realms of mind over matter."

688   Cameron, James. "Ask the Rabbi." *New Statesman*
       91 (April 9, 1976), 472.

       Summarizes *The Thirteenth Tribe* without
       judgment.

689   Grossman, Edward. "Koestler's Jewish Problem"
       Commentary 62 (December 1976), 59-64.

       Perceives that Koestler has "an extra-scholarly
       axe to grind" in *The Thirteenth Tribe*. Argues
       that there is no evidence that German Jews
       "could not have migrated in sufficient numbers
       into Poland in the 16th century." Maintains that
       "there is really much uncertainty among historians
       as to how many Khazars became Jews and stayed
       Jews." Rejects what he takes to be Koestler's
       thesis: that if the Jews are mostly descendants
       of Khazars, then Koestler is vindicated in his
       long-time argument that Jews should either go
       to Israel or assimilate.

690   Huttenbach, Henry R. "Appointment in Khazaria."
       New York Review of Books 23 (December 9, 1976),
       62.

       Replies to Wieseltier's review of *The Thirteenth
       Tribe* (see No.700). Applauds Wieseltier's attack
       on Koestler's scholarship, but argues several
       points about the history of Khazaria, eliciting
       a response from Wieseltier.

691   "Lost Empire." *Economist* 259 (April 24, 1976),
       121.

       A brief summary of *The Thirteenth Tribe*.

692   Maccoby, Hyam. "The Khazars and the Jews." *The
       Listener* 95 (April 8, 1976), 450.

       Praises Koestler's account of the Khazars but
       claims he is wrong in believing that establishing

them as the ancestors of Polish Jewry will harm
the idea of a chosen race. ("There has never been
a 'Chosen-Race' doctrine in Judaism.") Jews, instead, have regarded themselves as a "chosen
people." Concludes that *The Thirteenth Tribe*
"represents one more stage in his struggle to
exorcise his own Jewishness."

693   Majeskie, Jane. "Chutzpah." *National Review* 28
          (November 12, 1976), 1248-1249.

          Describes *The Thirteenth Tribe* as "a poorly
       researched and hastily written book."

694   Mason, Philip. "The Birth of the Jews?" *Spectator*
          236 (April 10, 1976), 19.

          Hopes that *The Thirteenth Tribe* will help edu-
       cate against anti-semitism.

695   MacLean, Fitzroy. "*The Thirteenth Tribe.*" *New
          York Times Book Review* (August 29, 1976), 4.

          Praises *The Thirteenth Tribe* as "excellent,"
       "readable," and "thought-provoking."

696   Meyer, Karl E. "Conversion in Khazaria." *Saturday
          Review* 3 (August 21, 1976), 40.

          Judges *The Thirteenth Tribe* an "important and
       rigorously argued book."

697   Raphael, Chaim. "Chosen Peoples." *TLS* (June 11,
          1976), 696.

          Calls *The Thirteenth Tribe* "a delight." Asserts
       that in terms of race it makes no difference
       whether or not Jews are of Khazar origin. "The
       Jews have always known that *physically* they are
       a mixed people."

698   Schechner, Mark. "All the Difference in the
          World." *The Nation* 223 (November 20, 1976),
          535-536.

          The Thirteenth Tribe is weakest in Koestler's
       not making more of his conclusions.

699   Toynbee, Philip. "Who Are the Jews?" *The Observer Review* (April 4, 1976), 27.

Judges *The Thirteenth Tribe* a "fascinatingly controversial book" in which Koestler "marshalls his argument with great skill." Finds the weakest link in Koestler's argument to be his claim that there is no such thing as a Jewish racial type: "I know many people who could not be anything but Jewish." Concludes that even though "the case is strong," *The Thirteenth Tribe* is a "mischievous book" because it destroys the Jews' sense of a unique heredity.

700   Wieseltier, Leon. "You Don't Have To Be Khazarian." *New York Review of Books* 23 (October 28, 1976), 33-36.

In *The Thirteenth Tribe*, "Koestler has merely reproduced Abraham Poliak's allegations and garnished them with a medley of quotations from better-known historians, all of which combine to make him appear learned." The book is "a barely veiled and singularly defeasible argument about the character and prospects of the contemporary Jewish community." Concludes that "only a Jew would have taken so much trouble to come up with an alibi for his own self-effacement." (See Huttenbach's response in No. 690.)

701   Booker, Christopher. "Sci-fi Sage." *Spectator* 240 (March 4, 1978), 20-21.

Discerns in *Janus* the flavor of cheap "sci-fi sensationalism." "Here is a poor little fox, baying at the moon, and talking pure gibberish."

702   Cort, David. "The Twilight Zone." *The Nation* 226 (May 6, 1978), 547-548.

Finds that much of *Janus* is "engaging."

703   Gould, Stephen Jay. "Koestler's Solution." *New York Review of Books* 25 (April 20, 1978), 35-37.

Likes the general metaphor of a hierarchy of interacting levels in *Janus*, but regards Koestler's

"'theory' of the human condition as singularly
unconvincing and full of irony and contradictions."
Criticizes Koestler at length, concluding that
"Koestler, to support his specific theory of human behavior, has cast his lot with the very perspective he rejects in his general vision."

704   Jonas, Gerald. "Seeing the Universe Whole." *New
       York Times Book Review* (April 2, 1978), 9, 16.

       Janus is valuable in teaching laymen "not to
       understand science too quickly."

705   Mason, Michael. "Two Cultures?" *New Statesman* 95
       (February 24, 1978), 255-256.

       Janus is "hag-ridden" by antagonisms and fears,
       and it reveals Koestler's "deep hatred of science."
       All of Koestler's arguments against determinism
       fail.

706   McConnell, Frank. "*Janus: A Summing Up*." *New
       Republic* 178 (May 13, 1978), 34-36.

       Koestler is "one of the best second-rate minds
       of his generation" who excels as an "*explainer*."
       He is in "the tradition of the polymath *manqué*."

707   Warnock, Mary. "Enter the Holon." *The Listener*
       99 (February 23, 1978), 251.

       Reviews *Janus*, remarking that "the secret of
       writing like this is to be careless of the chasm
       between theory and evidence."

M

REVIEWS OF WORKS ABOUT KOESTLER

708 Pritchett, V.S. "Absolutitis." Review of Atkins
(No. 277). *New Statesman and Nation* 52 (August
18, 1956), 189-190.

Atkins's book is "a rambling, slapdash study."
Koestler has "always been able to clunk around
with a noisy tincan collection of psychological,
political, scientific and philosophical jargon."
Koestler's value is in his "getting to the centre
of current political experience." Koestler and
Orwell have taken the places of H.G. Wells and
G.B. Shaw in English polemic writing. Still maintains that *The Gladiators* is better than *Darkness
at Noon* because "obsessions narrow the mind."

709 Harris, Harold J. "*Chronicles of Conscience* by
Jenni Calder." (See No. 280.) *Modern Fiction
Studies* 16 (Summer 1970), 242-243.

Praises Calder for her literary criticism.

710 "*Astride the Two Cultures: Arthur Koestler at 70.*"
(See No. 285.) *The Observer* (December 14, 1975),
19.

A brief review.

711 "Bridge-Builder. *Astride the Two Cultures: Arthur
Koestler at 70.*" (See No. 285.) *Economist* 256
(September 6, 1975), 122.

A "learned and interesting collection," but it
is not unified.

712   Cameron, James. "Walnut. *Astride the Two Cultures:*
      Arthur Koestler at 70." *New Statesman* 90
      (September 5, 1975), 283.

      Generally favorable, but critical of the writing
      of American academics.

713   Fuller, Edmund. "Arthur Koestler's Philosophical
      Ideas." Review of Harris (No. 285). *Wall Street*
      Journal (March 6, 1976), 22.

      A favorable review of *Astride the Two Cultures.*

714   Medawar, P.B. "Doing the Honors. *Astride the Two*
      Cultures: Arthur Koestler at 70." (See No. 285.)
      Saturday Review (March 6, 1976), 22, 24.

      Praises Koestler as a "superbly accomplished
      journalist." Accepts Koestler's notion of hier-
      archical organization but rejects Koestler's
      general thesis that tiers of hierachies are
      "homonomous" in Koestler's sense. Doubts that
      Koestler understands "the *kind* of intellectual
      performance that is expected of somebody who
      propounds or defends a scientific or philosophic
      theory."

715   Pearson, Gabriel. "Abreast of Both Worlds."
      Review of Harris (No. 285). *Guardian* (September
      4, 1975), 12.

      Identifies the most productive issue in Koest-
      ler's thought as the question "whether science
      is inherently deterministic and excludes con-
      sciousness and freedom."

716   Sargant, William. "Materialist. *Astride the Two*
      Cultures: Arthur Koestler at 70." (See No. 285).
      Spectator 235 (September 13, 1975), 348.

      "The book itself seems to me in the nature of
      a long publisher's blurb." "Although Koestler
      may not achieve much except *Darkness at Noon* in
      his own lifetime, he will continue to stir people
      up sufficiently to broaden their vision."

717   Kramer, Hilton. "Casanova of Causes." Review of
       Cynthia Koestler (No. 749) Mikes (No. 292).
       New York Times Book Review (October 7, 1984),
       11-12.

       Judges Mikes's book "sentimental and not very
       revealing." *Stranger on the Square* is "a poignant
       and revelatory fragment."

718   Pearce, Edward. "With Koestler." Review of Good-
       man (No. 283). *Commentary* (August 1985), 67-70.

       Comments on the topics mentioned in Mamaine
       Paget Koestler's letters (e.g., Malraux, The
       Congress for Cultural Freedom), expressing warm
       admiration for Mamaine Koestler and high regard
       for Arthur Koestler as an anti-Communist.

MISCELLANEOUS

719 "Arthur Koestler." *Current Biography*. New York: Wilson, 1944. Pp. 398-401.

720 Astorg, Bernard d'. "Arthur Koestler: Prix Nobel 1960." *Esprit* 126 (October 1946), 378-398.

Unexamined.

721 Avi-Schaul, Mordechai. *Lo Yogi ve-lo Komisar*. Tel Aviv, 1946.

Unable to locate.

722 Bartlett, Norman. "'The Hairy Image': Underground in London." *Meanjin Quarterly* 29 (September 1970), 381-393.

Cites Koestler (see No. 262) in support of the thesis that we are in the last desperate phase of romanticism.

723 Beaton, Cecil, and Kenneth Tynan. *Persona Grata*. New York: Putnam, 1954. Pp. 63-64.

A one-paragraph note, describing Koestler's battle as "between the individual good and the general good--between the Yogi and the Commissar."

724 Beauvoir, Simone de. *Force of Circumstance*. London: Deutsch, 1965. Pp. 106-111, 139-141.

Hostile view of Koestler in post-war Paris.

725 Beauvoir, Simone de. *The Mandarins*. Cleveland: World, 1956.

An unfriendly portrait of Koestler in this novel.

726   Bertalanffy, Ludwig von. "Evolution: Chance or
      Law?" In *Perspectives on General Systems
      Theory: Scientific-Philosophical Studies*.
      New York: Braziller, 1975. Pp. 137-148.

      Refers to Koestler's theory of open hierarchical
      systems.

727   Boveri, Margaret. *Treason in the Twentieth
      Century*. London: MacDonald, 1961. P. 27.

      "Koestler had wandered in and out of allegiance
      to so many ideologies that he had become a kind
      of virtuoso."

728   Brandt, Sabine. "Chronist des Jahrhunderts:
      Arthur Koestlers Lebenserinnerungen." *Die Zeit*
      (Hamburg) 25 (September 25, 1970).

      Unable to locate. (See Merrill and Frazier's
      note under their No. 544.)

729   Brien, Alan. "Afterthought." *Spectator* 213
      (November 20, 1964), 690.

      Recalls two meetings with Koestler. Sceptical
      of Koestler's interest in semi-mysticism and ESP.

730   Buchynski, Thomas. "Tuning in on the Twilight
      Zone." *Psychology Today* 11 (August 1977),
      38-44.

      Not really about Koestler except to support
      his interpretation of the creative sleepwalker.

731   Byrne, John. "The Going Rate for a Title." *TLS*
      (March 1, 1985), 243.

      Points out that "*Darkness at Noon* is one of
      the most elusive of all modern first editions
      (one suspects that many copies were destroyed
      in the blitz)."

732   Cahn, Edmond Nathaniel. "*Reflections on Hanging*:
      Preface for Americans." In *Confronting Justice:
      The Edmond Cahn Reader*. Ed. Lenore L. Cahn.
      Boston: Little, Brown, 1966. Pp. 305-314.

      Discusses Koestler's ideas as they apply to
      American law.

733   Chalmers Mitchell, Sir Peter. *My House in
       Málaga*. London: Faber and Faber, 1938.

       Describes the dramatic arrest of Koestler at
       Chalmers Mitchell's house during the Spanish
       Civil War.

734   Conquest, Robert. *The Great Terror: Stalin's
       Purge of the Thirties*. New York: Macmillan,
       1968.

       Refers frequently to Koestler and describes
       the account of Rubashov's trial as "extremely
       well founded on the facts."

735   Crewe, Quentin. *A Curse of Blossom: A Year in
       Japan*. London: Weidenfeld and Nicolson, 1960.
       Pp. 112-121, 149-153.

       Describes his travels in Japan, part of which
       were in the company of Koestler.

736   Dahm, Erland. "Den unge Arthur Koestler."
       Horisont 15, No. 4 (1968), 11-13.

       Sketches Koestler's early life.

737   Day, Frank. "Arthur Koestler." In *Critical
       Survey of Long Fiction*. Ed. Frank Magill.
       Los Angeles: Salem Press, 1983. Pp. 1547-
       1555.

       Provides a brief introduction to the novels
       and gives synopses.

738   Day, Frank. "Arthur Koestler." In *Research
       Guide to Biography and Criticism*. Ed. Walton
       Beacham. Washington: Research Publishing,
       1985. Pp. 666-669.

739   Detweiler, Robert. "The Moment of Death in Mod-
       ern Fiction." *Contemporary Literature* 13
       (Summer 1972), 269-294.

       Comments briefly on the execution of Rubashov.

740   Downing, Frances. "Koestler Revisited: The
       Character Gletkin in *Darkness at Noon*."
       Commonweal 53 (February 9, 1951), 444-446.

       "Communism is more than an enemy in Korea."

741   Drilhon, Frédéric. "Arthur Koestler mon voisin."
       Nouvelles Littéraires (February 9, 1961), 1, 5.

       An interview, pretty well summed up in the
       following exchange:
       Drilhon--"Quel espoir nous laissez-vous?"
       Koestler--"Il est possible qu'une nouvelle
       génération devienne sourde aux vieux slogans et
       s'immunise contre les idéologies qui sont nôtres.
       Elle mettre peut-être fin à l'(âge du paradoxe).
       L'espoir est maintenant de survivre dans un
       monde naturellement standardisé et par là assez
       fade."

742   Eastman, Fred. "A Reply to Screamers." *Christian
       Century* 61 (February 16, 1944), 89-90.

       Repudiates Koestler's arguments in "The Night-
       mare That Is a Reality" (No. 104).

743   Eichholz, Armin. *Buch am Spiees*. Munich: Scherz
       Verlag, 1964. P. 67.

       Includes Koestler among satirical sketches of
       writers.

744   Goertzel, Victor, and Mildred D. Goertzel.
       Cradles of Eminence. Boston: Little, Brown,
       1962.

       Refers frequently to Koestler's childhood.

745   Green, Peter. "Aspects of the Historical Novel."
       In *Essays by Divers Hands* (Royal Society of
       Literature). N.s. 31. London: Oxford University
       Press, 1962. Pp. 35-60.

       "*The Gladiators* is very sharp reminder of how
       Marxist theories of dialectic and history could
       transform a traditional historical picture."

746 Grey, Anthony. "Anthony Grey discusses his ex-
     perience of solitary confinement, and compares
     notes with Arthur Koestler." *The Listener*
     (July 1, 1971), 9-11.

     Grey spent 806 days in solitary confinement in
     Peking in the 1960s. He and Koestler discuss
     the psychological aspects of prison life.

747 Gültig, Heinz. *Suti, oder Das ibolithische Ver-
     mächtnis: Ein literarisches Gesellschaftspiel.*
     Zurich: Diogenes-Verlag, 1959.

     Includes a brief humorous sketch of Koestler.

748 Hall, Elizabeth. "In and Out of Jail with Arthur
     Koestler." *Psychology Today* 4 (June 1970), 64.

     Unexamined.

749 Hartt, Julian N. *The Lost Image of Man.* Baton
     Rouge: LSU Press, 1963. Pp. 76-79.

     Praises the "recoil" against "Marxist man" in
     Darkness at Noon.

750 Hoehl, Egbert. "'Sonnenfinsternis' in Mannheim."
     Christ und Welt 6 (February 12, 1953), 8.

     "Die Regie (Paul Riedy) mengte der Schwarz-
     Weiss-Zeichnung der Autoren keine freundlicheren
     Farbtöne bei. Trotzdem boten die sich Ursprüng-
     lich weigernden Schauspieler beachtliche Leist-
     ungen vor einem düstern Rundhorizont."

751 Hughes, Langston. *I Wonder As I Wander: An Auto-
     biographical Journey.* New York: Standard Book
     Company, 1956. Pp. 101-191.

     Describes his friendship with Koestler in Rus-
     sia. Koestler's account is given in *The Invisible
     Writing* (No. 12).

752 Jelenskie, K.A. "The Literature of Disenchant-
     ment." *Survey* 41 (April 1962), 109-120.

     Unexamined.

753   Johnson, Paul. *Modern Times. The World from the
       Twenties to the Eighties*. New York: Harper and
       Row, 1983.

       Refers briefly (p. 83) to Koestler's "brilliant
       novel, *Darkness at Noon*," but rejects the impres-
       sion it gives that Stalin's victims "were induced
       to collaborate in their own mendacious testimony--
       even came to believe it. Nothing could be further
       from the truth."

754   Junod, Dr. Marcel. *Warrior Without Weapons*.
       New York: Macmillan, 1951. Pp. 105-106.

       The author was a delegate of the International
       Committee of the Red Cross. Recalls his role in
       negotiating a prisoner exchange during the
       Spanish Civil War: Koestler for the beautiful
       wife of a Spanish Nationalist airman.

755   Kahn, Lothar. "Zionist Attitudes of Some Euro-
       pean Writers." *Herzl Year Book*, Vol. 6. New
       York: Herzl, 1965. Pp. 113-117.

       See No. 345.

756   Kalb, Bernard. "Arthur Koestler: Biographical
       Sketch." *Saturday Review* 33 (September 27,
       1952), 10.

       Very brief.

757   Kardorff, U. von. "Dichter und Journalist."
       Stuttgarter Rundschau 2, No. 2 (1947), 17.

       Praises Koestler as "einer der meist genannten
       und meist umstrittenen Publizisten der Welt."

758   Koestler, Cynthia. "A Koestler Memoir." *Paris
       Review* (Summer 1984), 202-227.

       An excerpt from *Stranger on the Square*.

759   Kvastad, Nils B. "Arthur Koestlers livsaskadning."
       Samtid och Framtid 21, No. 2 (1964), 99-102.

       Brief outline of Koestler's career.

760   Leary, Timothy. "You Have to Go Out of Your Mind
       to Use Your Head: Arthur Koestler's High Climb."
       In *High Priest*. New York and Cleveland: World,
       1968. Pp. 135-155.

       Describes a psilocybin experience at Cambridge,
       Massachusetts, with Koestler and Charles Olson.

761   Leboutet, Lucie. "La Créativité." *Année Psycho-
       logique* 70 (1970), 579-625.

       Refers briefly to Koestler's theory of bisoci-
       ation.

762   Lerner, Max. "Shall We Lay Down Our Arms?" In
       *Public Journal: Marginal Notes on Wartime
       America*. New York: Viking, 1945. Pp. 386-389.

       Criticizes Koestler because "he seems weary."

763   Levin, Bernard. "Note." *The Observer Review*
       (December 14, 1975), 19.

       Recommends among the "Books of the Year"
       Astride the Two Cultures: Arthur Koestler at 70.

764   Lilienthal, Alfred M. *The Zionist Connection*.
       New York: Dodd, Mead, 1978. Pp. 731-733.

       Accepts Koestler's thesis about the Khazarian
       origin of East European Jews in *The Thirteenth
       Tribe*.

765   Lindman-Strafford, Kerstin. "'Kott och blod' i
       idéroman." *Nya Argus* 59 (June 1, 1966), 153-156.

       Discusses Koestler briefly along with Sartre,
       Malraux, Mann, and Camus.

766   L.W.H. "Farewell to Arms? A Reply to Mr. Arthur
       Koestler." *The Canadian Forum* (March 1944),
       273-274.

       Laments, from a socialist's perspective, the
       "marked tendency to defeatism and pessimism" in
       Koestler.

767   Macrae, Donald. "Man and Cosmos." *The Observer*
       (February 19, 1978), 33.

       Unexamined.

768   Mikes, George. "Remembering the Koestlers." *The
       American Scholar* (Spring 1984), 219-224.

       Mikes is a Hungarian journalist living in exile
       in London. He met Koestler in 1952 and they be-
       came close personal friends. He comments here on
       their friendship, their shared interests in Hungar-
       ian poetry and football, and Koestler's last
       ailing years. (See No. 292.)

769   Moss, Norman. "Choosing to Watch a Great Decline."
       London Times (February 21, 1977), 5.

       Short critical essay.

770   Moss, Norman. "Koestler in Wonderland." *London
       Sunday Times Magazine* (October 14, 1973), 96.

       Short discussion of *The Challenge of Chance.*

771   Neumann, Robert. "Besonder Finsternis: Nach Ar-
       thur Koestler." In *Mit fremden Federn: Paro-
       dien 2* Vienna: Verlag Kurt Desch, 1955. Pp.
       217-221.

       Parodies Koestler's style.

772   Padev, Michael. "The Invisible Complex; Being
       Further Extracts from the Memoirs of Arth*r
       K**stl*r." *Punch* (July 28, 1954), 149-150.

       Parodies the two volumes of Koestler's auto-
       biography, *Arrow in the Blue* and *The Invisible
       Writing.*

773   Polonyi, Karl. "Correspondence." *New Statesman
       and Nation* 30 (July 21, 1945), 41-42.

       Challenges what Koestler says in *The Yogi and
       the Commissar* (No. 13) about the punishment of
       juveniles in the Soviet Union.

774   Prabhakar, M.S. "Two Inconsistencies in *Darkness at Noon.*" *Notes and Queries* 209 (October 1964), 387-388.

Which of Ivan's legs was amputated? What kind of chair does Rubashov sit in?

775   Reid, Robert. "Koestler at 70." *New Scientist* 67 (September 4, 1975), 536-537.

A brief tribute.

776   Robinson, Donald. "Arthur Koestler." In *One Hundred Most Important People.* Boston: Little, Brown, 1952.

777   Stace, W.T. *Mysticism and Philosophy.* New York: Macmillan, 1960.

Defines (pp. 86-87) the ontrovertive mystical experience as a condition in which the self divests itself of the stream of consciousness, leaving the "pure ego" by itself as "the bare unity of the manifold of consciousness from which the manifold itself has been obliterated." Classifies (pp. 120-123) Koestler's mystical experience as described in *The Invisible Writing* as a "partial and incomplete" instance of the "classical introvertive type." Judges Koestler's chapter on his mystical experience as "highly valuable and important for any student of mysticism."

778   Steiner, George. "Koestler's Quest." *London Sunday Times* (August 31, 1975), 23.

Unexamined.

779   Todorov, Tzvetan. "A Dialogic Criticism?" *Raritan* 4 (Summer 1984), 64-76.

Recalls briefly his first meeting with Koestler.

780   Ulc, Otto. "Koestler Revisited." *Survey* 72 (Summer 1969), 108-122.

Unexamined.

781   Uren, Ormond. "Change of Heart." *London Review*
      of Books (October 3, 1985), 4.

      Recalls in a letter a meeting in 1942 or 1943
      with Koestler and the Count and Countess Karolyi,
      and of his impression of Koestler as a "sinister
      arch-reactionary."

782   Waugh, Evelyn. "The Jesuit Who Was Thursday."
      Commonweal 45 (March 21, 1975), 558-561.

      Mentions Koestler in the last paragraph.

783   "Wenn die Russen kommen." *Der Spiegel* 7 (February
      11, 1953), 31-32.

      Describes the circumstances of the Mannheim
      production of *Darkness at Noon*.

784   Winegarten, Renée. "Arthur Koestler as Witness."
      Mainstream (Communist Party, Great Britain)
      12 (February 1966), 71-77.

      Unexamined. (Very hard to get.)

O

DISSERTATIONS

785 Borchert, Donald Marvin. "A Discussion Relating
to Humanization: The Means-End Program of
Karl Marx Analyzed on the Basis of His Major
Works; The Means-End Program Criticized from
the Standpoint of Arthur Koestler's Life and
Thought; The Post-Communist Criticism of Arthur Koestler Viewed from a Christian Theological Perspective." Unpublished Doctoral
Dissertation, Princeton Theological Seminary,
1966.

Unexamined.

786 Calder, Jenni. "Imagination and Politics: A
Study of George Orwell and Arthur Koestler."
Master's Thesis, University of London,
1966.

Unexamined. (See No. 280.)

787 Grazyte, Ilona. "Arthur Koestler as a Novelist."
Unpublished Doctoral Dissertation, Université
de Montréal, 1960.

Unexamined.

788 Huber, Peter Alfred. "Koestlers Werk in literar-
ischer Sicht." Doctoral Dissertation, Zürich
Universität, 1962.

Unexamined. (See No. 286.)

789 Keim, Arthur. "Arthur Koestler's Quest for the
Political Absolute." Unpublished Master's
Thesis, University of Washington, 1961.

Unexamined.

790   Levene, Mark Joel. "Themes and Techniques in the
      Work of Arthur Koestler." Unpublished Doctoral
      Dissertation, University of Toronto, 1975.

      Unexamined.

791   Mandelstam, Paul. "The Freudian Impact upon Con-
      temporary Political Thinking: An Analysis of
      the Political Ideas of Sigmund Freud, Arthur
      Koestler, Harold D. Lasswell, and Abram Kar-
      diner." Unpublished Doctoral Dissertation,
      Harvard University, 1953.

      Unexamined.

792   Pick, Aline. "The Quest for the Absolute: Eschat-
      ology in the Works of Arthur Koestler, Andre
      Malraux, and George Orwell." Unpublished
      Master's Thesis, Columbia University, 1962.

      Unexamined.

793   Sperber, Murray A. "The Uses of Apocalypse: A
      Study of Arthur Koestler's Life and Writings."
      Unpublished Doctoral Dissertation, University
      of California at Berkeley, 1974.

      Unexamined.

794   Webberley, Roy. "Education and the Work of
      Arthur Koestler." Unpublished Doctoral Disser-
      tation, Dublin University, 1974.

AUTHOR INDEX

SUBJECT INDEX TO PRIMARY SOURCES

INDEX OF PRIMARY TITLES